Anglican Church School Education

Also available from Bloomsbury

Faith Schools and Society, Jo Cairns
Is Religious Education Possible?, Michael Hand

Anglican Church School Education

Moving Beyond the First Two Hundred Years

Edited by

Howard J. Worsley

B L O O M S B U R Y

LONDON • NEW DELHI • NEW YORK • SYDNEY

Bloomsbury Academic
An imprint of Bloomsbury Publishing Plc

50 Bedford Square	175 Fifth Avenue
London	New York
WC1B 3DP	NY 10010
UK	USA

www.bloomsbury.com

First published 2013

British Library Cataloguing-in-Publication Data
A catalogue record for this book is available from the British Library.

ISBN: HB: 978-1-4411-2513-2
ePub: 978-1-4411-0815-9
PDF: 978-1-4411-0140-2

Library of Congress Cataloging-in-Publication Data
A catalog record for this book is available from the Library of Congress.

Typeset by Newgen Imaging Systems Pvt Ltd, Chennai, India
Printed and bound in Great Britain

Contents

Acknowledgements

This book has been written to honour the vision of Joshua Watson and that true servant of the Church would in turn direct that attention to God. He would say that without the advent of Christ, the story of schooling in Britain would be very different today.

I wish to thank each of the fourteen contributors who, in my view, are the most accomplished scholars in the field of Anglican education at this point in time, numbering five professors as well as two new writers to the host of experienced researchers. If faults are to be found in the text, they are most likely to be those of the editor as in places I have had to cut the original writing in order to conform to a standard volume.

The Watson Symposium, at which all these chapters were presented, is itself indebted to the sponsorship of the Keswick Hall Trust and the Hockerill Foundation, as well as to the backing of the National Society and the Association of Anglican Directors of Education.

Without a doubt, apart from the huge debt that I always owe to my wife, Ruth, and my family and friends for accepting me for suddenly vanishing to 'complete a thought', my greatest debt is to my colleague, Sheila Barker, who has constantly kept up with my editing and otherwise kept the administrative show on the road. She is a true friend.

My hope is that this volume will be well used in the professional development of church school headteachers (and the new range of church school leadership programmes) as well as in the ongoing education of clergy, governors or school researchers. May it be one of many voices on a subject that brings theology into context and which connects the Church to society in meaningful encounter.

Foreword

Paul Butler, Bishop of Southwell and Nottingham

When Augustine began his mission to these islands, one of the very first things he decided to do was establish an educational centre. The Kings School, Canterbury traces its roots to this foundation. So from the very outset of Christianity and the Church, education was regarded as a crucially important part of how the Church would engage in the mission of God. In the centuries that followed many educational institutions were founded by the Church, or church leaders. The explosion that came about through the creation of the National Society in 1811 was the conviction of Joshua Watson, and others, that education should be for all, most notably for the poor. In this Watson was building on the work of Robert Raikes who, a few years previously, was credited as being the original founder of the Sunday school movement.

Two hundred years of Church of England schools, seeking to serve the poor, was rightly celebrated across the land in 2011. It was my honour to share in a number of celebrations locally and nationally. In my own diocese of Southwell and Nottingham, we had a fantastic 'Candle Journey' around all our Church schools culminating in an amazing celebration, 'Burning Brightly', in the beauty of Southwell Minster. In every diocese there were creative ways of celebrating these 200 years. Nationally, I loved being with around 2,000 children and teachers in Westminster Abbey for the main national celebration. It was also my privilege to play a small part in helping the Watson Symposium to take place. Persuading such a distinguished range of educational experts to write and deliver papers all on one day in St John's, Hackney was a phenomenal achievement. It happened largely due to the determination and drive of Howard J. Worsley. The day itself was truly memorable for the range of attendees and for the quality and challenge that came from the papers delivered. All who attended had to make hard choices as to which papers they would hear. It is wonderful that the whole collection has now been drawn together for wider readership.

The history of these 200 years is inspiring, but it is not all glowing. There has been a danger of a drift towards gentrification and the challenge to hold to the original vision of serving the poor remains. The challenge also of what sharing the Christian faith as the Church of England understands and teaches it in a very different faith climate is very big. Proper assessment and reflection on the history is a vital part of ensuring that Church schools of the present and the future are the best that they can be.

We are all acutely aware of how much change there has been in recent years in the world of schools. Church schools, of all denominations, have been very much a part of this change. The changing has not stopped; it has moved on even since the symposium took place. If Church of England schools are to be effective as part of the mission of the church then a continual practice of reflection and evaluation, with honesty about hard research findings, is an essential part of our work. Several contributions in this volume offer such careful critical reflection; it is not always comfortable reading.

Then there must always be an eye to the future. Christians are people of hope, convinced that the future is God's and that the reign of God is coming in all its fullness one day. As we look to that fullness we have to constantly seek to see where the next steps might be in all of life, including education. Just what should be the priorities for schools in the years ahead? How might we work to bring these into reality? The chapters in this volume offer a wide range of thoughts and possibilities. Together they offer stimulation to further thought, debate, and ultimately action. In their varying ways every chapter keeps asking the proper questions about what is truly distinctive about church school education, and in particular Church of England school education. Many offer input into what this contribution is in an ever more plural society of many faiths, and none (though arguably there is no such thing as no faith). There is much which also speaks to all schools not simply those with a Church of England foundation.

It is my hope that this volume will be very widely read by educationalists of all views, and not only those who serve in these islands. There is a great deal here to help all educationalists ponder the lessons from history, the development of education through time, the priorities and ways of schooling in the present, and ideas and directions for the future. I hope it will be read and used by headteachers, teachers, governors, clergy and those who have political responsibility for education nationally and locally; it will stimulate thought and debate.

The Church of England's engagement in education remains a very high priority. This is not simply about the church's own schools but is about education as a whole. There is a special responsibility for the schools with a church foundation but there is a commitment to the education of all. The church believes education matters for our society and our world; we have been at the forefront of education throughout our history and across the world. We have every intention of continuing our commitment to schooling for all and see our own schools as a vital and distinctive part of that contribution.

Joshua Watson was a pioneer in his day. The Watson Symposium offered some fresh pioneering for our own time. Just as Augustine, Watson and the Hackney Phalanx rose to the challenge of their own times, may the Church of England, along with our sister churches, rise to the challenge of our time.

List of Contributors

Jeff Astley
Jeff Astley has worked in parish ministry, university chaplaincy, teacher training and higher education. Since 1981, he has been the Director of the North of England Institute for Christian Education, UK, and since then has taught and supervised in the Department of Theology and Religion and School of Education of Durham University, UK. He has held the title of Honorary Professorial Fellow in Practical Theology and Christian Education in the Department of Theology and Religion since 1997, and is a Visiting Professor at Glyndwr University and York St John University. Jeff Astley has authored and edited over 30 books, including *The Contours of Christian Education* (1992), *The Philosophy of Christian Religious Education* (1994), *Critical Perspectives on Christian Education* (1994), *Christian Theology and Religious Education* (1996), *The Fourth R for the Third Millennium* (2001), *Children, Churches and Christian Learning* (2002), *The Idea of a Christian University* (2004), *Education and Adolescence* (2005) and *Peace or Violence: The Ends of Religion and Education?* (2007).

Alan Brown
Alan Brown is currently Senior Lecturer in Education Studies at the University of Worcester, UK, and is a consultant for religious education for the Worcestershire Standing Advisory Councils on Religious Education (SACRE). He was the Schools (Religious Education) Officer for the Church of England Board of Education from 1980–2001 and Deputy Director of the National Society from 1995–2001. He also ran the National Society's Religious Education Centre in London from 1985–99. He has written a number of books and articles on religious education and related topics including a range of booklets on Church schools for the National Society during the 1990s. He, with colleagues trained most of the Anglican school inspectors during the 1990s and is a Statutory Inspection of Anglican Schools Inspector having inspected over 500 schools.

Priscilla Chadwick
Priscilla Chadwick worked in senior management in both secondary schools and higher education, leading schools at times of significant change in both state and independent sectors. As a theologian, she has taken a particular interest

in religious education, religious broadcasting and ecumenical initiatives and chaired the Dioceses Commission for the Church of England. She is Chair of Governors of one of the new Anglican academies in the London Diocese, having been a Trustee in Southwark of the only Anglican City Technology College. At South Bank University, UK, she was responsible for the quality of teaching and learning across one of the United Kingdom's largest universities and later successfully restructured two public schools into a centre of excellence in the independent sector, being elected the first woman to chair the Headmasters' and Headmistresses' Conference (HMC) in 2005. She also chairs St Gabriel's Trust which supports teachers of religious education nationally and is a member of the Church of England Board of Education

Trevor Cooling

Trevor Cooling is Professor of Christian Education and Director of the National Institute for Christian Education Research at Canterbury Christ Church University, UK. Previously, he was the Director of the Transforming Lives Project, an interdenominational initiative that promotes teaching as a Christian vocation. Trevor has been active in education for over 30 years as, at various times, a teacher, Head of Religious Education in a secondary school, Chief Executive of the Stapleford Centre, Principal Lecturer in Theology at the University of Gloucestershire, UK, Schools Adviser for the Anglican Diocese of Gloucester, UK, with forays into spells as a curriculum developer, author and government adviser. He has a Ph.D. in Religious Education from the University of Birmingham, UK, although his first degree is in Biology. He has written widely on education in both books and journals. His most recent publication, *Doing God in Education* (2010) is a robust defence of the Christian contribution to publicly funded education.

Tim Elbourne

Tim Elbourne has been Director of Education of the Diocese of Ely, UK, since 1998 and is a very part-time assistant priest in a group of five rural parishes in that diocese. He is a member of the Council of the National Society for Religious Education and currently chairs the Grove Education Series, the Keswick Hall Trust and the Chaplaincy Council of Anglia Ruskin University, UK. In 2011, on behalf of the National Society and the Association of Anglican Directors of Education, he convened the first ever consultation for educationalists from across the Anglican Communion which issued the 'Cambridge Declaration', resolving to establish a worldwide network for people involved with Anglican schooling. He has been a parish priest and in-service training officer for clergy in West Yorkshire, UK, and was University of York chaplain for six years after his curacy in Tottenham, UK. He has chaired the network of Diocesan Directors of Education and been training officer of its Association.

Helen Everett

Having taught Chemistry in English Secondary Schools for 12 years, Helen decided a change of direction was necessary and undertook an MA in Comparative Education at Institute of Education, University of London, UK. Her dissertation, 'A Comparison of Evangelical Christian and Islamic Independent Schools', focused on the reasons why these two groups should feel it necessary to found independent schools. This led to her interest in faith schools and inspired her Ph.D. study looking at faith schools and how in their desire to nurture the faith and form a religious identity they may impact negatively on their students' attitudes of tolerance to diversity. Helen was awarded her doctorate in 2012 as this book was going to press.

Leslie J. Francis

Leslie J. Francis is Professor of Religions and Education within the Warwick Religions and Educational Research Unit, University of Warwick, UK, and Canon Theologian at Bangor Cathedral, UK. He has been researching and writing about Church schools since the early 1970s, giving particular attention to quantitative studies concerned with pupil attitudes and values.

David W. Lankshear

David W. Lankshear was Schools Officer of the Church of England Board of Education and Deputy General Secretary of the National Society from 1991 to 2003, having previously been a Head of a Church of England primary school, UK, and a Diocesan Director of Education, UK. Since 2003, he has been working as a consultant and researcher in the field of Christian education. He currently holds a Research Fellowship at the Warwick Religions and Education Research Unit at the University of Warwick, UK. He is also an Honorary Research Fellow at Glyndwr University, UK and the St Mary's Centre, UK. From 2006 to 2009, he was Research Officer and from 2007 Secretary to the Church in Wales Education Review, whose report was published in 2009. He is currently Secretary of the Inter-European Commission on Church and School.

Gemma Penny

Gemma Penny is Research Associate with the St Mary's Centre, UK, and is undertaking doctoral research within the Warwick Religions and Education Research Unit, University of Warwick, UK.

Julian Stern

Julian Stern is Professor of Education and Religion, and Dean of Education and Theology, at York St John University, UK. He was a school teacher for 14 years, and worked in universities for 16 years prior to coming to York St John University in 2008. Julian is widely published, with 11 books and over 30 articles, including *The Spirit of the School* (2009), *Schools and Religions: Imagining the Real* (2007) and *Teaching Religious Education: Researchers in the Classroom* (2006).

Ian Terry

Ian Terry first worked for the Anglican Church, in the Church of the Province of Southern Africa, teaching in an Anglican High School in Lesotho from 1975 until 1978. He returned to England to train for the Anglican Priesthood at the College of the Resurrection, Mirfield, UK. While there, he travelled to Geneva to research the World Council of Churches, and was part of an international consultation, 'Christ, Liturgy and Culture', at the Ecumenical Institute, Bossey, Switzerland. Since those early days, Ian has taught in a further three Anglican Schools, inspected many Church of England schools as a SIAS Inspector, researched the themes of ethos and values within Anglican Schools at doctoral level, and worked as Herefordshire's Diocesan Director of Education, UK, between 2002 and 2008. He is currently Team Rector of Bournemouth Town Centre Parish, UK, and researching the spirituality of children and young people.

Paddy Walsh

With a background in philosophy and theology, Paddy Walsh moved over from secondary school teaching in Dublin, Ireland, and London, UK, to teacher education and research. He was a curriculum specialist and consultant and an educational philosopher for more than 30 years at the Institute of Education, University of London, UK, where, now semi-retired, he retains a role as Deputy Director of the Institute's Centre for Research and Development in Catholic Education. His best-known publication is *Education and Meaning: Philosophy in Practice* (1993), which won an SCSE education award in 1994. Over the years, he has engaged with Catholic and joint-Church schooling as pupil, teacher, parent, member of working parties, researcher (in several countries), doctoral supervisor and examiner, writer and governor.

Robert Wickham

Robert Wickham feels it is a great privilege to be the current Rector of Hackney, UK. He is aware of the incredible work of his predecessors (and their families) and their influence is all around him. He has been ordained for over 13 years, having served in Willesden, Kings Cross, UK, and now in Hackney. He has a passion for recognizing Jesus at work in the heart of the City, seeing the immense contribution that our Churches make, and for the Church's role in Education.He studied Geography at Durham University, UK, and has just completed an MA in Theology, Politics and Faith-Based Organisations at King's College London, UK. Both these Institutions were shaped and moulded by Joshua Watson.

Howard J. Worsley

Howard J. Worsley is the convener for the group of writers who came together to form the Watson Symposium and to write this book. He has been a secondary school teacher, a Scripture Union schools worker, a vicar and a theological college tutor before becoming a Diocesan Director of Education, first in Nottinghamshire, UK, and then in London, UK. He is Senior Lecturer in Christian Education at Christchurch Canterbury University, UK. His ongoing research interest considers how children access faith and his recent writings have focused on children's insights into the Bible. He is passionate to connect what is best about the Church to the next generation.

Andrew Wright

Andrew Wright is Professor of Religious and Theological Education at King's College London, UK. He has written extensively in the fields of critical religious education, Christian theology of education and Anglican schools, and is currently researching the pedagogy of teaching and learning in religious education classrooms. His recent publications include *Spirituality and Education* (2000), *Religion, Education and Post-Modernity* (2004), *Critical Religious Education, Multiculturalism and the Pursuit of Truth* (2007). His latest book, *Christianity and Critical Realism: Truth, Ambiguity and Theological Literacy*, will be published next year.

List of Abbreviations

AADE	Anglican Association of Directors of Education
AASSH	Anglican Academy and Secondary School Heads
BFBS	British and Foreign Bible Society
BFSS	British and Foreign Schools Society
DBE	The Diocesan Board of Education
DFE	The Department for Education (1992–5 and 2010–)
DfEE	The Department for Education and Employment (1995–2001)
DfES	The Department for Education and Science (2001–2007)
ECM	The Every Child Matters Report (2002)
EU	European Union
NS	The National Society
Ofsted	The Office of Standards for Education
PGCE	Post Graduate Certificate for Education
QCA	Quality and Curriculum Authority (1997–2012)
SACRE	Standing Advisory Council for Religious Education
SIAS	The Statutory Inspection of Anglican Schools
SPCK	The Society for the Propagation of Christian Knowledge
VA	Voluntary Aided (School)
VC	Voluntary Controlled (School)

Introduction

Howard J. Worsley

This book, broadly titled *Two Hundred Years of Anglican Church Schools*, is made up of the 14 chapters presented to the Watson Symposium, a one-off gathering of academics and educationalists in 2011. As a part of the national celebrations marking 200 years of the Church of England's contribution to education, the Watson Symposium called together leading writers and researchers in church school education on behalf of the National Society and the Anglican Association of Directors of Education.

The Symposium met on 20 October 2011 and was successful in attracting over 100 delegates from all over the country to hear the freshly researched articles. The venue chosen for this event was always going to be the large Victorian Church of St John's, Hackney, where Joshua Watson's tomb can be found (and where his brother was the parish priest).

The event was hosted by the Bishop of Oxford, the Right Revd John Pritchard who was the Chair of the National Board of Education for the Church of England. It was convened by myself, ably assisted by Sheila Barker, Assistant Director for schools in the Diocese of Southwell and Nottingham, UK.

Due to the generous contributions made by the Keswick Hall Foundation and the Hockerill Trust, the symposium was able to subsidize the cost of the conference, charging each delegate only a modest entry fee, and ensuring that all participants were equipped with a memorable conference pack as well as being sumptuously dined (inclusive of a glass of wine in true Hackney Phalanx tradition).

What you now have in your hands is a volume that is long overdue. It is strange that the Church of England has not made more of its historic legacy of bringing schooling to Britain through its establishment of the National Society (led by Joshua Watson), but this work goes a small way to correcting the record.

As will be apparent from the contents, the 14 chapters for the Watson Symposium have been gathered into four parts which reflect on the past, the present and the future of Anglican Church schools. The first part is titled 'The Historical Story', and details the background to the establishment of the National Society, with Robert Wickham's chapter detailing the political battle surrounding education in the nineteenth century and my own chapter showing it as an ecclesiastical struggle of the era. Priscilla Chadwick then offers insight into how Anglican Church schools not only survived in the following century but were to flourish against the odds. Finally in this part, aware that the story of Anglican education often overlooks the impact made by the Church in Wales, David W. Lankshear resets the balance with his chapter detailing the Welsh story and the effect of education as mission.

The next two parts involve reflection on the current context of church school education. Reflection on current policy and philosophy brings the insights of our only Catholic contributor, the philosopher Paddy Walsh, who discusses the three areas of personhood, love and historical awareness as being fundamental for the Christian school. Jeff Astley then boldly considers how the Church has attempted to maintain a preferential option for the poor in education against a wider background of commodification. The specifically Anglican contribution, made by the Church of England leaving its distinctive touch upon education is discussed by Ian Terry. This is in sharp contrast to the following empirical research of Leslie J. Francis who offers statistical evidence from the point of view of those adolescents who attend Anglican secondary schools.

The subsequent reflection (the third part) on current practice moves from a more conceptual and attitudinal framework to one that considers the tasks of safe engagement, learning and cultural transformation. Alan Brown points to 'The Bright Field' of faith in a safe space as being the aspiration for the Church school, away from the fortress of segregated religious identity. The vision of distinctively Christian learning is then proposed by Trevor Cooling with Andrew Wright developing a reflection on how Church Schools might either affirm, challenge or transform the culture in which they exist.

The fourth and final part considers how Church schools might be influential in shaping future thinking. Both Helen Everett and Julian Stern pose tough questions to Anglican education, Everett questioning the extent to which Church schools are different from their community counterparts in showing tolerance and Stern questioning the rhetoric of inclusive service and mission. Finally Tim Elbourne's chapter details the current context of change, explaining how after the resurgence of confidence following the Dearing era, that Church schools need to reflect theologically in order to find their next phase of mission.

At the end of the book, I have again taken up my pen for a final chapter that focuses the symposium findings back onto vision for the Church school. After the significant process of reflection allowed by the symposium, it is essential that the practical implications are made from a professional and a personal point of view.

It has become clear that the various contributions do not all fit perfectly into one neat package offering a single view of education. What has been gathered at the Watson Symposium is an example of genuine scholarship with some contributors showing a more positive vision for Church schools and others offering a more cautionary critique. It seems that the empirical findings are sometimes at variance with the theoretical vision and that different theological perspectives create a range of educational impact.

As such, this collection will provide stimulation for both students considering the nature of Anglican education and for practitioners reflecting on their distinctive contribution in their own context. To make it easier for wider study, each chapter offers some keywords after an initial abstract. A final index is also included after a general bibliography at the end of the book. If the individual chapters are to be used for seminar work, suggested 'key questions', posed by the writers, have been offered at the end of each chapter.

As a final aid to understanding the complexities of 200 years of the Church of England's contribution to education, I offer below an overview of the history of Christian education in these islands. Knowing that I run the risk of being overly simple, I endeavour a bird's eye view of schooling in Britain, but one which has been significantly influenced by the contribution made by the National Society over the past 200 years.

Historical context

Educational literacy grew as a direct result of the spread of Christianity in England. Initially Christianity was one cult among many arriving on British shores with Roman artisans and traders, but when Constantine became a Christian in the fourth century, the faith became more visible, even surviving the departure of the Romans until Augustine arrived in AD 597. The immediate result of the conversion of King Ethelbert was for land to be offered on which Augustine built a monastery and subsequently a school for training Anglo Saxon priests.

Christianity then rose from being a minor cult to demonstrate its potential as a major religion but was curtailed by Viking invaders. Of particular tragic note was the plundering of Lindisfarne in AD 871, exemplifying the destruction of the church which was both the learning centre and the focus of power.

King Alfred the Great (r 871–99) noted that education and faith literacy declined after the initial conversion of the Anglo-Saxons. In his preface to his translation of Gregory I's *Cura Pastoralis*, he set out his intention to educate the people of England by not only making them literate but also by getting the Bible translated. His victory over the Viking Guthrum at the Battle of Eddington was a marker in encouraging Christian learning.

However, history was to show that widespread education was not to take place until after the Norman Conquest when Christianity was finally to take root in the new building projects, with stone churches being available for use as schools as well as markets and places of worship. Alongside the churches, monasteries grew up as centres of Christian learning and these were to remain until the time of the Reformation.

Schooling was not widely available, though a useful internet search of 'oldest schools in the UK' shows that after the oldest school claimed its foundation in the sixth century (King's School, Canterbury, a claim which is not without contention), a smattering of schools trace their origins to every century until the fifteenth century. In that century, 21 schools were recorded to have been set up and then in the sixteenth century over one hundred schools were named. It is noteworthy that of these schools, many were established with the initial intention of being a benefit to the poor but ended up being funded as schools for children from families with access to wealth. These old 'academic' schools taught Latin and religion, whereas other schools set up by guilds were for apprentices to learn trade skills.

More recently, the churches in England may claim to have made an even greater contribution to 'education for all' children by their establishment of societies with the aim of widespread schooling. Beginning with the foundation of the Society for the Propagation of Christian Knowledge (SPCK) in 1698, nineteenth-century societies (listed below), contributed to the development of a wide curriculum, including Religious Education and the work of Church Colleges for training teachers.

1800–70

Two hundred years ago the battle for widespread education was fought in post-Industrial England, with the churches emerging to pick up the baton as providers of elementary education for local children. The following voluntary societies were set up to do this:

- in 1808 – the foundation of the Royal Lancasterian Society (later renamed the British and Foreign Schools Society in 1814) (*Protestant*)
- in 1811 – the foundation of the National Society (*Church of England*)
- in 1838 – the foundation of the Wesleyan Education Committee (*Methodist*)
- in 1847 – the foundation of the Catholic Poor School Society (*Roman Catholic*).

These four societies received funding from their various member churches and local benefactors and then relied upon the government for grant assistance.

The full title of the Church of England's society was 'The National Society for Promoting the Education of the Poor in the Principles of the Established Church throughout England and Wales'. This will be the focus of the study of this book as it marks 200 years since the National Society began.

As a result of the government's ability to grant 50 per cent of all building costs, churches were able to set up schools in church halls and vicarages and to establish teacher training colleges alongside. Anglican schools grew rapidly after 1811. By 1815, every diocese was consulting the National Society and 100,000 children were going to school. By 1835, that number had grown to 1,000,000. Religious instruction was central to the curriculum and Her Majesty's Inspectors (HMIs) were set up (Anglican HMIs needed approval from the Archbishops).

1870–1902

After this period of expansion, it became clear that further provision to cover the country would need funding greater than was being realized by voluntary subscription and the government was required to act, resulting in the 1870 Education Act.

The 1870 Education Act

This initial act created School Boards whose job was to provide schools (board schools) in places where the churches were unable to do so. This was done by the levying of rates. An enduring part of this act was a clause defining the nature of religious instruction in board schools (or any subsequent school without a religious character). Board schools were not required to provide religious instruction but normally did, the requirement being that 'No religious catechism or religious formulary which is distinctive of any particular denomination shall be taught in the school.' In other words, board schools could teach the Creed, the Lord's Prayer, the Ten Commandments and doctrine as long as they did not use the actual words of the catechism. The creation of board schools paralleling voluntary schools has generally been known as 'the dual system', an example of the Church in partnership with the State.

1902–44

Within another generation it became clear that education in voluntary schools needed to be further enabled by a coordinated system of elementary education, resulting in the 1902 Education Act.

The 1902 Education Act

This act created Local Education Authorities (LEAs) that were to replace School Boards and had the overall responsibility for funding a common system of elementary education in a local area. At this point in time, just after the Boer War, it was clear that the nation needed its voluntary schools and that it could not afford to replace them. Churches were required to bring their school buildings up to a higher standard. Accommodation was worked out at 8 sq. ft per child up to around 1900. By 1909, it was 10 sq. ft (a size that would now be considered pitifully small).

Under huge controversy, Church schools became funded by the rates. Many Free Churches took this moment to hand their schools over to the LEAs who were generally able to provide a better standard of building and a higher level of teacher pay. At a time when it seemed possible that church school provision would end, the Anglican and Roman Catholic churches fought strongly for their retention.

During the period before the next educational landmark act of parliament in 1944, secondary education (which was for fee payers and scholarship pupils) began to be developed by the LEAs. Although the 1936 Act allowed for Special Agreement Schools which were senior elementary schools, the churches could not afford to further invest in secondary education while also bringing their junior schools up to government standard.

1944–80

Directly after the Second World War there was a united vision to reconstruct education and the skilful conversation between Rab Butler, the prime minister and William Temple, the Archbishop of Canterbury, resulted in the 1944 Education Act.

The 1944 Education Act

Central to this act was the division of education into Primary, Secondary and Tertiary stages. There was also the possibility for two different statuses for Church schools: Voluntary Aided (VA) schools being principally governed by church appointed managers (governors who had to find a contribution to building costs but had greater control of appointments and religious education) and Voluntary Controlled (VC) which were equally governed by church and LEA governors (but which had to find 'no new money for school building, did not employ the teachers but could, if parents wished, provide religious education according to the trust deed'). The churches, in cooperation with the LEAs had to decide which status they desired for their schools and which age group they would serve.

The Church of England in most dioceses opted for a mixed provision of VA and VC status, reflecting the tension of control versus partnership and the balance between religious nurture and service provision. Considerable variation can be seen between different dioceses as to which status choice was made (e.g. the Dioceses of Blackburn and London opted almost exclusively for VA status while the Diocese of Oxford opted mainly for VC status). Most Anglican schools became primary.

The Roman Catholic Church opted only for VA schools but managed to develop a balance of provision between Primary and Secondary schools, reflecting their greater interest in religious nurture and in recruiting Catholics to all teaching posts.

The act also made new provision for religious education requiring every LEA to create an Agreed Syllabus for use in all, except the VA schools. Churches became stronger partners in the process of defining curriculum development. Collective worship was now held in all maintained schools and religious education was compulsory.

At the age of 11, children sat a system of tests (the 11-plus examination) which was a deciding factor in how they would next be educated. Secondary provision was divided into the three categories: grammar schools (with a more academic curriculum for the top 25% in the 11-plus exam), technical schools (with a more practical curriculum) and modern schools (both providing a mixture of provision for the 75% who were not selected for grammar school streaming and who were not deemed to be practical).

Year	Anglican	Roman Catholic	Anglican	Roman Catholic	Anglican Overall	Roman Catholic Overall
	Primary %	Primary %	Secondary %	Secondary %	All Pupils %	All Pupils %
1949	22.5	8.8	3.8	2.9	16.9	7.0
1959	18.8	9.7	3.1	4.4	12.9	7.7

The 1965 Circular 10/65

It soon became apparent that the tripartite secondary education system was a divisive system that did not offer equal benefit to all children. It was then that the Circular 10 appeared requesting LEAs to reorganize secondary education on comprehensive lines (i.e. a single secondary school for all children between the ages of 11 and 18 that became known as the comprehensive school). To achieve this, school sizes had to grow and in 1972 the school leaving age was raised to 16. This caught the churches out as they had been busy building small secondary modern schools to balance the existing grammar schools.

Year	Anglican	Roman Catholic	Anglican	Roman Catholic	Anglican Overall	Roman Catholic Overall
	Primary %	Primary %	Secondary %	Secondary %	All Pupils %	All Pupils %
1969	17	10.2	3.0	7.9	11.6	9.4
1979	16.6	9.0	3.7	8.8	10.6	8.9

It might be noted that Roman Catholic secondary school provision continued to expand to catch up with its stakeholding in primary provision while Anglican provision remained static.

The education acts between 1988 and 1996

Various education acts towards the end of the twentieth century continued to focus on governance, admissions, curriculum reform, inspection and localized LEA provision within the national system. The church continued to show commitment to its schools, developing its own church school inspection under the Section 23 measure. Religious education syllabuses now began to move from a 'confessional' to a more 'professional' delivery in a more pluralist culture. Church representatives remained deeply involved in the development of the religious education syllabus.

The Education Reform Act of 1988 brought in the National Curriculum, SATs, Local Management of Schools, Grant Maintained Schools and Open Admissions. The Conservative government brought new levels of accountability with Ofsted (Office for Standards in Education) inspections coming in 1992 and the church Section 13 inspections (later called Section 23 and then 48 inspections).

By the mid-1990s, most pupils were remaining in full-time education until the age of 18, a majority passing GCSEs and more going on to sit A levels. Standing Advisory Councils on Religious Education (SACREs) became compulsory for all LEAs to identify a locally agreed religious education syllabus to reflect the world faith of the area in the provision of appropriate religious education. the 1988 Education Act was memorable for its insistence that all worship was to be '*broadly* Christian' where it had previously been 'Christian'. This was built on the prior framework established in the 1944 Act that all pupils had to attend a daily act of worship.

The advent of a new Labour government in 1997 brought about a period when education was high on the public agenda, the new prime minister saying that his priorities were 'education, education and education'. The agenda was to usher in new reforms for schools. New Labour believed that 'Standards mattered more than structures.'

The education acts 1997–2010

The 1998 law clarified that 'schools with a religious character' (VA, VC or Foundation schools) were to be part of the menu of choice for parents selecting the best school for their child. The profound effect of this Act was to reduce infant class size. New Labour proceeded to show a strong support for the development of different schools with a religious character and new schools included those from wider faiths than Christian.

In 1998, the Church of England's General Synod commissioned Lord Ron Dearing to make recommendations for the development of Church schools, boldly stating that 'Church Schools stand at the centre of the Church's mission to the nation.' The resultant Dearing Report ('The Way Ahead Report', 2001) was to recommend targeting the building of 100 new church secondary schools, particularly in areas of deprivation, that Church schools should be both 'distinctively Christian and inclusive' and that focus should be made on how to attract Christian teachers into teaching.

Year	Anglican	Roman Catholic	Anglican	Roman Catholic	Anglican Overall	Roman Catholic Overall
	Primary %	Primary %	Secondary %	Secondary %	All Pupils %	All Pupils %
1999	17.7	9.6	4.8	9.8	12.4	9.7
2002	18.2	9.6	4.8	9.7	12.4	9.6

During this period, the New Labour administration was to leave a legacy whereby money was put into refurbishing and re-equipping schools, where teaching assistants became a common feature in schools, where class sizes decreased and where expansion was made in Early Years, Sure Start and Children's Centres but where testing and results became more dominant, causing open competition between schools. Ofsted grew in power as the final judge of 'outstanding, good, satisfactory or failing' schools. The National Society mirrored this by the creation of a SIAS (Statutory Inspection of Anglican Schools), with the Section 48 measure replacing the old Section 23 measure in 2005 to assess a school's Christian ethos, religious education, collective worship and leadership and management. Over time, it also became apparent that Diocesan Boards of Education (DBEs) were going to be required to be providers of service and to be held accountable for school improvement.

A positive feature of this period was New Labour's creation of the Academy Programme overseen by Lord Adonis, whereby the most deprived educational areas in the country were identified as being places where new investment could take place by the creation of new secondary schools that were sponsored by an investor who would also supply fresh thinking and impetus. The Church of England was quick to engage with this as a means of adding to its secondary school stock in accordance with the Dearing Report recommendations. Other Christian sponsor bodies to do so were the Oasis Trust and the United Learning Trust.

Overview statistics of public education: Comparing Church of England, Roman Catholic and voluntary schools

	1870–1		1900–1		1925–6		2010–11	
	Schools	Pupils	Schools	Pupils	Schools	Pupils	Schools	Pupils
Church of England	6,724	1,439,428	11,734	2,811,956	9,992	2,081,458	4,600	959,455
Roman Catholic	383	113,490	1,054	400,546	1,141	413,575	2,001	725,225
Other voluntary	1,681	459,761	1,532	517,049	493	125,925	228	119,515
Total voluntary	8,788	2,012,679	14,320	3,729,551	11,626	2,620,958	6,829	1,804,195
Board and Council/Community	0	0	5,806	2,884,295	9,101	4,419,066	13,360	5,596,195
TOTAL	8,788	2,012,679	20,126	6,613,846	20,727	7,040,024	20,189	7,400,390
Church of England voluntary (%)	76.5	71.5	81.9	75.4	85.9	79.4	67.3	53.1
Church of England total (%)	76.5	71.5	58.3	42.5	48.2	29.6	22.7	13.0

However, the Roman Catholic Church did not commit to the Academy Programme, deeming the independent nature of each academy to be contrary to its policy in education (as each Academy no longer related to the local authority but directly to the Secretary of State for Education via a Board of Trustees, a relationship which was considered to be a possible threat to the school's link to the diocese).

2011 onwards

The celebration of 200 years of Anglican contribution to the maintained system of education has taken place under a cloud of uncertainty offered by the educational policy of a new coalition government elected in 2010. The first act through parliament was an Academies Act that broadened the concept of 'Academies' from being needy schools experiencing new investment to all outstanding schools as measured by Ofsted, a status for all schools to aspire to. The new wave of Academies encouraged all schools to explore independent status, those currently judged as outstanding being the first to convert and those failing being thrust into new sponsorship. At the same time, parent and teacher groups were invited to bid to open new Academies called 'Free schools', where they felt that the local authority was not meeting the needs of their children. The drive towards individual school autonomy seems to be designed to leave the local authority to whither as a partner and to allow new private educational services to emerge. While the English Baccalaureate (without religious education) has been introduced, there has been a cut in PGCE places for religious education, and a National Curriculum review and an HE White Paper are on the horizon.

Part One

The Historical Story

1

The Political Theology of Joshua Watson

Robert Wickham

Abstract

The founder of National Society in 1811 was Joshua Watson, a lay businessman who devoted much of his life and money to the development of societies which adhered to impeccable high church principles, determined by the Church–State relationship.

This chapter will use the narrative theology of the ethic of conviction to discern Joshua Watson's legacy. It will particularly explore the theme of establishment and education, with specific reference to the origins of the National Society, and the 1830's political, democratic, educational and ecclesial reform.

Keywords
High church, Hackney Phalanx, reform, establishment, the National Society

---

Setting the scene: The high church movement and the Hackney Phalanx

The high church movement, of which the Hackney Phalanx was a major component, began in the late seventeenth century. High church emphasized the political and Catholic nature of the Church of England, rooted within the divine basis of the relationship between the Church and the State, the importance of the divine rights of both Monarchy and Episcopacy and a great dedication to the importance of liturgy, sacraments and the catechism as an expression of these divine rights.

In the eighteenth century, the key players among the high churchmen were George Horne, William Jones and William Stevens. They gloried in the term 'Catholic', spoke vociferously against the schism suggested by dissenters and espoused the theology that there is no salvation outside the Church of England, while referring to others as schismatic's, infidels and apostates (Matheson, 1923,

p. 9). Indeed, with the growing calls for the emancipation of the Roman Catholic Church, which was eventually achieved in 1829, there was much to shout about, and much to be threatened by.

The high church movement worked in the shadow of widespread political and industrial revolution. Most notably the American War of Independence and the French Revolution both demonstrated the overthrowing of political and ecclesial orders and both left the late Hanoverian political nation and church 'shaken and stirred' (Burns, 2000, p. 200).

In France, the French Revolution confirmed the worst suspicions of the ultimate aims of radical politics. *The Times* newspaper reported in September 1789 that the French revolutionaries had ordered all church plate to be melted down for coinage as a bold and wise regulation which would 'not hurt anyone' (Varley, 2002, p. 27). Then between 1793–4, church property was looted, church buildings were desecrated, and bishops and clergy were driven into exile, imprisoned and killed, for they were seen as an extension of power and the dominant state.

As a response, William Stevens, as a high churchman, fought in the propaganda war against the revolution. He suggested that the State could only be understood when seen under the lordship of God, emphasizing the importance of the relationship between the two, but that in no way was the Church a department of the State. He even brought shelter for those in exile.

For the high churchmen, the divine relationship between the Church and the State was essential. Fuelled by the teachings of John Hutchinson (1674–1737) as opposed to those of John Locke (1632–1704), their 'orthodox' political theology (associated with the Caroline Divines) embodied a critique of the apparently secular theories of government (Nockles, 1994, p. 45). Such secular theories were dismissed as undogmatic moralism, which celebrated the self as an expression of Pelagianism as opposed to recognizing the sovereignty of God. As Archdeacon Daubeny stated, 'When the State came into being, these two separate Kingdoms became united in the same civil society, but in this case, the Union, being an accidental circumstance, did not affect the original independent right of either party.' In other words, both were in an exclusive relationship with each other, but this did not mean they had become merged or shared the same identity (as opposed to that perceived in France).

Such a high view of State and monarchy was derived from scripture (Isaiah 49.23), which arguably enshrined royal supremacy. This reflects the sacred, quasi-religious character of the Office of the Monarchy, as mentioned in the Coronation service, which stated that the Church must be protected by the monarch. Indeed, this Jure Divino basis of monarchy, along with its constitutional order was linked to that basis of episcopacy and ecclesiastical order. This was a view held by King George III, who exercised his Royal prerogative enshrined in the Coronation Oath by refusing to support the Bill for Roman Catholic emancipation, overruling the Prime Minister Pitt the Younger in 1801. Indeed, for the high churchman, the calls for disestablishment were seen as a desecration of the State, because of its quasi-sacred qualities.

In addition, the high churchmen also championed the apostolic nature of the Church of England, as opposed to the claims of evangelicals, who championed the principles of sola scriptura and private judgement, or the claims of the Roman Catholic Church whose claims lay in the authority of the Pope. Principal characters such as Daubeny and Van Mildert argued that through the principal of Apostolic Succession, the Church had the right to interpret Holy Scripture, and as such advocated that the Book of Common Prayer be used as the churches response to scripture. In addition to its emphasis on the divine basis of the threefold ministry, and the linked succession of the Apostles in the line of the succession of bishops, the Church of England represented the via media between the rival theories of Rome and Geneva.[1] The established national church was therefore both Protestant and Catholic, for in reality the two were compatible. Such ecclesiology highlighted those churches which had disregarded Episcopal government as dissenters, separatists or at worse schismatic, for the Episcopal orders were an essential mark of the True Church.

However, the beginnings of the nineteenth century saw a number of deaths of the pre-eminent high churchmen. Boucher died in 1804, Horsley in 1806 and William Stevens in 1807, and the mantle of the high church theology and mission naturally fell upon Joshua Watson who became the focus of the group. Hackney became the centre of the group's activities, with the development of the Hackney Phalanx. It became concerned with nurturing ecclesiastical and civil contacts, encouraging and criticizing the literary activities of colleagues, and promoting the reform of the Church of England along impeccable high church lines. As the influence of the Hackney Phalanx grew, so did a concern for practical piety and practical charity. The Phalanx saw themselves as loyal servants of the Church and her leaders. In the light of this, the relationship between Church and State was played out in a variety of ways, the provision of education, church buildings, and various printed publications and through changes in government.

Introducing Joshua Watson

Joshua Watson expounded the virtues of wisdom, knowledge and joy (Churton, 1855, p. 12). Indeed, he was an eminently good man, demonstrating many qualities, including an innocence of life, a single hearted sincerity, a gentleness of word and conversation, duty through selfless acts of mercy 'to be unobserved in the eyes of good men'. According to Churton, Watson's biographer, Watson demonstrated disinterestedness towards himself, and a pure independence of character, where he desired only works of piety, and sustained charity. Furthermore, he adds that 'Watson would never pronounce, or use the pronoun I'.

Watson's influence was to be felt both nationally and internationally, and his words of wisdom were appreciated by many. Vernon Harcourt (Archbishop of York 1807–47) stated that 'When we were in doubt we asked for Joshua Watson, and what he said, we did.'

Indeed, following Watson's death in 1855, the Committee of the National Society (founded by Watson) described him in the following way:

> The Committee must also record their sense of severe loss which the Church of England has sustained in the death of Joshua Watson Esq. who not only took a leading part in the formation of the Society, but also acting as its Treasurer during a period of 31 years; and was, both by his wise counsels and his munificent gifts, a most effective promoter of its interests. (Rivington, 1867, p. vi)

As a man of theology, Watson spoke with a degree of reverential dread against all dogmatizing on the higher mysteries of the faith, and his desire was that his acceptance of the faith as the Church of England taught it led to his spirit of practical duty. As was stated in his Eulogy:

> Let the sense that you are engaged in your present duty free you from your anxiety. While thus engaged you may have an entire conviction that whatever happens is for the best. And whatsoever is good for any of the ends which we are bound to serve, is doing God's work. (Rivington, 1867, p. 24)

Joshua Watson was born on 9 May 1771 at Tower Hill, City of London, the second son of John Watson, a wine merchant of Tower Hill. Joshua's elder brother, the Revd John James Watson (1767–1839), was both Rector of Hackney and Archdeacon of St Albans, and the two brothers became prominent national churchmen of the day. Joshua and Mary Watson had two daughters; the first died unmarried, but the second, Mary, married Henry Michell Wagner (1792–1870), vicar of Brighton, in 1838 (Nockles, 2004, p. 36).

From an early age, Watson was seen to be a calm and content child. Having been observed playing by George III, the monarch was heard to have said, 'Who is that happy boy?'

Between the ages of 13 and 15, Watson attended the City of London Commercial School, and then in 1786 he entered into his father's wine business in the Counting House, where he learnt many skills concerning philanthropy and good governance. The wine trade flourished as a result of a series of government contracts associated with the Napoleonic wars. These factors became an important formation in Watson's financial and political acumen.

Watson's main passion was his works of piety and charity. For most of his life, his aim was to employ his wealth, and still more his time, his labour, and indeed all his powers of mind and body in the service of the giver. When Watson died, it was reputed that he had given over half his wealth away in charitable donations.

This conviction of carrying out God's work shaped the rest of his life, and Joshua Watson formed close friendships with numerous like-minded people in the Hackney Phalanx. The most prominent members included: Henry Handley Norris (1771–1850); Joshua's elder brother, the Revd John James Watson (1767–1839); William Van Mildert (1765–1836), Rector of St Mary le Bow, City of London (afterwards Bishop of Llandaff and Durham); and Christopher Wordsworth (1774–1846), Master of Trinity College, Cambridge.

Watson and the Phalanx worked hard to oversee their various religious, educational, missionary, and philanthropic activities. These were shaped by their high church principles, and were grounded in their ideology for the Church of England's unique relationship with the State. These societies included: the National Society (from 1811–42), the Society for the Propagation of the Gospel in foreign parts (SPG), the SPCK (from 1797–1833), the Clergy Orphan Society (from 1814), the Additional Curates Society (from 1837) and the Incorporated Church Building Society (from 1817). Furthermore, they shaped the first British package of International Aid to those, in Leipzig, Germany, who had suffered at the hands of Napoleon in 1814.

In addition, Watson and the Phalanx also helped to shape the ecclesiology, theology and missiology of the Church of England. This was determined through the appointment and developing of new bishoprics in different parts of the world, through the Colonial Bishop's Fund from 1841, through Higher Education (in developing Kings College London and Durham University), and through a series of periodicals such as the *British Critic* (from 1811) and the *Christian Remembrancer* (from 1818).

In 1814, Watson retired from the wine trade, and devoted himself fully to these activities and societies. On account of this charitable work, he received many gifts and accolades, including ornamental presents from the kings of

Prussia and Saxony, and a diploma of honour at the University of Hamburg, was elected a member of the Hamburg Patriotic Society for the Encouragement of the Liberal and Useful Arts, and was awarded a Doctor of Law degree from the University of Oxford, which he tried to refuse. Although he never personally crossed the English Channel, Watson assumed that the fledgling Anglican Communion was his concern, although the issue concerning Watson's motives are unclear within a contemporary debate surrounding the wider influences of colonialism.

Watson's later years were beset by domestic hardship. His wife, Mary, died in 1831 and his brother died in 1839. These losses, along with that of his daughter, Mary, in 1840, forced him to sell his Westminster house in 1840, and move back to Clapton to live with his sister-in-law, Mrs J. J. Watson. He also made regular visits to his friend the Revd Edward Churton, his later biographer, at Crayke, near York.

Watson was regarded as a shy, reserved, and self-effacing man, but he had a great gift for gaining and retaining friendships. His friends found him a 'conversationalist of wit and charm, never short of amusing stories and anecdotes, especially relating to his favourite author, Dr Samuel Johnson'. He remained active until the end of his life. He died at Clapton on 30 January 1855, and was buried on 7 February in the family vault at St John at Hackney church.

The battle for ecclesial and secular politics

Many changes occurred during Joshua Watson's lifetime, which threatened the perceived validity of the theology of the high churchmen and those engaged within the Hackney Phalanx. These included Roman Catholic emancipation in 1829, the rise of dissenting churches, the threat of revolution from abroad and the liberal agenda in English politics from 1830 onwards.

The period of greatest political and ecclesial upheaval was between 1828 and 1835. These changes were not planned for, but occurred organically as a result of overruling political circumstances. Ertman names these as a series of general elections, a series of defeated coalition governments, wider European pressures, increasing sense of power from dissenting Christians, and the development of the rights of religious minorities. Each of these influences led to a fundamental break in the constitutional order within the United Kingdom, and significantly reduced the role of the Established Church, which seriously dented its confidence of its sense of purpose.

Even though the political influence of the Church of England became diluted, and church attendance and affiliation became a matter of personal choice, the Church remained Established, and retained certain legal rights, responsibilities and political powers. As an example, in August 1833 the Whig government, which seemed to be so sacrilegious and anti-clerical, rejected a radical motion which would have ended the system of voluntary education and replaced it with a centrally organized State. Instead it voted for an annual subsidy to assist the endeavours of the Church to provide for the education of the poor in Great Britain.[2] Such a vision for education kept the position of the Church of England as a national provider of religious instruction, and therefore became a key argument in the failure of the calls for disestablishment. Had it not been for the enterprise and vision of Joshua Watson in founding the National Society 22 years earlier, the Church may have lost its relationship with the State completely.

The battle for education

Prior to 1811, charity schools, and small private educational establishments that were overseen by the Church of England, provided the State with the education which it required. There was no provision for any national, comprehensive vision of education. Indeed, the State was apathetic in relation to the role and form of education. However, the opposing political and ecclesial forces which played out in the early nineteenth century were felt very acutely in the development of British education. The ever growing urban population, migrating from parts of England, Ireland and beyond, highlighted the problems of illiteracy and poverty. In London alone the population grew from 959,000 in 1801 to 2,362,000 in 1851(Dennis, 1984, p. 22). This population was mixed and unsettled, and the Church of England struggled to keep up with such population changes. In addition, the evangelical revival movement, realized in the work of the Clapham Sect, began to flex its muscles in education. Initially, this took the form of the Sunday school movement, which realized new patterns of work brought about by the increasing demand for child labour precluded children from school attendance. The evangelical movement was able to recruit its volunteers from the many middle-class converts who had a passion for rescuing the children of the poor. In 1787, there were just 201 Sunday schools educating 10,232 children in England. By 1803, this figure had raised to 844,728 children in England attending Sunday schools.

In 1804, Sir Thomas Bernard, through the Society for Bettering the Conditions of the Poor began research on how to develop an educational system. He discovered that most day schools were charging 3d per week for the education, which precluded many very poor children from receiving it. This was despite some schools receiving huge endowments. His conclusions were presented by Samuel Whitbread as a Private Members Bill to parliament, which introduced the proposal to levy local rates upon the growing populations by vestries or magistrates to provide elementary education for poor children (between the ages of 7 and 14), through an extension of the Poor law (Murphy, 1971, p. 3).

To the forefront of the debate for providing a system of elementary education stepped two principal characters, Joseph Lancaster, pursuing a Monitorial system of Education and Andrew Bell, advocating the Madras System, learned while studying in India. Their ecclesiology differed, as did their vision for the place of religion in schools. Lancaster, a Quaker, favoured a non-denominational scheme, with an insistence on the use of the Bible, but no catechism or peculiar religious tenets were to be used. In addition, children were to be encouraged to attend church with their parents. From 1808, his followers became known as the Royal Lancasterian Society, and then from 1815 as the British and Foreign School Society (BFSS). The BFSS had the aim of promoting 'the education of the Labouring and Manufacturing Classes of Society of every religious persuasion'.

In contrast, Bell, as a committed member of the Church of England, published a sketch of a 'National Institution for Training up the Children of the Poor'. This included an insistence upon instruction of liturgy and catechism, and attendance at Church of England churches on Sundays (Burgess, 1958, p. 20).

The ecclesiology which Bell demonstrated was drawn to the attention of the Hackney Phalanx, and in the summer of 1811, Joshua Watson, Henry Norris and John Bowles met to discuss a Church of England response to the challenge of widespread non-Church of England education, which seemed to threat not only the position of the Church as the nation's educator, but also the very relationship of how the State related to Christian educators other than the Established Church.

On the 16 October 1811, under the chairmanship of the Archbishop of Canterbury, Charles Manners Sutton, the National Society for the Education of the Poor in the Principles of the Established Church (the National Society) was born. 'The sole object of the Society shall be to instruct and educate the poor in suitable learning, works of industry and the principles of the Established Religion according to the Established Church.'

The rationale behind this was laid out in the introduction of the first Annual Report:

The National religion should be made the foundation of National education, and should be the first and chief thing taught to the poor, according to the excellent liturgy and catechism provided by our church and for that purpose, must be admitted by all friends to the Establishment; for if the great body of the Nation be educated in other principles than those of the Established Church, the natural consequences must be to alienate the minds of the people from it, or render them indifferent to it, which may, in succeeding generations, prove fatal to the Church and to the State itself. (Rivington, 1812, p. 5)

John Bowles further described such a relationship between the National Society and the State as 'an establishment interwoven with the Constitution of the Country'.

Once set up, the National Society moved quickly to raise funds for the creation of schools through private means. Just one week later, on 21 October 1811, the plea went out for financial support from the public, to all who were 'attached to the Constitution of Church and State', for such religious duty as an early discipline was of great importance in terms of happiness and welfare of the poor. Indeed, such exposure to liturgy and catechism were both 'powerful instruments' for infusing into the minds good knowledge and forming them to good habits. The very lowest classes of society would benefit and the vision might become universal. However, the plea continued. This could not be done without the general cooperation of the higher and middle classes of society, for their affluence would furnish the means and their attention and inspiration must forward the execution and bring it to perfection.

The Society itself was constructed to exacting high church ideals concerning monarchy. Despite the Lancasterian Society using the term 'Royal', the Royal Charter of Incorporation of the National Society from 1817 was signed by King George III. The Charter stated that the Society had been created in the best interests of the Realm, to promote and encourage the moral and religious education throughout all classes of people.

Episcopal ecclesiology and inherited Church–State ideology were at the heart of this expression of establishment. The Archbishop of Canterbury was recognized as the President, the Vice President would be the Archbishop of York, and all other diocesan bishops of both York and Canterbury Provinces. Furthermore, ten other persons, either Temporal Peers or members of the Privy Council would be further Vice Presidents. The Charter named Joshua Watson as its first Treasurer, a role which was to 'continue during his natural life', or until he should decline to continue in such office, or be removed following a decision by the committee. The Society also acted with the full support of the Prime Minster,

Earl Liverpool, who vouched to appoint peers who were blameless in character, with irreproachable orthodoxy.

By 1813, the subscriptions to the National Society were increasing, including £210 from the Prince Regent, £500 from each of the Universities of Oxford and Cambridge, and numerous £1 subscriptions. In the first year alone, some £22,000 was raised, and the task of creating a new school in every parish in the land had begun.

Grants were initially issued after applicants had satisfied three categories. First, only a proportion of the sum required would be issued, forcing the local parishes to find match funding from local sources, although larger grants were offered to poorer areas. Secondly, the school had to open free from debt, and would be required to write a statement to this end. Finally, there needed to be a secure tenure of the land for the schools. Freehold was not a specific stipulation, but the committee did insist that any leases should be long-term leases.

Three further stipulations stated that only specific forms of liturgy were used, that children must attend Divine Service, and that any books used had to be taken from a specific and recognized list given through SPCK, in order to regulate the teaching material against any dissenting ideology.

The grants issued were to be strategic, and governed by geographical and sociological rather than denominational reasons.

By 1815, with the growth in the numbers of the school, the Third and Fourth Annual Reports make it clear that the Society needed to be reshaped. One arm of the Society was to relate to the processes of education, and help towards the shaping of policy and teacher training, while the other would dedicate itself exclusively to the building of new schools.

As influence of the National Society grew, new committees across dioceses were created, along with the creation of new Diocesan Boards for schools. The Central School was in Baldwin Gardens in London, and international links in Nova Scotia and the Netherlands were also developed. The number of English and Welsh schools also grew, with some 360 schools being mentioned in 1814, with over 60,000 children receiving the benefits of religious instruction, all overseen by this relationship between Church and State.

By 1815, 564 schools had been created, supporting 97,920 children, and with many more in the pipeline, the National Society had soon reached its first milestone of over 100,000 children attending its schools. In addition, now every diocese in England was consulting the Society.[3]

Despite the great success of the National Society schools, parliament refused to initially endorse their form of education.

In 1816, Lord Brougham reported to parliament that a very large number of poor children were wholly without means of instruction. However, following the emancipation of the Roman Catholic Church in 1829, and then the Great Reform Act of 1832 the relationship between Church and State became far tenser, as described in the preceding chapter, and education became a battleground.

The new Whig government of 1830 however did recognize the huge numbers of people attending schools through the churches provision, and decided to get involved to develop further this elementary vision of education, despite the many calls for disestablishing the Church of England.

In 1842, Joshua Watson decided to resign as Treasurer of the National Society, stating both ill health and that he felt that the National Society had sold out on its principles in that it had finally agreed to receive conditional state aid. The relationship between Church and State in education had gone too far, and his beloved National Society would, from now on need to respond to the State rather than the other way round. He felt that the Society should only be subject to her bishops, and he preferred to retire rather than join in an act which would virtually subject them to the House of Commons. This moment was recorded in the Annual Report of 1842, in the following statement: 'Your committee have enjoyed the benefits of his enlightened council and unwearied application.'

Joshua Watson was held in very high esteem by his colleagues at the National Society, as this statement demonstrates, and he never fully retired from his association with the Society. For example, in 1848, the Bishop of Norwich suggested that in order to access a great legacy, and further funding, the National Society should make optional the catechetic element of the curriculum. Watson responded with the words, 'You must bid much higher, if you expect us to sell the Churches catechism.' He remained resolute in his beliefs to the last.

Four years before Joshua Watson's death in 1855, the national census in 1851 revealed much about the nature of religious observance in the United Kingdom. It was reported that over 2 million children attended something in the region of 17,000 Church schools which were formally registered (Dennis, 2001). This was an incredible legacy incepted at a meeting just 40 years previously at Joshua Watson's home in Hackney.

These developments eventually led to the 1870 and the 1944 Education Acts, which enshrined in law the centrality of religious instruction and acts of worship, but also set up the dual system of education which exists today. Both VA and community schools operate in adherence to their deeds of governance.

The schools of the National Society, and the Society itself had worked through several years of turbulence. The Society had been forced to compromise in a number of its principles, such as insisting that the bishop oversaw every school, and its unique position as the established sole education provider in England. However, in our present day system of education in 2011, the vision of Joshua Watson can still be seen. The National Society continues to work with DBEs and through the work of the Department for Education.

Conclusion

Joshua Watson's legacy can be felt in many parts of the Church of England. Indeed, it can be argued that the very established nature of the Church of England remains as a result of this legacy. He was driven by his simple theology, by his desire for better conditions and education for the poor, and for his distinctive ecclesiology. This legacy also extends far beyond education, but it reaches into the very heart of government, international relations, justice, and how one driven individual uses his own financial means in his causes. It is no wonder that he was, in his day, described as the greatest layman in England.

Key questions

1. How might we learn from Joshua Watson for our Mission Today?
2. Is Joshua Watson's worldview relevant for the Church and Church schools today?
3. Is the Church of England still established, and what does this look like?
4. Should the Church of England develop liturgy purely for schools?
5. To what extent are bishops overseers of Christian education?

Notes

1 Referring to both the Roman Catholic Church and Protestant Calvinism.
2 Canon Charles Smyth, Fellow of Corpus Christi College, Cambridge, on the occasion of the One Hundred and Fiftieth Anniversary of the Foundation of the Society, on 12 October 1961, found at: www.churchofengland.org/media/1243126/microsoft%20word%20-%20150th%20anniversary%20lecture.pdf (accessed 3 August 2011).
3 'The Story of the National Society Pamphlet' taken from *Pamphlets in Education*, vol. 17, 1950–65, Church Army Press.

2

High Church and Evangelical Legacies to Mission in Church Schools

Howard J. Worsley

Abstract

This chapter stems from an observation that Church schools in the twenty-first century evidenced the partnership of both the high church (Catholic) and the low church (evangelical) wings of the Church of England. That observation has led to an historic investigation as to the primal influences of those ecclesiological groups and then a theological reflection on their resultant mission. It is written in two sections.

The first section explores the historical context of schooling in the nineteenth century, detailing how both the high church Hackney Phalanx and the low church Clapham Sect were both initially involved in bringing mass education, working with their respective figureheads Joshua Watson and William Wilberforce.

The second section reflects upon the historical legacy, considering how the high church influence became gradually more dominant in its missional impact. Observations are made that the nineteenth century brought the combined energies of low and high church thinking to bear on education and thereby produced a balance of which the political effects were strategic and effective.

Keywords
Legacy, high and low church, theology of mission

Prior to 1811, schooling was not widely available, although the wealthier classes had access to public schools (many of which had originally been set up to provide a service to the poor) and the lower classes had sporadic access to the charitable schools loosely coordinated by the SPCK. Those without financial resources might otherwise have attended one of the various Sunday schools pioneered by Robert Raikes and colleagues or one of the newly formed 'ragged schools'.

The establishment of the National Society in 1811 was aimed at providing a controlled system for the whole country whereby every parish had a school that was run by a trained teacher. Their particular focus was to be on the poorer classes as was apparent in National Society's full name, the National Society for Promoting the Education of the Poor in the Principles of the Established Church.

The nineteenth century evidenced the struggle for influence in educational provision in which the two main providers of Church schools were eventually to be the Church of England and the Roman Catholics (who were to set up the Catholic Poor School Committee in 1847). Before this, in the early stages of the battle for education, there was support from the dissenters (the term given to non-conforming Protestants) who were also interested in offering education to poor children. This stake in education was largely handed over to the State by the dissenters in 1870, when a new education act promised better teacher pay and a higher standard of school building for board schools not under the control of the Church. Apart from a small number of Methodist primary schools still in operation, this policy has continued to the present.

This chapter, written 200 years after the formation of the National Society, is an examination of the competing ecclesiological influences that were in England, particularly in the Church of England in the nineteenth century, and how the various church factions responded theologically and practically to the opportunities in education. A discussion on the legacy of this influence is then made on how the Church of England is currently engaging with the school network in the twenty-first century.

General political context of the early nineteenth century

The social climate of the early nineteenth century was a hotbed of unrest as influences from the continent were felt on class structures, on industrialization, on population migration and on education. In his earlier book detailing the religious attitudes of lay people in the period leading up to this, W. M. Jacob (1996, p. 16) details:

> Religion permeated every area of people's lives. The ringing of the church bell for curfew or to call people to prayer or work ordered the day in most towns and villages.

His subsequent work, *The Clerical Profession in the Long Eighteenth Century* (2007), shows the relative education of Anglican clergy and their engagement in providing education for the people for whom they lived and worked.

In the late eighteenth century, the upper classes generally had little interest in educating the cultural development of the working class and the effects of the revolutionary spirit in Europe served to reinforce attitudes that were unsympathetic to developing the critical faculties of the population at large. There was also a growing fear that a lack of education might provide social ferment just as much as a provision of education would cause dissatisfaction. It might be noted that the second half of the nineteenth century did see the increase of crime, pauperism, riots and strikes.

Similarly, the working classes had little appetite for education in that the widespread employment of children for labour was deemed to add financial benefit to poorer homes. Indeed, child labour continued to increase until after 1850.

This general state of inertia was further compounded by the sense that the voluntary school system that had evolved was adequately successful and needed no intervention from parliament. Into this scenario, the Church's interest in education was not without problems as it was hindered by internal friction and denominational competition. An example of how religious conflict delayed the establishment of a national educational system was the failure of the 1843 Factory Bill when non-conformists and Catholics joined forces to oppose legislation limiting child labour and providing initial education. Their objection was that the children would have to be taught by headmasters from the Church of England, have the catechism as a part of the syllabus, be present at liturgical services and be required to attend Sunday services.

Against this state of stalemate between competing factions however, there was a general cultural awareness of poverty and the need to address it. This was exemplified by the Poor Law Bill brought in by Samuel Whitbread in 1807, the first part of which dealt with education, suggesting that every parish be responsible for the provision of at least two years of education for every child between the ages of 7 and 14. Similarly, the Factory Acts of 1833, 1844 and 1867 all contributed towards a national policy for education and put restrictions on child labour and offered alternative opportunities of education for children.

Stronger academic thinking was also beginning to emerge, evidenced by Samuel Coleridge's last and seminal book, *On the Constitution of the Church and State*, published in 1830, four years before his death. His ideas on education were to be hugely influential to subsequent Anglican thinkers as they strove to offer a free education for all. His romantic vision was for a partnership between his idea of the National Church and his idea of the State in responding to Roman Catholic emancipation. He argued for 'a law of balance' between the two forces of permanence and progression within the State which would allow for a creative tension in which national educational programmes could operate.

General denominational context of the early nineteenth century

Within the Church of England, the influence of emergent Roman Catholicism was a growing concern. Anti-Catholic feelings were still stirred by the stories of the burnings of Cranmer, Ridley and Latimer and the executions of Thomas More and John Fisher remained within the collective memory. The Irish migration, particularly to Liverpool and London, began after the Irish rebellion of 1798 and this brought a steady stream of Catholic labourers willing to accept lower wages and to live in contained areas. Many Protestants were also confused by the profound effects of the high church, seen in the workings of the Hackney Phalanx who were to develop into the Tractarian movement which began to publish high church thinking from the 1830s. Against this backcloth, in the half century between 1778 and 1829, parliament systematically dismantled the structure of anti-Catholic legislation that had developed since the Reformation. It has been estimated that in 1770 there was about 80,000 Catholics in England and Wales but by 1850 it had increased tenfold to about 750,000 (Morris, 2008, p. 15). Coleridge's *On the Constitution of the Church and State* (1830) was written in response to one of the several Catholic Emancipation Bills of the 1820s which proposed to open the Houses of Parliament to Roman Catholics. Coleridge was anxious to support the granting of Catholic Relief, but only if it were accompanied by securities to protect the national institutions from any attempt by Rome to establish a political base in England.

In those days, the Church of England's aspiration was to be a national church, expressing it's ministry with that of the universal Church Catholic. Prior to the Reformation it had obviously operated as the Catholic Church in England and afterwards it saw itself as a main stream of reform not of division (Chadwick, 1994, p. 10). Only the radical Protestants wanted a sect or 'a gathered Church' ministering exclusively to committed believers. Therefore, incorporated into the Church of England were the ranks of Anglican high churchmen and the evangelical low churchmen.

Specific Anglican context for the development of Church schools in the early nineteenth century

For the purposes of this brief chapter, there are two groups to be noted, the one being from an evangelical ecclesiology, the Clapham Sect and the other, the Hackney Phalanx (or the Clapton Sect), from a high church perspective. The Clapham Sect (c.1790–1830) was an influential evangelical group operating in Clapham in London at the beginning of the nineteenth century. In his book, *The Clapham Sect: How Wilberforce's Circle Changed Britain* (2010), Tomkins describes them as:

> a network of friends and families in England, with William Wilberforce as it's centre of gravity, who were powerfully bound together by their shared moral and spiritual values, by their religious mission and social activism, by their love of each other, and by marriage.

While being well known for their successful social reform in their role in abolishing slavery, they also founded several missionary and tract societies.

By contrast, the Hackney Phalanx was a loosely defined group of Anglican high churchmen who were similarly bound together to form a pressure group on the religious and political measures of the nineteenth century. They too were largely related by blood or marriage and 'remained to the end a body of friends, rather than an ecclesiastical or a religious party' (Webster, 1954, p. 18), linked around Joshua Watson. In his book, *Joshua Watson: The Story of a Layman 1771–1885*, Webster notes how it was Watson who breathed new life into SPCK before the formation of the National Society. Up until this point SPCK had been a catalyst for the spectacular growth of the charity school movement, offering advice to local groups in helping set them up and run them. It provided sets of rules, sample curriculum and training in best practice in the classroom.

In his scholarly work on Van Mildert and the high church movement of the nineteenth century titled *The Last of the Prince Bishops*, Varley (2002) details how it was that the relationship to SPCK was the organization around which church education policy was to be set up.

SPCK drew its membership from both the Clapham Sect and the Hackney Phalanx until the Religious Tract Society was established in 1799, taking the evangelical members with it who were disgruntled by SPCK's slow response to print a Welsh Bible, a deliberate action that portrayed their lack of interest for enthusiasm. It was at this point that the Clapham Sect joined forces with the dissenters and asked the memorable question, 'If Bibles were to be printed for

Wales, why not for the British Empire and the world?' They were then to go on and form the British and Foreign Bible Society (later called the Bible Society) in order to achieve this aim, in which they were not backed by the Hackney Phalanx.

This question of putting the Bible into the hands of all people was seen as naïve by the Phalanx who considered the project to be irresponsible due to interpretative issues and so got involved in the public debate, distancing themselves from the Bible Society and identifying themselves more closely with the work of SPCK. In the SPCK board meeting of January 1811, Joshua Watson made his first public speech to this effect, which resulted in the Phalanx's further identification with the SPCK in financial and administrative dealings. From this vantage point, working alongside Bishop Samuel Horsley, he moved to tidy up the work in school education in which SPCK was involved. This was to see the launch of the National Society.

Prior to this, Horsley's concern had been with the mixed provision of charity schools and Sunday schools where,

> The minds of the children of the very lowest orders are enlightened – that is to say, taught to despise religion and the laws of subordination. (1813, p. 157)

He wanted to stop the sporadic and unprofessional practice of independent education available through the voluntary providers and he had a vision for the Church of England to respond with a solution, offering their clergy as managers of the process.

SPCK now gave its long-term foothold in education over to Watson who established a committee called the National Society in opposition to the Royal Lancastrian Institution (RLI) who used the notion of royalty to describe the aspirations for their educational endeavours (Varley, 2002, p. 72). The RLI had been set up by a quaker called Joseph Lancaster (1778–1838) in 1808, in Borough Road, Southwark, where Lancaster had established a school in 1798 which was supported by the Clapham Sect, drawing mainly on evangelicals and dissenters. His methods were written up in a pamphlet titled *Improvements in Education* (1803), a document which drew heavily on the work of Andrew Bell.

The teaching method developed a monitorial system whereby older or more able children were put in charge of other pupils. The monitors were taught early in the day by the teacher, before the other children arrived. The Lancastrian system operated on a system of rewards and punishments, pupils would receive badges for good conduct or work, which when collected together could be traded for a toy. If their behaviour was less satisfactory, the countermeasures were the 'dunce's cap' or the more extreme measures of the pillory, being suspended from the ceiling in a basket or being forced to wear a wooden log around the neck. This system of elaborate punishments was designed to encourage children to feel a sense of shame and was considered preferential to causing physical pain.

The RLI was thus forced into direct rivalry with the National Society because of their common interest in educating the poor and their interest in doing so as an aspect of Christian commitment. The more politically astute Watson, however, was able to distance himself from the low church and the dissenters by appealing to the authority of the Established Church rather than a more diffuse Christian engagement. In the first report of the National Society, this was clearly defended by saying that, 'national religion should be made the groundwork of national education' (Churton, 1861, p. 91).

This thinking became widespread among those who supported the Hackney Phalanx and both bishops and Cambridge divines were canvassed for support.

At its inception, the National Society adopted as policy that schools would be run on the original Bell system (as opposed to the Lancastrian system beloved by those less committed to the Church of England). Andrew Bell (1753–1832) was a more influential figurehead than Lancaster, not only because it was him who had pioneered the monitorial system but also because he was an ordained priest. He developed his educational practice in 1787 when he was a chaplain in Madras in India to a number of British regiments for whom he oversaw an orphan asylum for the illegitimate and orphaned 'sons of officers'. He would say that he had observed some Malabar children teaching others the alphabet by drawing in the sand and so he developed a system where more able children would teach others less advanced. He was valued for being an able administrator and he regarded 'unsectarian religious teaching' to be a contradiction in terms.

Drawing on Bell's System, the National Society adopted a policy first to collect subscriptions and to build schools and secondly to encourage parishes to open their own schools. The first report of the National Society (Churton, 1861) further stipulated that,

> schools should be under the immediate inspection and government of those whose local knowledge would be likely to make better provision for each case, and who will naturally take a livelier interest in that which they have instituted and conducted themselves.

The new society then approved a motion whereby schools could use books only from the SPCK catalogue.

The SPCK remained a constant backcloth to the National Society, it's Bartlett's Buildings headquarters the meeting place and administrative centre for the Phalanx. It was this that led to ongoing workings with the evangelicals in that the more politically minded and pragmatic William Wilberforce remained in contact with SPCK. Indeed, Wilberforce showed huge appreciation for the National Society and gave generously to its funds as well as attending a number of their public meetings. In his diary in July 1814, after he had been to a meeting at the Central National School, Wilberforce wrote:

> children admirably taught, and general spirit delightful and animating – the difference between them and the Lancastrians very striking – exemplifying the distinction between church of England and Dissenterism – the intelligence, and fixed but not apparently nervous or feverish attention pleased me much. (1838, vol. 4, pp. 22–3)

This preference by Wilberforce for the National Society over the RLI continued after 1815, the point at which Lancaster finally broke away and called his Society the British and Foreign Schools Society, with Wilberforce as the Vice President. Wilberforce was persuaded to join the dissenting group. This popularity was shared with success in that by 1833, the National Society had 690 schools whereas the British and Foreign Schools Society had only 190 schools.

As the National Society accelerated forwards gaining widespread support across the country, Wilberforce continued to seek the support of the Phalanx for his cherished interest in the evangelization of India in which his involvement drew him to support the great Baptist missionary William Carey and the evangelical chaplains to the East India Company, but this non-establishment endeavour proved to be beyond Watson's ability to support and again the Phalanx parted company with evangelical vision. Commenting on Watson's politics, Varley (2002, p. 80) makes the appreciative and yet critical comment about this single-minded focus:

> Combined with his formidable administrative skills, this unassuming layman played a crucial role in revitalising his beloved Church of England. However, it is easy to criticise Watson's vision as narrowly High Church, parasitic on the creative energies of the Evangelical and Dissenting pioneers.

In this, of course, Watson was shaped by political circumstances as well as by his own convictions.

The theology of mission for the Clapham Sect and the Hackney Phalanx

The parting of the ways between Wilberforce and Watson was between two sects that were both involved in engaging nineteenth-century society with the Christian gospel via the Church's involvement in education. Both men sat on the same committees attending the same meetings but their theology of mission was different.

The term 'theology of mission' first appeared in print in an essay by Gerald Anderson (1961) that presented a tripartite diagram to represent his idea. In simple terms, it was the way in which the biblical text interacted with the faith community and the missional context, focused with an integrating theme. The theology of mission is concerned with those underlying principles of the faith which determine the methods and strategy of mission.

For both Wilberforce and Watson, the integrating theme was education and their missional context was schools focusing on the young and the poor but their understanding of the biblical text was different as was their understanding of the church universal.

For Wilberforce, as an evangelical, his fundamental understanding of the Bible as the Word of God led him to the conviction that it needed to be made available to all people as widely as possible. As a young MP, in the autumn of 1783, he read the New Testament on a journey to France and said afterwards

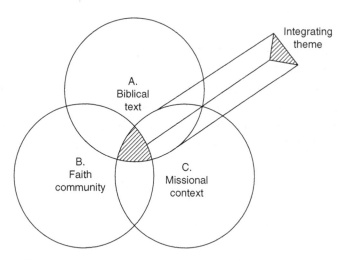

Figure 2.1 The tripartite nature of theology of mission (C. E. Van Engen, 1994)

that he 'became a new man as a result'. It was this Protestant zeal to remove any mediation from the scriptures that prompted Wilberforce to align himself with that group which withdrew from SPCK to set up the British and Foreign Bible Society in 1804. Thus he distanced himself in public debate from those who were less enthusiastic to print Bibles in Welsh or for the far corners of the world. He was one of the speakers at the first general meeting of the British and Foreign Bible Society on 2 May 1804.

Conversely, while Watson had a high view of scripture, he had greater concern as to whether the translation was authorized and whether the interpretation of it was authentic.

This was what led Watson to first respond publicly at the SPCK board in 1811, because he felt that the Bible Society, by promoting widespread usage of scripture, with multiple interpretations, would induce schism in the Church and effectively adulterate the Word of God. Therefore, alongside other high churchmen like Van Mildert and Herbert Marsh, Watson opposed the Bible Society. At this period in time, the Phalanx sponsored various open letters to the London clergy, one titled, 'Reasons for Declining to become a Subscriber to the British and Foreign Bible Society', written by Christopher Wordsworth in 1810 and another titled, 'A Practical exposition of the tendency and proceedings of the British and Foreign Bible Society', written by Henry Norris in 1814. (see Varley, 2002, p. 68).

This difference over their handling of the Bible was reflected in the different ecclesiological mind-sets of both men. Wilberforce was a cradle Anglican who as a member of the upper class would have adopted a vogue Latitudinarian viewpoint in an age when scepticism and religious apathy were widespread. As was culturally normative for a member of the Established Church, Wilberforce was brought up to despise enthusiasm and to see the new movement of 'Methodism' as a cause for mockery. It was somewhat to his surprise therefore that on his journey to the continent in 1784 he was challenged for ridiculing of the views of Methodists by his travelling companion, Isaac Milner. They discussed the matter further and both read the book *The Rise and Progress of the Soul* by Philip Dodderidge (famous for writing the hymn 'O happy day') and this in turn led Wilberforce to see himself as 'a nominal Christian'. Two years later, in 1786, Wilberforce moved from a stage of spiritual restlessness into the comfort of an evangelical conversion and in 1797 he published *A Practical View of the Prevailing Religious System of Professed Christians in the Higher and Middle Classes in This Country Contrasted with Real Christianity.*

In these ways, Wilberforce renewed his faith but in so doing also embraced that greater strand of individualism that comes with personal pietistic experience and which has characterized the Protestant faith expressed in evangelicalism. The locus of such authority becomes the self, validated by that community of people who have also had a similar experience. The Established Church can be seen to be the inhibitor of experience or of personal expression to such a way of thinking and true to the script, the Monthly Review dismissed Wilberforce's book as an example of enthusiasm from as early as 1797 (Bayes, 1994).

By contrast, Watson had no interest in conversion, kept no spiritual diary comparable to Wilberforce and had a faith founded in the Bible and liturgy which was stable despite the vagaries of the emotions. Along with the Hackney Phalanx, he had a high doctrine of the Church and of the State, which led him to claim that all Christian citizens were in the relationship of children to their mother, the Church of England, even if they belonged to non-conformist churches (Webster, 1954, p. 20). He never wavered in his belief that the Church of England alone was the reformed Catholic Church of the land. He went so far as to play a leading part in ending the employment of the Church of non-episcopally ordained missionaries and in preventing the SPCK from publishing Watt's Catechism because the author was a non-conformist. This view seems equally extreme to a twenty-first-century Anglican, let alone to a post-modern thinker in its trust that authority and institution are correct.

Such divergent views on the relative authorities of the Bible and the Church led to quite different understandings of the human condition, of Christ's atonement and therefore of mission. The evangelicals insisted on a deep acceptance of the sinfulness of the human and the sufficiency of Christ's sacrifice. Wilberforce wrote:

> We must be deeply conscious of our guilt and misery, heartily repenting of our sins, and firmly resolving to forsake them: and thus penitently flying for refuge to the hope set before us, we must found altogether on the merits of our crucified redeemer our hopes of escape from our deserved punishment, and of deliverance from their enslaving power. This must be our first, last, our only plea. (*A Practical View*, 1797)

Justification was by faith alone, expressed through conversion, not via the baptism of the Church nor the sacraments.

Conversely, the Hackney Phalanx came from a tradition that emphasized the Catholic heritage of the Church, regretting the destruction of the Reformation while not denying its need. They looked to Jeremy Taylor, the seventeenth-century theologian who pointed to the incarnation rather than the atoning death of Christ as being the central dogma of the faith. They exalted the place of the Church in salvation seeing it as,

> a society of divine institution assembled under ecclesiastical government, and holding communion in Christian fellowship and in the public services of religion after the apostolic pattern. (*British Critic*, 1818, vol. X, p. 117, citing Archdeacon Daubeny)

In terms of mission outcomes, it is hardly surprising that the Clapham Sect showed initial engagement with schools but that they withdrew over time when a higher churchmanship began to dominate. By 1870, the dissenters had lost interest in running schools and the British and Foreign Schools Society were happy to leave the task of education to the State. By and large this was also true for the Methodist engagement in education, even though they had been so involved with the poor. However, with a focus that was more on personal redemption and sanctification achieved through righteous living, the great evangelical achievements were to be the abolition of the slave trade, the revival of overseas missionary work and the spread of humanitarian ideals.

By contrast, the Hackney Phalanx were to find a political compromise with the parliament working with the Church. They expected the State to work through the Church and that the Church could find the resources and the vision to claim her right to educate the nation. By 1815, every diocese in England was consulting the National Society and 100,000 children were attending school. By 1835, over 1,000,000 children were being educated.

The twenty-first-century context of Anglican schools

Two centuries have now passed since the National Society was established as a subcommittee of the SPCK, to organize a systematic schools system. Since then, the free churches, with their more evangelical form of Protestantism have largely disengaged from the public organization of church education and the Roman Catholic Church has entered the frame, accelerating their stake in education to match their Anglican counterparts. It is a useful cause for reflection as to why a more Catholic theology has better prioritized the maintenance of their stake in public schooling whereas evangelical theology has been more prepared to delegate that trust to the State. It could be because the nineteenth-century emphasis within evangelicalism was on individual responsibility and personal salvation which caused it to prioritize the home and the Church rather than the public sector (although Wilberforce was a classic exception to this.)

It can be observed that evangelical Christian outreach to children in the Church of England has focused on the development of the Sunday school (though even this has moved from an original general education using the Bible, to nurture young children biblically during adult service time (Griffiths, 2009)). Evangelical influence has also concentrated on holiday club outreach to children.

Conversely, within Anglicanism there has been less emphasis in the Catholic tradition on general children's ministry other than through the teaching of the catechism or integration into ritualistic service. However, the tradition of strong school engagement has been maintained.

Within the free churches of England (the natural successors of the nineteenth-century dissenters), school engagement has tended to be via parachurch movements like Scripture Union or Youth for Christ who have supported Christian outreach in schools. Free church involvement in setting up schools has tended to be with a view to nurturing children of the faith, as is seen in the rise of the Christian independent schools (see the Christian Schools' Trust, www.christianschoolstrust.co.uk).

Aware of such historical wrestling of theological understandings, it is interesting to reflect on what the Dearing Report meant when it spoke of school education as being missional and for 'Church schools to be at the centre of the mission of the Church' (Dearing, 2001). In this context, it is helpful to consider the definition of mission offered by David Bosch in his seminal work, *Transforming Mission* (1994). He wrote:

> We have to distinguish between mission (singular) and missions (plural). The first refers primarily to the 'Missio Dei' (God's mission), that is, God's self-revelation as the One who loves the world, God's involvement in and with the world, the nature and activity of God, which embraces both the Church and the world, and in which the Church is privileged to participate. 'Missio Dei' enunciates the good news that God is a God-for-people. Missions (the 'missiones ecclesiae', the missionary endeavours of the Church), refer to particular forms, related to specific times, places, or needs, of participation in the 'Missio Dei'.

In these terms, it might be suggested that in 1811, there was a fusion between 'Missio Dei' and 'missiones ecclesiae', a coming together of mission and missions, a fusion of concept and action and of high and low churchmanship. Subsequently, lived experience, two centuries later, suggests that a more Catholic understanding of mission as 'Missio Dei' has been better able to live with the broad aim of education as partnership with State and has maintained its stakehold whereas a more evangelical understanding of mission as 'missiones ecclesiae' has been more effective in mission projects. This observation might be further researched but arises from lived observation in the twentieth century.

To return to Bosch's opus maximus (1994) (subtitled, *Paradigm Shifts in Theology of Mission*) he traces the different New Testament models of mission into their Roman Catholic missionary paradigm in the medieval period and into their Protestant missionary paradigm of the Reformation. The former period showed the early emphasis of salvation being individualized and yet also the gift of the Church (pp. 214–19) breeding a colonial zeal which was territorial and the latter bringing a new pietism and then Puritanism. Moving into the nineteenth century, his observation is that evangelical missions began to serve the interests of the Empire but that they succeeded 'in putting their stamp on all aspects of British life' (p. 282). The emergence of a post-modern paradigm has left a context in which a raft of elements can be seen at work in mission, models of mission being seen as liberation or as witness or as inculturation, to name but a few. While Bosch never considered schools, nor the educational system as a focus of his thinking, it has been developed elsewhere.

Astley (2002) offers further insight by identifying the three principle models of Christian education to be: (1) education into Christianity, (2) education about Christianity and (3) education in a Christian manner. His observation is that the latter is most predominant in educational thinking in Britain where there is a notion of teaching and learning Christianity. It can also be observed that Roman Catholic school education places more emphasis on the nurture and Christian development of the child and that Anglican school education places more emphasis on service to the community. These compatible strengths have been encouraged to unite in the Dearing Report (2001) which has a vision for Church schools being 'distinctively Christian and inclusive'.

In 2005, a group of Anglican Diocesan Directors of Education convened to explore models of mission in 'The Way Ahead Report' which were also identifiable in the influential Archbishop's Council Report on mission titled *Mission Shaped Church*. Their findings identified three models or metaphors which were in dynamic tension, namely (1) 'the family' working with 'the tribe', (2) the 'ark of salvation' also being the 'vehicle of outreach' and (3) the 'prophetic presence' wrestling with a notion of 'partnership with state'. Running through them all was the observation that Church schools were in a threshold place whereby people of faith or of no faith were in transition (Worsley, 2006).

Reflections on history as a means to move forward in mission

At the time of writing, in 2011, Britain is facing a new paradigm shift in education as a coalition government encourages the development of independent academies, each competing for individual distinctiveness in the market-place of education. The Catholic and Anglican school authorities now have to consider how to preserve their influence in education with the trend being for them to develop their role as providers.

Against this backdrop, a report by the Office for National Statistics (ONS) and Tearfund in January, detailed that although the majority of Britain says it is Christian (72%), only 32 per cent attend church. By contrast, of the far smaller percentage of Muslims, 80 per cent go to the mosque. When asked about schooling however, 30 per cent of Christians say their religion affects their choice of school, compared to 21 per cent of Muslims. In other words, Christian schooling is seen to be a part of the legacy of Christian thinking that is surviving better in the current age.

Is this because education is a meeting place for Church and State? Is this because the mission in schools is one which unites both high and low church and which calls for a uniting of values? Is this because a residual trust remains in the Christian faith as being relevant and important in the nurturing of children?

Whatever the case, the nineteenth-century legacy remains intact as holding some credence in the national consciousness and needs to be carefully reworked if the future of the Church of England is to be assured. History demonstrates that there is impact when the evangelical and Catholic wings of the Church come together in missionary enterprise.

Maybe the next stage will be the development of other faith schools alongside existing provision, as was most recently the case with the rise of Catholic schools in the twentieth century. Assuredly the key issue will be that the Church has sufficient faith and hope through which to encourage Church schools not to shrink from the complexity of engagement. They must wrestle with the ancient authorities of scripture, church tradition and reason to be part of the future of mission in the nation and must be assured that their concern is to focus on the poor.

Key questions

1. Historically, what were the main theological reasons that caused evangelicals to become involved in Church schools? What do you think of these reasons?
2. Historically, what were the main theological reasons that caused the high church to become involved in Church schools? What do you think of these reasons?
3. Looking at your Church school (or one with which you are most engaged) what is the theological legacy (from evangelical or high church tradition) that is most evident in the school?
4. What is it from this legacy that is most helpful or unhelpful to the mission of the school?
5. How can evangelical and high church traditions join together in developing the mission of a Church school?

3

Conflict and Consensus in the Dual System

Pricilla Chadwick

Abstract

Although by the start of the twentieth century, the Anglican Church was recognized as a significant partner with government in the 'dual system' educating the children of England, over the following hundred years, this relationship came under marked pressure from many different directions. As schools expanded through the decades, the financial commitment of the church to its schools was seriously tested. Wartime coalitions helped consolidate the churches' role in England's postwar educational provision and church secondary schools expanded in partnership with local authorities, but the controversies over religious education continued to be dangerously divisive in an increasingly secular society.

It was the reforms of the Thatcher and 'New' Labour governments that began systematically to dismantle the 'dual system', encouraging greater autonomy for schools. The churches continue to face the dilemma: should they seize the opportunity to become more distinctively Christian as parental demand for Church schools remains high; or should they retain their historic Anglican commitment to the nation as a whole and offer a less exclusive policy on pupil admissions?

Keywords
Church schools, dual system, partnership, religious education, grant maintained status, autonomy, agreed syllabus, Cowper-Temple clause

Reflecting from a twenty-first-century perspective on the development of Church schools throughout the twentieth century, it seems remarkable that Anglican schools not only survived the political vicissitudes of the various governments' education policies but even flourished and expanded, enhancing their position as major contributors to the nation's well-being and academic success. How did this come about?

Church schools have always been a contentious issue. The Church of England aimed to offer an ecclesiastical *via media* between Roman Catholics who looked to Rome for authority and the Puritan dissenters who eschewed the establishment. So too in its education policy, the Anglican establishment looked both ways, seeing its schools first and foremost to be educating the nation but also educating children in the doctrines of the Anglican Church. By contrast, the Roman Catholics primarily created schools to protect their interests as a minority discriminated against in a society that distrusted its loyalty to the Crown; and the dissenters or non-conformists opposed any kind of denominational teaching in schools funded by the nation's rates, relying on their Sunday schools to nurture their children in Protestant teaching. The Anglicans' commitment to the education of the nation paved the way for the 'dual system' whereby the Church would work in partnership with the State to provide education for the nation's children (the majority of whom could be described as Anglicans), a partnership which was to experience significant upheaval as British society evolved and governments changed throughout the twentieth century.

The nineteenth-century background

The work of the Church of England's National Society from 1811, alongside other charitable bodies, had pioneered education for the poor and, with the extension of the popular franchise following the 1832 Reform Act, the State offered the first building grant of £11,000 for the National Society's 690 schools in 1833. Further financial support was only accepted after a 'concordat' in 1840 allowed the Church right of veto over government inspector appointments. In 1847, the National Society was divided on the issue of allowing laymen to sit on school boards, the majority being reassured in that the parish incumbent remained as chairman, but the Tractarians were concerned about 'creeping erastianism' as the State's influence on Church schools increased.[1]

Yet, even though it had increasing influence, it was not until the 1870s that the State finally accepted its responsibility to run schools. The Forster Education Act, concerned to ensure a better educated workforce to create 'industrial prosperity', recognized that Church schools and non-denominational state schools could work alongside each other in a 'dual system', thereby papering over the cracks of a society divided by sectarianism and religious protectionism. The Act set up board schools where needed and by 1884 the Church of England had willingly transferred control of over 600 of its elementary schools to school boards. Meanwhile, the Cowper-Temple clause had guaranteed that 'in schools hereafter established by means of local rates, no catechism or religious formulary which is distinctive of any particular denomination shall be taught.' In effect, this limited religious education to Bible stories in state-funded schools, but the acrimonious debates in parliament (one lasting for four consecutive nights) eventually contributed to the Liberal government's election defeat in 1874.

In spite of these tensions, Anglicans embarked on the twentieth-century confident that their contribution to the nation's education was valued, yet increasingly dependent on government financial support for its schools and wary of government interference in its policies. It could be argued that nothing much has changed over the past hundred years, since such issues continue to resonate into the third millennium. This inference, however, would be misleading because during the twentieth century the social context and political ideologies shifted significantly, altering the relationships between Anglican schools and their partners in the national educational enterprise.

Balfour and Birrell

Controversy arose early on as the gulf between state and voluntary provision widened and it became clear that more state aid was essential if the voluntary sector was to survive, let alone flourish. Balfour's 1902 Education Act, offering state aid to Church schools in return for allowing government inspection of standards and local authority representation on management boards, might have been seen as paving the way for the eventual abolition of the dual system, as advocated by the non-conformists. However, the latter were entrenched in their opposition to 'Rome on the rates' (as they saw it) and, when the 1902 Act was finally passed after 57 days of debate, many non-conformists refused to pay their rates; 38,000 summonses were issued and 80 protestors jailed.

Therefore, Augustine Birrell, President of the Board of Education in the new Liberal government of 1906, proposed a Bill to abolish the divisive dual system, encouraged by atheists and secularists as well as the non-conformists to bring all schools under full state control. Such a proposal, however, then rallied the Churches to the cause, the Archbishop of Canterbury, Randall Davidson, arguing persuasively in the House of Lords the injustice inherent in confiscating 14,000 schools and demolishing their trusts by radical secularization. The fall of the 1906 Birrell Bill, which educationalist Cruickshank later regarded as 'unquestionably the great missed opportunity of the twentieth century' (1963, p. 103), was followed by several further unsuccessful attempts in 1908 and 1918 to resolve the problems of the dual system. As pressure grew with the expansion of schools and the raising of the school leaving age, the Churches' position became even less secure. Nevertheless, the Bishop of Durham, Herbert Hensley Henson, commented perceptively in 1939:

> The Dual System as it now exists, obstructs the complete triumph of the secularising tendency. It affirms an educational ideal which is larger in range, more intelligently sympathetic in temper, more congruous with human nature, than that which secularism embodies. (1939, p. 204)

Butler's postwar compromise

The virulent debates around the 1906 Birrell Bill certainly made Winston Churchill reluctant[2] to bring forward legislation during the Second World War. However, the proposals leading up to Butler's 1944 Education Act were underpinned by the realization that the democratic values, for which so many had sacrificed their lives fighting Nazism, were largely based on England's Christian heritage. As the *Times Leader* (17 February 1940) noted: 'More than ever before, it has become clear that the healthy life of the nation must be based on spiritual principles . . . Education with religion omitted is not really education at all.' William Temple, Archbishop of Canterbury, went further: 'We must take steps to ensure that the corporate life of the schools is Christian' (1942, p. 93).

However, the Church of England's school buildings were in a parlous state, 399 of the 700 condemned by government being Anglican foundations. Temple acknowledged later: 'I was doing a rather elaborate egg-dance, and some of the eggs were such as it be most important not to break, because the smell would be awful' (Iremonger, 1948, p. 572).

The government recognized the churches' financial difficulties, offering 50 per cent grants to bring voluntary school buildings up to standard and the creation of VC status for schools willing to be managed by LEAs which would assume responsibility for all buildings maintenance. Some Anglicans wanted to retain control of all their denominational schools, as did the Roman Catholics who demanded at least 70 per cent capital grants for their schools.[3]

Non-conformists meanwhile stood by their convictions on state schools for all, with the Cowper-Temple clause guaranteeing non-denominational religious education. Following the 1943 White Paper, William Temple took the wider view:

> Let us not give the impression that our concern as church people is only with the adjustment of the dual system: we ought as Christians to be concerned about the whole of educational process. I am quite sure that the raising of the school leaving age will of itself do more to make permanent the religious influence of the school than anything that can be done with directly denominational purpose. (Iremonger, 1948, p. 573)

Such a view reflected Anglicans' confidence in their position as the Established Church of a nation determined to reconstruct its postwar education system. The mutual respect between Temple and Butler undoubtedly facilitated the final compromises needed to pass the 1944 Education Act, which included the continuation of the dual system modified by offering a choice for VC or VA schools. The government would provide all the running costs; local authorities would manage VC schools with some church representation and offer denominational instruction if requested by parents; and the churches would retain their control of VA schools supported by 50 per cent state capital grants. The government (Butler, 1971, p. 101) correctly predicted that the majority of Anglican schools could only afford to opt for 'controlled' status even if, as Archbishop Fisher, Temple's successor, thought, 'aided' status was preferable (Carpenter, 1991, p. 431). Although Butler had to compromise his ambition for a single national system, he felt that one publicly funded system was at least a step in the right direction.

Yet, again the issue of religious education threatened to rock the fragile political boat: Chuter Ede, Butler's parliamentary secretary in the coalition government described the negotiations as 'a knife-edge with precipices on both sides' (Butler, 1982, p. 160). Based on the 1870 Cowper-Temple clause framework, local authorities (such as Cambridgeshire in 1924) had devised agreed religious syllabuses which Butler thought were 'not intended to be a form of State religion but are the beginnings of the teaching in the literacy of faith' (Address to the World Conference of Faiths, June 1943). Butler's proposals for his Bill incorporated the five points first put forward by the Archbishops in 1941: the school day should begin with a collective act of worship; every maintained school must provide religious instruction according to a local agreed syllabus (though parents could withdraw children even in voluntary schools); religious instruction would have equal status with other curriculum subjects, be taught at any time of the day and be open to inspection.

The Anglicans, unlike the Roman Catholics, welcomed the proposals, commending the new provisions for worship and religious instruction at their 1948 Lambeth Conference. The Butler Act undoubtedly papered over the fissures of the dual system and allowed the postwar governments to focus attention on providing free secondary education for all, 'comprehensivization', raising the school leaving age to 15 (and later 16) and developing a national examination system.

The Fourth R: The Durham Report on Religious Education, 1970

These issues later came under closer scrutiny in the 1970 Durham Report under the chairmanship of Bishop Ian Ramsey. During the 1960s, the theological world was challenged by more liberal interpretations such as Bonhoeffer's 'religionless Christianity' and Robinson's 'Honest to God', questioning the validity of traditional religious teaching. Similarly, paedological research such as Goldman's 'Religious Thinking from Childhood to Adolescence' (1964) argued that denominational instruction was wholly inappropriate at primary level and rarely acceptable in secondary schools.

The changes in postwar Britain, overshadowed by the nuclear threat and with classroom pupils less respectful of authority, meant that religious education (as it became called) also had to adapt from instruction through Bible stories to a more relevant engagement with issues of interest and concern to contemporary society, where young people expected their own views to be taken seriously. New pedagogical trends increasingly advocated more participatory active learning, encouraging religious education lessons to explore moral values and Christian ethics (e.g. war and pacifism, abortion and euthanasia) alongside Bible teaching. Another significant change in postwar Britain was the arrival of Commonwealth immigrants, many of whom were Christian while others were from Muslim, Hindu or Sikh backgrounds. It became increasingly important for social cohesion and mutual understanding that the pupils' religious education curriculum included the study of world religions. These changes were generally incorporated into the LEAs' agreed syllabuses as the SACREs set up by the 1944 Act reflected the local communities they served.[4] Reflecting on these changes, the Church of England Board of Education and the National Society decided in 1967 to establish a commission to re-examine both religious education and the place of Church schools in contemporary society, aiming to 'inaugurate changes no less significant than those which have characterized the whole century since Mr Forster's Elementary Education Act' (p. xiii).

The Durham Report's analysis (1970) still resonates more than 40 years on. The continuation of the dual system was being challenged by those who thought it divisive, segregating children 'according to their parents' religion' (p. 224); Anglican schools were confused as to their *domestic* role in nurturing Anglicans and their *service* role to the local community in educating the nation's children; they were not always linked into their local parish churches and often created difficulties by being the only school available in 'single-school' areas; they were dependent on state financing, yet reserved teaching posts (particularly headships) for practising Anglicans. In addition, the financial commitment to their schools was a significant burden on the Church of England, which saw little 'pay-back' in church attendance figures or improved religious knowledge.

Yet, the Durham Commission was confident that Church schools still had an important role to play, even with a more open approach to teaching and learning: 'It is where the shared assumptions of the members of the school's staff coincide with the assumptions of the parents of the pupils that the educational potential of a church school can be most fully realised' (Durham Report, 1970, p. 228). Even if the percentage of Anglican schools had declined from the almost 50 per cent of all schools in 1944 as the postwar state system had expanded, it argued that the Church should retain its stake in the national system, giving 'full opportunity for expressing its beliefs about education' with authority derived from its direct experience of involvement in schools.

> The Church of England sees in the Dual System an important opportunity to express in direct service its concern for the general education of the young people of the nation. It also recognises the importance of a continuing opportunity for community-building . . . focused on the local church. (p. 252)

Clearly VA schools with their close links with the local Anglican Church were in a strong position to respond to the latter task; but the Report felt that VC schools made a valuable contribution particularly to the former task, where school governors could oversee good quality religious education (not just denominational teaching) and the parish incumbent develop a general pastoral role in the school; and, if the local community desired a stronger partnership with the church, the school might even seek to transfer to aided status.

In all these areas, the Report argued, diocesan education authorities had a critical role to play, notwithstanding the need for the churches to work with the LEAs and parish communities. The haphazard nature of planning for contraction (falling pupil rolls in the 1980s) or expansion (in the 1990s) in the number of Church schools nationally, let alone the financial constraints for capital projects, led the Commission to recommend greater strategic direction from the dioceses and the Church of England as a whole. Diocesan advisers, especially for religious education, were encouraged to offer their services to the local authority, as well as their Church schools, emphasizing that religious education's purpose was non-denominational, 'to explore the place and significance of religion in human life and so make a distinctive contribution to each pupil's search for a faith by which to live'. Such an approach to religious education meant that HMIs might be permitted to inspect religious education alongside other curricular subjects, freeing up diocesan staff to support the quality of learning in the classroom.

Interestingly, a key recommendation of the Durham Report was that ecumenical cooperation between Anglicans and Roman Catholics could lead to joint research and advisory services as well as joint schools and colleges. It recognized that such ventures, while complex, were best developed where the churches already worked together, but 'we look forward ultimately to the development of a nation-wide pattern of ecumenical aided schools' (p. 268). Such an aspiration reflected the greater optimism following the Second Vatican Council's decree on ecumenism (*Unitatis redintegratio*, 1964) and the Church in the Modern World (*Gaudium et spes*, 1965, see Flannery, 1981) that Christian unity was at least desirable if not immediately possible. Some comprehensive schools with Christian foundations moved tentatively to create the first joint schools in the 1970s and 1980s. However, the Roman Catholic Church tended to support such initiatives only as a second best option where necessary to preserve Catholic education in a community, rather than as a first choice.[5]

As is already evident, *the Fourth R* had much to say about the Anglican contribution to the nation's education and the future role of Church schools. Some of its recommendations required urgent action to ensure the dual system continued to flourish; others pointed to challenges in the future yet to be taken up. The 'blueprint' laid down in 1970 was to influence Anglican policy for many years to follow. Nevertheless, in the increasingly secular society of the second half of the twentieth century, various attempts to abolish religious education and especially collective school worship, despite triggering public cries of protest (e.g. *Times Leader*, 31 October 1984), led to apprehension that the delicate compromises of 1944 might be undone. Perhaps, only a brave or foolhardy government would dare to risk that.

Baker and the conservative reforms

The 1944 Education Act had been built on a partnership between central and local government, Church and State, teachers and parents. As Robert Waddington pointed out in 1984, 'The English school is unique in operating within a fine balance between political, church, community, parental and professional interests' (p. 14). That balance was about to change. The rise of Thatcher's 'market-driven' ideology in the 1980s was to have a profound influence on education into the twenty-first century.

The 'One Nation' Conservatives and the Labour politicians in the decades following 1944 were both committed to improving educational opportunities by expanding comprehensive schools for all. Anglican diocesan officers worked in partnership with local authorities to ensure that Church schools received appropriate support, both financially and educationally. In 1963, Archdeacon Mayfield reflected: 'A partnership in terms undreamed of only 25 years ago has been set up between Church and State; it penetrates the whole field of education' (p. 170).

A central aspect of the partnership was that local authority agreed syllabuses provided pupils with a basic understanding of Christianity and were often used by Anglican VA as well as VC schools. In 1985, the Church of England's Board of Education Report to General Synod emphasized 'the importance of working even more closely with local authority partners, particularly in the case of admissions policies and staffing for Church schools'.

Anglican schools still had to watch their backs. Of their 21.3 per cent stake in maintained schools, 12.5 per cent were voluntary controlled where church foundation governors were only in the minority. LEA reorganization plans (e.g. creating sixth-form colleges) often affected Anglican schools, as did LEA funding for pupils' school transport threatened by financial cuts in the 1980s.[6] Nevertheless, the partnership with local authorities undoubtedly received a boost when the Bishop of London, Graham Leonard, defended the Greater London Council against Thatcher's abolition plans in 1985, since Church schools benefited from its support network: the reprieve was however only temporary.[7]

Church schools also benefited from being part of an Anglican diocesan family. Diocesan officers could offer valuable guidance on religious education and collective worship, both of which in aided schools were inspected by diocesan rather than LEA inspectors. Diocesan advice on pupil admissions encouraged schools to reflect their local communities as well as their parish congregations.

Yet, it was the Churches' relationship not with local authorities but with central government which was to alter radically following Thatcher's third election victory in 1987. Her focus on 'standards', the market and parental choice paved the way for much greater autonomy for school governors in pupil admissions, budget prioritizing and even in deciding whether to adopt 'grant maintained status' (GMS) by opting out of their LEA completely. The government's assumption had been that Church schools, especially aided ones, would welcome these initiatives since their very existence was predicated on the principle of parental choice for denominational education; their parents already contributed money voluntarily to the school's budget and they exercised some independence from their LEAs.

The government's political strategy to reduce local control, however, had unforeseen consequences for the 'forgotten' partner, namely the churches. The Chairman of the Anglican Board of Education regretted that '"partnership" seems to have slipped out of the Government vocabulary' (Adie, 1990) but Thatcher's Secretary of State for Education, Kenneth Baker, was 'surprised that the Churches should criticise this extension of choice' (*Times*, 1 February 1988). Baker's 1988 Education Reform Act in practice gave the Secretary of State an additional 175 centralized powers and the later 1993 Education Act another 50, leaving observers to note 'the heaviest centralised controls that the schools system has ever experienced' (Bridges and Husbands, 1995, p. 2). The government was determined to marginalize any authority, including diocesan authorities, which threatened the move to greater autonomy for schools (cf. Baker, 1993, Carlton Club seminar, 31 January 1988). Nevertheless, Baker later commented in his autobiography:

> When it came to the Church of England, the person I dealt with was Graham Leonard, the Bishop of London. I enjoyed our relationship since we were both High Anglicans, though at times the advice Graham received was, I thought, neither High nor particularly Anglican. (1993, p. 218)

Both Anglican and Roman Catholic education spokesmen opposed these developments, though for rather different reasons. The former had valued the historic relationships of dioceses with locally elected governments, fearing the overweening power of the State to abolish Church schools if sole control fell into the hands of central government. The latter recognized that their Catholic schools, built by the significant financial sacrifices of their parishes across the country, looked to episcopal authority to ensure their freedom from State interference. By undermining the influence of both the LEA and the dioceses, the government had stirred the churches into a stronger ecumenical lobbying partnership across the Reformation divide.

This left many Church schools with the problem of divided loyalties. The initial financial incentives to adopt GMS were very attractive to parents whose Church schools lacked resources and some were happy to be rid of LEAs unsympathetic to denominational education or the administrative inconveniences of the historic dual system. Yet, Church schools valued their distinctive Christian ethos and the attraction of church affiliation to parents in the educational market-place. One Anglican diocese warned:

> For Christians, there are not only political and pragmatic considerations but also an ethical dimension to the decision to apply for GMS which cannot be ignored. For example, the preferential funding which GM schools receive … can be seen as being at the expense of neighbouring schools. (Blackburn Diocesan Board of Education, 1994)

The Anglican national education spokesman, Geoffrey Duncan, while appreciating the attraction of GMS for church school governors threatened by reorganization plans or closure, thought that GMS was 'a gift … on a plate to some future administration that wants to get rid of church schools'. His suspicions were well-founded in that the Grant Maintained School Trust claimed that 'we wouldn't differentiate at all between aided, controlled or county schools once they're GM' (Chadwick, 1997, p. 58). Indeed, the Department for Education and Employment (DfEE) held no record of GM schools' previous status as Church schools until it was forced to collect this data following a parliamentary question on 11 May 1994. The sudden announcement in September 1995 by Thatcher's successor, John Major, without any prior consultation, that Church schools could become 'grant maintained' without the previous requirement of a parental ballot, outraged the churches and that plan was quietly dropped by early 1996.

On the other hand, there were Christian voices such as that of Frank Field MP, arguing that GMS offered the chance to safeguard or even restore the role of Christianity in a predominantly secular society. His anti-erastian, high church views naturally chimed in with the desire for church independence from government. An Anglican governor of a GM Church school commented: 'the truth is that our "churchness" has been strengthened by opting out' (*TES*, 8 May 1992). John Gay of the Culham Institute thought that Church schools' relationship with their diocesan boards could be strengthened as schools looked to them for support instead of to LEAs.

Religious education and the National Curriculum

The Conservative government in 1988 also introduced their radical reform of the school curriculum. Kenneth Baker and his civil servants knew enough political history to realize that controversy over religious education must be avoided at all costs in any curriculum review, so his 1987 proposals for a National Curriculum were careful to ensure that the legal arrangements for religious education were not amended in any way. What he had not reckoned with was that, by recommending major changes to all other subjects taught in schools, Baker was radically altering the context in which religious education was taught and, in effect, marginalizing the subject. It was not long before the churches once again became involved in political controversy about education.

It could of course be argued that such ecclesiastical intervention was unwarranted: diocesan religious education syllabuses could after all be used in VA Anglican schools. Nevertheless, the churches sensed their schools would be required to reduce the time allocated to religious education in order to accommodate the demands of the National Curriculum and, from a broader perspective, felt obliged to stand up to what they considered a serious threat to the spiritual dimension of education in the nation's schools as a whole. Cardinal Hume had warned that Baker's Bill 'offers us an educational system and curriculum at the heart of which is spiritual emptiness' ('No Room for Religion', *The Times*, 13 February 1988).

Baker came under increasing pressure, realizing that he would need the support of the bishops in the House of Lords if his Bill was to pass smoothly into law. The Bishop of London again played a crucial role in steering a difficult course between the traditionalists, mainly evangelicals such as Baroness Cox, who wanted more explicit reference to Christianity and those who hoped the basis of the 1944 Act (especially the agreed syllabus framework) was sufficiently flexible to adapt to the multifaith nature of late twentieth-century Britain. Graham Leonard eventually negotiated with national religious and educational representatives to produce an agreed formula, namely that each agreed syllabus should 'reflect the fact that the religious traditions in Great Britain are in the main Christian, whilst taking account of the teaching and practices of the other principal religions represented in Great Britain'.

Baker was greatly relieved: 'It was touch and go right up to the Third Reading in the House of Lords on 7th July . . . The religious aspects of education had certainly been strengthened' (1993, p. 209). Religious education was to be firmly placed in the 'basic' curriculum of every maintained school and all LEAs had to constitute a SACRE. The Church of England had made a significant contribution to the final outcome for all schools.

Such consensus, however, did not last long. Two-thirds of LEAs were slow to establish SACREs under the 1988 Act and further government legislation was required in 1993, emphasizing that 'Christianity is the main cultural and religious heritage of our children.' As Leonard had feared, this led to formal complaints from the Muslim community. The Archbishop of York, John Habgood, speaking in 1992 at the Way Ahead Conference, regretted the shortage of curriculum time for religious education and the lack of qualified religious education teachers:[8] he advocated a national rather than local framework for religious education, a proposal taken up by the government's School Curriculum and Assessment Authority (SCAA) when it produced national model agreed syllabuses in 1994. These were launched by Sir Ron Dearing, Chairman of SCAA, who expressed his satisfaction that the faith groups were helping stem 'the ebb-tide of religious knowledge' and reiterated his 1993 recommendation that religious education should have a minimum of 5 per cent curriculum time at KS4.

As the new Ofsted school inspection system was introduced after 1992, Church schools were permitted their own diocesan inspection framework (initially under Section 13), allowing both religious education and their Christian ethos to be inspected and reported to parents and the community. In 1995, government ministers announced the introduction of the religious education short course GCSE which became a highly successful KS4 programme for both secular and Church schools. However, the national concern about religious education continued as children's lack of religious knowledge became more evident.[9] The *Times Leader* writer commented:

> The truth is that while we may reject or ignore Christianity . . . to teach it poorly in our schools is to rob children of the most essential education of all: the knowledge of who and what we are. (30 June 1995)

One journalist, Clifford Longley, criticizing the Churches' tendency to attract the best religious education teachers into Church schools, went further:

> The argument concerns the Churches' self-interest. They also have a responsibility towards the whole nation. The Church of England admits as much without being sure what to do about it. (*Daily Telegraph*, 30 June 1995)

More recent debates about the exclusion of Religious Education from the *English Baccalaureate* proposed by the coalition government in 2011 led to two Early Day motions in parliament and significant lobbying by the churches. Although the government refused to amend its proposals, the outcry suggested that these issues were far from dead.

In the meantime, the *spiritual and moral* dimension of education, written into Baker's 1988 Education Act and included in the Ofsted framework for school inspections, had come under closer scrutiny in the 1990s. Public confidence in society's moral values had been seriously undermined by the murders of 2-year-old James Bulger and headmaster Philip Lawrence, for example. Christopher Price wrote:

> Throughout a century of argument between church and state about the 'dual' system of secular and religious schools in England, the rhetoric assumed the centrality of moral and religious education in both traditions. Now with the churches and the great education authorities sidelined, such arguments are no longer deployed. . . . The 1988 Act was grossly unbalanced; it led to too much testing and too little space for values. (*TES* 'Opinion', 20 October 1995)

The Archbishop of Canterbury led a debate in the House of Lords on 5 July 1996 highlighting the dangers for society inherent in 'the privatization of religion'. Viscount Tonypandy pleaded:

> If society has lost its way, don't put the blame on the schools. If society has lost its way, it's because it has lost its faith.[10]

Yet teachers' hesitation in advocating unequivocal moral standpoints or spiritual guidance in the classroom seemed to reflect the uncertainty of a society at the end of the twentieth century which paid mere lip-service to its Christian heritage, whose moral values had been steadily undermined by moral relativism and in which teachers, faced with a diversity of school pupils' religious beliefs or life-stances, felt confused and unsupported. It was perhaps not surprising therefore that parents, seeking clearer moral guidance for their children, wished increasingly to enrol their children in Church schools, leading to greater demands for Christian schools and Academies.

Conclusion

Bishop David Young, speaking on the fiftieth anniversary of the 1944 Education Act, noted that the challenge to this country is:

to articulate a vision for our nation in a fast-changing world, a vision which embraces the pluralism of multi-culture and multi-faith, which builds on values shared, which gives energy and purpose to our economic and social life. Such a vision was there in 1944. It cannot simply be replicated: a new vision must be discerned. (*Fifty Years Forward, TES* and Institute of Education Conference, May 1994)

In the twenty-first century, 200 years after Joshua Watson, that new vision still remains to be explored in a number of ways. The contribution of the Church of England to the nation's education system, far from being marginalized or undermined, seems to be expanding particularly through the academies programme. New Christian charitable trusts such as Oasis, Woodard or the United Learning Trust, have taken on responsibility as sponsors for state schools across the country. As the resources and education responsibilities of local authorities are being reduced[11] and the churches need to manage their limited resources carefully, academies and voluntary schools, both controlled and aided, are increasingly working together, supported by diocesan education officers.

However, it will be interesting to see if, in the process of gaining more independence, Church schools have inadvertently made themselves more vulnerable to a future government whose policies might be less sympathetic to Christian education. The need for responses to short-term government policy often deflects attention from the need for a clear long-term Church of England strategy. There remains some apprehension under the current government, as seen with previous ones, that the legal framework of Church schools is not always well understood by legislators and the Church of England has constantly to alert ministers and civil servants to the sometimes unintended consequences of educational reform for the 'dual system'.

Yet, the Anglican Church remains a significant partner with government in the enterprise of educating the nation's children for the twenty-first century. As Bishop Graham Leonard clearly articulated:

The concept of partnership in education is more than just a cliché or bureaucratic device. . . . The Christian vision of education . . . sees human beings as partners with God in the work of creation. . . . For the Church to exercise its important responsibility in education, we may have to disturb and invigorate the ecclesiastical and educational structures and expectations. (General Synod Index 1995–2000, Speech to General Synod, 8 July 1995)

Key questions

1. How do Anglican schools resolve the tension between responding to parental choice and serving the wider community?
2. To what extent does the 'dual system' have a future?
3. Is the move towards greater autonomy for schools a threat or an opportunity?
4. What kind of relationship should an Anglican school have with its local churches and diocese?
5. To what extent should Anglican schools contribute to the national debates on religious education?

Notes

1 High church Anglicans in the mid-nineteenth century published 'tracts' advocating the separation of church and state: this issue was influential in Newman's decision to secede from Anglicanism.

2 He was 'horrified to see that an educational dispute charged with religious issues could so split the nation that the Conservative Party lost the next election' (Butler, 1982, p. 148).

3 The Roman Catholics were correct in their demands for capital support and the grant was raised to 75 per cent by 1959. Their conviction about the Cowper-Temple clause being 'Protestant and so denominational' made for great tensions in the negotiations with Butler: 'We fear that any hint of our readiness to compromise on our religious principles would give the secularists in the government a handle for the abolition of our schools' (Heenan, 1944, p. 148).

4 Apart from the public outcry in 1974 when Birmingham unsuccessfully attempted to include Humanism and Marxism in its agreed syllabus, the legal framework survived relatively uncontroversially into the Thatcher era.

5 The national furore in 2000 caused by the Archdiocese of Birmingham in withdrawing from the successful joint school in Oxford (leading to its closure in 2003) may ironically have encouraged other dioceses to consider this issue more positively. In Liverpool, for example, there have been several new ecumenical schools established in recent years.

6 In 1991, the Audit Commission recommended the withdrawal of this discretion on economic grounds (*Home to School Transport: A System at the Crossroads*). A challenge in the High Court to the decision by several local authorities in 2011 to abolish free transport to Church schools was strongly supported (*Tablet*, 20 August): in one local authority which retained academic selection, free transport was offered to grammar schools but not to Church schools.

7   Graham Lane of the Association of Metropolitan Authorities previously described Church schools disparagingly as 'independent schools on the rates' but had later been more supportive, impressed by the professionalism of church educationalists in the post-1988 period.

8   After intensive lobbying, the Teacher Training Agency eventually agreed by October 1995 to designate religious education as a 'shortage subject', though it did not offer any financial incentives for recruitment.

9   The 1996 survey by the Secondary Heads' Association revealed that 48 per cent of comprehensive schools had less than 3.5 per cent curriculum time allocated to religious education.

10   Such issues were voiced again after the race riots in 2001 and the city disturbances in 2011.

11   Over the past few decades, local authorities have tended to merge responsibilities for education, children's services and leisure under one executive.

4

Anglican Education in Wales

David W. Lankshear

Abstract

The report of the Church in Wales Educational Review was adopted by the Church in Wales Governing Body at their meeting in September 2009. Among the recommendations was the adoption of 'Serving Christ through Education in Wales' as the mission statement of the Church in Wales' work in education. From the start, the review had sought to ensure that its recommendations and the outcomes of the review should be driven by research. This chapter presents an overview of the story of Church schools in Wales followed by a consideration of the research conducted on behalf of the review and will consider the extent to which the research evidence supports the adoption of such a mission statement as both realistic and challenging.

Keywords
Church in Wales, policy, research, primary schools, ethos

Introduction

The story of Church schools in Wales has its roots more than a century before the foundation of the school in St Peter's Parish, Carmarthen. Griffith Jones (who began his work in about 1736) and the movement for the establishment of circulating schools brought education to the working classes in an unprecedented way and were widespread throughout Wales. The focus was on reading and the learning of scripture in order to 'save souls'. By the end of the eighteenth century, these schools had, to a large extent, died out. However, the Anglican Church's commitment to bringing education to the people was still very real. The National Society, devoted to the provision of schools and resources, was founded in London in 1811. The Church provided 230 schools in Wales by 1826 and 336 by 1831. The 1851 census showed that Anglican Schools provided instruction for 11,000 children between the ages of 3 and 10 years within Wales. This meant that the church was providing for one-third of the total number of children in education. The years after 1850 saw a strengthening in the power and fortunes of the Established Church as the governing classes of the coalfields and other heavy industry began to be associated with the church. The Church schools of the Llandaff diocese are still placed to the south of the M4 representing the Church domination in the south of the County of Glamorgan and the prevalence of non-conformity in the Valleys to the north. Very often these industrialists and wealthy landowners from all over Wales were the benefactors of Church schools as they sought to educate their workforce.

The Education Act of 1870, which sought to provide elementary education for all, meant that a concerted effort was made to provide education for all children under the age of 11. The number of schools provided by the School Boards rose rapidly. However, controversy arose when the government brought forward proposals to bring Church schools and board schools together under one system under the leadership of LEAs. The 1902 revolt was unique to Wales but very significant in terms of the place of Church education. At that time, the majority of schools were affiliated to the Church and there were at least 300 school districts where the only elementary education available was through the local Anglican schools. However, two-thirds of the population saw their religious allegiance as being non-conformist. Therefore, there was significant opposition to the Balfour Education Bill which related to the funding of schools. Many objected to giving money to support the work of the Church of England. This was a bitter battle and its legacy still prevails, most notably in the areas of Wales where there are very few Church schools. Disestablishment of the Church in 1920 went a small way to overcoming these issues.

The process of rationalization of school provision, begun following the 1902 Act was given further impetus in the process of implementation of the Education Act 1944. The Church in Wales has only been involved in the establishment of secondary schools in very limited numbers.

In the period since the Education Act 1944 was passed there have been many changes to the organization in Wales, including the introduction of comprehensive schools, but the basic structure created in 1944 has remained. In 1988, with the passage of the Education Reform Act, provision was made for a National Curriculum and for regular external assessment of pupils' progress. The way in which schools were managed financially was also changed. In 1998, the Schools Standards and Framework Act clarified the position of schools with a religious character within the overall provision of schools and created the category of Foundation schools.

Throughout this period, in order to be able to respond effectively to the changing nature of educational provision and the new understandings of children's needs that develop within the provision of education, all dioceses have a committee within their formal structures that has the oversight of the work with schools and other parts of the statutory provision. This committee is usually referred to as the DBE, but there is no consistent practice in the use of this title. For the purposes of our report we are using DBEs to cover the committee structure within the diocese dealing with these matters. It should be noted that the Diocesan Boards of Education Measure 1991 does not apply in Wales as it is legislation for the Church of England.

In 1999, the National Assembly for Wales was formed and a new era for education in Wales began with the development of new systems and a new curriculum for the country. Virtually all central government responsibilities for education and training were devolved to Wales at that point.

Background to the review

In 2001, the General Synod of the Church of England formally adopted the recommendations contained in the Report 'The Way Ahead: Church of England Schools in the New Millennium' (Dearing, 2001). The recommendations addressed the issues that faced both Church of England schools and the Church of England as a whole at that time, building on a significant body of work in the previous two decades (see Lankshear, 2003) and setting out a strategy for the future development of the Church of England's work within the state-maintained school system. The position of the Church in Wales at this time was anomalous in that it looked to the Church of England's partner organization, the National Society, for support in its work in education but much of the energy and resource available to the Society was focused on the implementation of 'The Way Ahead Report'. The Church in Wales also faced rather different circumstances from the Church in England. Until devolution, the education system in both countries had been covered by legislation which was passed by the parliament in Westminster and so almost all negotiations on the law of education could be conducted by the National Society's officers based there. With devolution the legislative and administrative focus increasingly was on Cardiff rather than London. A further difference was that while 'The Way Ahead Report' had provided a spur to the development of the number of Church of England secondary schools, the opportunities for new Church in Wales secondary schools was very limited and most of the Church in Wales' work would remain focused on its engagement in primary schools and its support for all schools within Wales.

In 2006, the six dioceses of the Church in Wales had responsibility for 63 VA primary schools, 1 Foundation primary school and 108 VC primary schools. Many of these primary schools are small: only 27 schools had over 201 pupils and 74 had 100 pupils or less. In Llandaff diocese there are 3 Church in Wales VA secondary schools. The only other secondary school in which the Church in Wales has a stake is in St Asaph diocese where there is a secondary school jointly held with the Roman Catholic Church.

Within the state-maintained system in Wales, it is possible for schools to use either Welsh or English as the medium of instruction. 18 per cent of Church in Wales primary schools used Welsh as the medium of instruction at KS1 and 7 per cent used both Welsh and English. 8 per cent of Church in Wales primary schools used Welsh as the medium of instruction at KS2 with 17 per cent using both Welsh and English. All other Church in Wales schools use English as the principle medium of instruction.

The review process

In November 2006, the Church in Wales began the work of producing its own review of its work in education in Wales. The group was made up of 11 members representing a range of experience and interests within Church education in Wales under the Chairmanship of Ian Miller at that time Chief Executive of Denbighshire County Council. From the first, the review group determined that the report should be based on research evidence and that it would take a broad view of the Church in Wales' engagement with the education system as a whole. To that end, it commissioned a range of research projects designed to inform its work and the debate that it wished to generate within the church and the education system in Wales.

The Church in Wales Education Review (Lankshear, 2009) was presented to the Governing Body of the Church in Wales in September 2009 and was adopted by an overwhelming majority of those present. Since 2009, considerable work has been undertaken to implement the recommendations. The first of these was that the mission statement 'Serving Christ through education in Wales' should be adopted. This statement had been identified by the review group as a reflection of what was already happening and also as clear challenge for the future.

Interpreting the mission statement and defining expectations

The recommendations of the review group were addressed to the Church at every level, the Church in Wales schools and to the Welsh Assembly Government and were presented within a five-year framework for implementation. The recommendation on the wording of the mission statement was the first recommendation and was addressed to the Church in Wales. However, it has clear implications for Church in Wales schools as well as for the Church in Wales Governing Body, the dioceses, deaneries and parishes. There will be many interpretations and expectations for the way in which the mission statement could be evidenced in the practice of the Church in Wales. Some of these are contained in the *Framework for the Inspection of Anglican Schools* (National Society, 2009). Others will be implied by publications on the development of vocation (e.g. Durka, 2002; Smith and Shortt, 2002), publications on the relationships between parishes and local schools (e.g. Lankshear, 1996) or within secular publications on school leadership (National Assembly, 2000).

The list of expectations that follows is not intended to be definitive but reflects issues that were at the heart of the review group's discussions and reflect a range of implications drawn from the report which it is hoped that the church will be addressing during the five-year implementation process.

1. Church in Wales schools demonstrate a clear understanding of their religious character and how this is interpreted within the practice and policies of the schools. They aspire to the highest possible quality of educational experience for all children in their charge.
2. Admissions policies in use in Church in Wales schools reflect a balance between service to the local community and service to the church community.
3. Clergy give time and energy to the service of the schools in their parish.
4. Parishes relate well to the schools within their parishes or which serve their parishes.
5. Teachers are supported in their Christian vocation to teach and are valued members of the church community.
6. Dioceses show a consistent lead to Church in Wales schools and those working within them – they acknowledge the importance of the Christian service provided by church members in schools and colleges of all types throughout Wales.

The first two expectations are focused directly on Church in Wales schools. Expectation 1 addresses the way in which Church in Wales schools can interpret the mission statement. It draws heavily on the *Framework for the Inspection of Anglican Schools*. The other expectation directly related to Church in Wales schools addresses the issue of admissions, which in some areas is perceived to be controversial. The debate is usually framed in terms of the preference that is perceived to be given to the children of churchgoing parents in the admission policies of schools with a religious character. This expectation challenges the church to understand how the needs of these children and the needs of the children living close to the school are held in balance across the admission policies and practices of Church in Wales schools as a whole.

The next three expectations are focused on the local church. Expectation 3 explores the work of the clergy and the way in which they relate to the schools in their locality as representatives of the church. Expectation 4 explores how the whole of the local church, clergy and people together relate to local schools and Expectation 5 explores the support offered by the local church to those of its members who understand their work within the education system as an outworking of their understanding of their Christian discipleship.

The final expectation focuses on the leadership within the church at diocesan level and how far these leaders may reflect the mission statement in their roles.

The mission statement was intended to both reflect the current practice of the Church in Wales and to provide challenges for the development of the practice in the future. The logical question is then how far are these six areas reflected in and identified by the research undertaken for the review and to what extent does the research support both intentions of the mission statement?

Testing the expectations

Methodology

The review group commissioned a variety of research projects all of which contribute to the assessment of the expectations listed above.

First, there was a collation of data already held by dioceses and local authorities that relates to Church in Wales schools. The main categories of data collected in this way were number on role, numbers of teaching and non-teaching staff employed in the schools, the school's status and the extent of nursery provision, if any, at the Church in Wales primary schools. This data was sourced from, local authority websites, the personnel within diocesan education teams and the records that they have created and, where the data could not be completed from these sources, the schools themselves.

Secondly, the school brochures published by Church in Wales schools were requested from all schools by letter. Schools are required by the 1996 Education Acts to make these available in response to any reasonable requests; although they are allowed to charge the cost of printing them where they feel that the request does not come from a person with an immediate interest in the information contained within the brochure. One hundred and thirty brochures were received from the one hundred and sixty eight schools (77%). The school brochures were used for four purposes:

1. as a source of data to complete the information collated under 1 above
2. as a source of information about the school's admission policy (for those schools which either failed to reproduce their admissions policy in their brochure or did not return their brochure, the full list of Church in Wales school admissions policies was established by reference to local authority websites)
3. to examine the extent to which the text of the brochures reflect the Christian identity of the school with clarity and coherence across the range of the school's polices and practice reflect in the brochure
4. to establish the medium of instruction at different key stages in the school.

Thirdly, semi-structured interviews were conducted with each diocesan bishop in the Church in Wales. These interviews, which each lasted around 1 hour, provided opportunities to explore the following issues with key leaders of the Church in Wales and focused on the following topics:

1. the place of Church in Wales schools in the mission of the diocese
2. their expectation of the attitude of parochial clergy to work in the schools within their benefice
3. the nurture of the Christian vocation to teach
4. their expectations of the review and its outcomes
5. their understanding of the leadership provided by the diocese to Church in Wales schools and to staff working within them.

Fourthly, semi-structured interviews were conducted with the diocesan director of each diocese. These interviews, which each lasted between 1 and 2 hours, provided an opportunity to explore the following issues with those charged with providing educational leadership within each of the Church in Wales diocese and focused on the following topics:

1. the place of Church in Wales schools in the mission of the diocese
2. their role (or roles) within the diocese and the resources available to them to undertake their responsibilities
3. the nurture of the Christian vocation to teach
4. their expectations of the review and its outcomes and how they understood that these might help and support them in their work
5. their understanding of the leadership provided by the diocese to Church in Wales schools and to staff working within them.

Fifthly, every Church in Wales priest of incumbent status was sent a questionnaire, which contained two distinct sections. The first concerned the commitment of the respondent to work in and with schools of all categories within their benefice. In particular it sought to establish:

1. the proportion of incumbents who have schools in their benefice and the types of school present
2. the proportion of the incumbent's working week that this work absorbed and the nature of the work undertaken.

The second section contained a range of statement about the work of Church in Wales schools and about education in more general terms and required the respondents to indicate their agreement or otherwise with these statements on a five-point Likert scale: disagree strongly, disagree, not certain, agree and agree strongly. The statements were drawn from or based on work undertaken in other studies of clergy attitudes to schools and education but were also reflective of the priorities of the review group.

The address list of incumbents was supplied by the Provincial Office of the Church in Wales. According to this list, there are 456 benefices within the Church in Wales of which at least 10 were vacant at the time when this questionnaire was distributed. Of the 446 incumbents who received questionnaires 275 returned them completed (61.7%). Four incumbents returned their questionnaires uncompleted citing as a reason for non-completion that the questionnaire was focused on the work of Church in Wales schools to the detriment of work in other types of schools.

Sixthly, a short questionnaire was sent to each parochial church council (PCC) secretary. The purpose of this questionnaire was to identify how the PCC understood and reflected the parish's engagement with and commitment to local schools. A further section sought data on the local church's engagement with children, young people and their parents. The address list of PCC secretaries was supplied by the Provincial Office of the Church in Wales. According to this list, there are 1,049 such office holders. Unfortunately, it is not possible to determine how many of these posts are vacant at any given time. Out of the 1,049 questionnaires distributed, 538 of these questionnaires were returned completed (response rate 51.28%). It is not possible to know how far this response rate should be adjusted upwards to allow for vacancies.

Seventhly, a survey was conducted to explore the reasons why parents, whose children attend Church in Wales schools, chose this school over others in their area. This questionnaire was distributed to parents through 21 Church in Wales schools (16 VA and 5 VC) in 2 Church in Wales dioceses. The schools approached to take part in the survey were in areas where parents were in a position to make choices about the school to which they wished to send their child or children, and 708 parents completed these forms. It is not possible to identify the response rate that this represents because of the difficulties in determining the definition of 'parent' and the precise number of 'parents' associated with each school.

Eighthly, as part of a wider project exploring the teachers' experience of the 'Christian vocation to teach', 205 teachers from a variety of schools in Llandaff diocese were asked to complete a questionnaire designed to identify:

1. the extent to which their reasons for entering teaching related to their faith
2. the extent to which they attribute their continuing commitment to teach to their faith
3. their sources of support in their work
4. their attitudes to education
5. the extent to which they might be displaying burn-out symptoms.

The questionnaire also included a short personality inventory. At the same time as this survey was being conducted in Llandaff diocese, 302 teachers in other parts of England and Wales had also completed the survey, making it possible to compare the teachers in Llandaff with teachers from a wider area.

Finally, with the approval of the Welsh Assembly Government, the Fisher Family Trust provided the review group with data at school level drawn from the results of the national attainment tests completed by Year 6 pupils in primary schools in Wales. As a result, it was possible to undertake some analysis of these results and to compare the general educational performance, in so far as this is measured by these tests, of pupils in Church in Wales schools with other schools in Wales. These comparisons were explored for results in English, Mathematics, Science and Welsh by local authority, diocese, urban and rural settings and by medium of instruction.

Within each of these areas of research the initial findings were communicated to the review group by a paper prepared by the review's research officer. Following receipt by the review group these papers were published on the review website. In some cases they were also considered by professional focus groups. In forming the review's recommendations both the results of the research and the subsequent discussions were used by the review group. Some of the results were considered sufficiently important to the main thrust of the review groups recommendations to be included in the final report of the review group.

Results

Within the confines of this chapter only a selection of those results relevant to the questions raised at the end of the introduction will be reported in this section.

Expectation 1

Church in Wales schools demonstrate a clear understanding of their religious character and how this is interpreted within the practice and policies of the schools. They aspire to the highest possible quality of educational experience for all children in their charge.

The examination of the school brochures demonstrated the extent to which Church in Wales schools made a clear presentation of the way in which the school's ethos was reflected in all aspects of the life of the school. In the event, the way in which this was done proved to be inconsistent. For example:

- 86 per cent stated their Church identity explicitly and correctly
- 85 per cent explicitly mentioned their links with the local church
- 43 per cent mentioned the value of the individual child but almost no brochures related this to their sections on special educational needs, child protection or bullying
- 85 per cent mentioned relationships but only 18 per cent related this to the Christian ethos of the school
- 93 per cent of schools mentioned school worship in their brochure but only 15 per cent mentioned the Anglican tradition within this context.

While this may only be evidence that schools are failing to ensure that their brochures properly reflect the practice within the school, the brochures are used as part of the documentary evidence for school inspection and it would be surprising if this were the case that inspectors have failed to draw governors' attention to this issue. If the brochures correctly reflect current practice then these findings may be identifying an area were further development needs to take place.

The data with which the review was provided for school performance indicated that Church in Wales primary schools provided higher levels of pupil performance in the core subjects overall than other primary schools in Wales; however, the performance data for Welsh was not as good as for other primary schools in Wales. These statements were true when groups of schools serving specific types of communities, such as urban or rural, were compared. These figures suggest that Church in Wales schools are meeting an expectation that they should be places where children achieve well, but given the rising expectations of what children should be achieving there exists a continuing challenge to maintain their performance compared with other schools in Wales.

Expectation 2

Admissions policies in use in Church in Wales schools reflect a balance between service to the local community and service to the church community.

These policies were analysed to identify which of two principle approaches to admissions do Church in Wales schools adopt. The results show that in 96 per cent of VC schools and 50 per cent of all VA or Foundation schools, geographical factors are given the highest priority, with the effect that the school will be serving its local community unless that community fails to produce enough children to fill the school. In the remaining schools, the highest criteria relates to the parental involvement with the church. Giving such a criterion the highest priority does not, of itself, imply that the school will be full of the children of churchgoing parents. Only if the membership of the local churches produces enough children to fill the school will this be the case. This is most likely to happen in those urban areas where there may be a significant number of parents living within reach of the school who attend church. Overall 77 per cent of Church in Wales schools give priority to admitting children from their local community; only 23 per cent may be admitting children of churchgoing parents before admitting other children from the local community.

The survey of parents conducted in schools in two of the dioceses indicated that parents considered 'high standards' and 'church character' when choosing a school for their child. This was true whether parents choose the nearest school for the child or whether they had chosen one other than the nearest school. The results of this survey are a reminder that even where church school admissions policies appear to give priority to church attenders over children living in the locality, some of the places allocated on the basis of church attendance may be allocated to children who would have received a place if geographical criterion had been given priority.

These figures demonstrate that Church in Wales schools are showing a clear commitment to serving their local communities. They also suggest that the debate on school admissions would benefit from research into the issues and monitoring of changing patterns in different areas.

Expectation 3

Clergy give time and energy to the service of the schools in their parish.

38.5 per cent of incumbents reported that they had a Church in Wales primary school in their benefice, 81.1 per cent reported that they had a community primary school and 13.5 per cent reported that they had a Roman Catholic primary school. 33.1 per cent of incumbents reported that they had a community secondary school in their benefice, 4.4 per cent had a Roman Catholic secondary and 1.1 per cent had a Church in Wales secondary school. Only 1.8 per cent reported that there were no schools in their benefice.

An incumbent may be involved in many different ways with the schools in his/her benefice depending on the quality of the relationships that exist and the talents of the particular incumbent. However, two roles appeared to be sufficiently common to merit specific enquiry. Table 4.1 shows the proportion of incumbents reporting that they served on the governing body of one or more

Table 4.1 Proportion of incumbents reporting membership of school governing bodies

	Incumbents who are governors (in %)	Incumbents who are chairs (in %)
Church in Wales schools	36.0	13.8
Roman Catholic schools	1.5	0.0
Community schools	33.8	5.5

types of school. It also shows the proportion of incumbents who not only are members of the governing body but also chair the meetings.

It is to be expected that the proportion serving on the governing bodies of Church in Wales primary schools should be equal to the proportion having such schools in their benefice. It is slightly surprising therefore that the number is slightly lower. This may be because a small number of incumbents have exercised their right not to take up their ex-officio place on the governing body of such schools. One in three of all incumbents responding to the questionnaire are governors of community schools and over 5 per cent of all respondents chair these governing bodies. This is a significant commitment to the management and welfare of community schools undertaken on behalf of the Church in Wales.

The other role which many incumbents would expect to play in schools in their benefice is that of contributing to the leadership of school worship. Table 4.2 shows the proportion of respondents who indicated that they undertake this role. It also shows the proportion of respondents who not only contribute to the general leadership of worship, but specifically preside at celebrations of school Eucharists.

Table 4.2 Proportion of incumbents who report involvement in school worship

	Incumbents leading worship (in %)	Presiding at Eucharists (in %)
Church in Wales schools	36.4	13.5
Roman Catholic schools	10.7	0
Community schools	62.9	0.7

As in the figures for membership of the governing body, the proportion of those leading worship in Church in Wales schools is very similar to the total proportion of incumbents reporting the presence of a Church in Wales school in their benefice. This is to be expected. The proportion reporting that they preside at schools Eucharists in Church in Wales schools must be presumed to represent the proportion of Church in Wales schools that hold such services. Within this table, the proportion of incumbents who report that they are making a contribution to the worship in Roman Catholic schools and in community schools represents a significant commitment to school worship beyond the Church in Wales sector.

The incumbents were asked to estimate the proportion of their working week that was spent in work with the schools in their benefice. Table 4.3 shows these proportions for the three different categories of schools.

Table 4.3 The percentage of incumbents committing different amounts of time per week to the three categories of school

	No time (in %)	Less than ½ day (in %)	½ day (in %)	Up to 1 day (in %)	1–2 days (in %)
Church in Wales schools	57.1	21.8	11.6	8.7	0.4
Roman Catholic schools	96.7	2.9	0.4	0.0	0.0
Community schools	22.9	55.6	15.3	4.4	1.5

The percentages given in the column referring to involvement with Roman Catholic schools when compared to the proportion of incumbents who say that they are leading worship in Roman Catholic schools suggests that there are some incumbents who are regularly involved with schools but the commitment is less than can be properly measured in terms of the proportion of a working week. It may be, for example, that they lead an act of worship every month, or visit the school once a term as a regular expression of interest and concern. Therefore, these figures are likely to represent an underestimate of the time committed to schools by incumbents in the Church in Wales. Nevertheless, they are an indication of a significant regular commitment.

These figures demonstrate that Church in Wales incumbents allocate significant time and energy to their work with schools in their benefices.

Expectation 4

Parishes relate well to the schools within their parishes or which serve their parishes.

In the survey sent to PCC secretaries they were asked to rate their church's contact with different categories of schools on a five-point scale from 'no contact' to 'very close contact'. Table 4.4 shows the PCC secretaries responses.

Table 4.4 The percentage of PCC secretaries rating their parish's contact with different types of schools as good or very good

	Primary (in %)	Secondary (in %)
Church in Wales schools	22.2	0.6
Roman Catholic schools	0.6	0.8
Community schools	34.6	6.5

It must be remembered that in some parishes the clergy in the benefice may have developed close links and commitment to schools at a personal or professional level, which are not yet reflected in the attitudes and understanding of the PCC or the lay people in the parish.

Comparing these responses with the proportion of parishes reporting the presence of different types of schools, there is potential support for the proposition that close contact between Church in Wales schools and the parishes in which they are situated is structured into the system, whereas the development of close contacts between other types of schools and Church in Wales parishes takes goodwill and hard work on both sides. The figures also draw attention to the difficulties that exist for parishes to establish close relationships with the secondary schools that serve their area, presumably because of the size of such schools and the wide range of community groups with which the schools have to maintain contact.

PCC secretaries were asked to rate contacts with teachers and school governors on the same five-point scale.

- 40.2 per cent reported that their parishes had close or very close contact with teachers
- 37.2 per cent reported that their parish had very close contact with governors.

The respondents were also asked about the presence of adults connected with schools on the PCC.

- 16.7 per cent reported that teachers were members of the PCC
- 44.8 per cent reported that school governors were members of the PCC
- 25.4 per cent reported that other adults employed in schools were members of the PCC.

There are at least two ways of understanding these responses. First, it will be clear that many PCC have, within their members, people who can contribute to any discussion on schools or young people from firsthand experience from working in or contributing to the life of schools. This should enable the ministry of the church to schools to be well focused and constructive.

Secondly, the church should take note of the large number of active church members who are serving schools in a variety of activities. This illustrates why those who emphasize the need for the church to ensure that the vocation to teach is actively supported feel so strongly.

These figures suggest that many parishes believe that they have good contact with the primary sector in education, but also support the argument that further work needs to be done to enhance the contacts between local churches and the secondary schools that serve their areas.

Expectation 5

Teachers are supported in their Christian vocation to teach and are valued members of the church community.

The survey on teachers' sense of vocation was conducted in both Church in Wales schools and community schools. It is not possible to be sure how far the sample is a true cross-section of all teachers and therefore the conclusions drawn from it must be cautious. 92 per cent of the teachers responding to the survey identified themselves as Christian with 36 per cent attending church once per week and a further 25 per cent reporting that they attended church at least once per month. 94 per cent identify themselves as 'dedicated to teaching' and 72 per cent indicate that they have a sense of vocation. This should at least be taken to indicate that there are significant numbers of teachers who are active Christians within the profession and that they have an understanding of their professional work as being motivated by a commitment to the task which draws on their religious beliefs. There is evidence within the data that teachers develop their sense of vocation and commitment as they exercise their profession. This implies that the association in some quarters of 'the vocation to teach' with recruitment of new Christian teachers may miss the importance of working with existing teachers to encourage their development.

61 per cent report that attendance at school worship helps to sustain them in their work and this proportion is significantly higher among teachers working in Church in Wales schools. Around one-third identify attending church worship (38%), the support of their faith community (34%) and knowing that others are praying for them (35%) helps sustain them in their vocation. Only about half this number identifies discussing their work with their local faith leader as being supportive (16%). Despite the limitations of this survey, the results should be encouraging and also challenging.

Expectation 6

Dioceses show a consistent lead to Church in Wales schools and those working within them – they acknowledge the importance of the Christian service provided by church members in schools and colleges of all types throughout Wales.

The interviews that were conducted with Diocesan Directors of Education provided clear evidence for the complexity of the tasks being undertaken by diocesan education teams. Those undertaken with diocesan bishops demonstrated a real appreciation for the work of diocesan education teams and of all those working within schools and colleges in Wales.

In general terms, it is the task of the diocesan education teams to support the schools which are achieving the aspirations held for Church in Wales schools and to encourage those schools that are working towards them. This includes preparing teachers for leadership roles in schools, supporting school governors, representing the church's interests in the process of appointing headteachers and other senior leaders in Church in Wales schools and then inducting and supporting them in their work. It also includes the support and development of Religious Education in Church in Wales schools. A major achievement of the teams working as a province has been the production and publication of the provincial syllabus (Kay, 2001). Further diocesan teams have the potential to make a significant contribution to the development of Religious Education in all schools, if only through the work of local SACREs and Syllabus conferences. Other tasks undertaken by diocesan education teams include the development of the spiritual and moral components of the curriculum, the development of school worship, the management of aspects of the inspection programme and the management of school buildings. In all these areas, elements of leadership are provided by members of diocesan teams in the service that they provide, their willingness to set and exemplify high standards and their advocacy. Every diocesan education team must maintain a network of relationships with the church structures within the diocese and ecumenically in its area in order to ensure that the vision for the church's contribution to education is maintained and enhanced. In addition, there are 22 LEAs in Wales. Each diocese must have the capacity to relate constructively to every local authority that falls within the borders of the diocese in whole or in part. In addition, acting together the dioceses must relate to the National Assembly Government and the national institutions concerned with education in Wales.

Most of this work is focused on administration and management issues and in these areas the overall impression is of much being achieved with very limited resources. In the more general role of leadership within education in the diocese and developing and sustaining a vision for the work, the situation was less clear. There was an impression that some of this work fell between the diocesan bishop and the Diocesan Director of Education, with each having expectations of the other which, given the pressures on both post holders were probably unrealistic. This was particularly clear in the area of inspiring, developing and sustaining the Christian vocation to teach.

This data support the argument that this expectation represents both a reflection of what is currently happening and a challenge for future development.

Conclusion

This chapter has suggested that the adoption by the Church in Wales of the mission statement 'Serving Christ through Education in Wales' would be justified should it be demonstrated that it was both realistic and challenging.

The chapter has presented research evidence that suggests that this statement is justified both as a reflection of current practice in a number of areas where there are expectations on the Church in Wales or on Church in Wales schools and as a challenge to further development in these areas.

Key questions

1. To what extent would the use of the research methodologies developed for the Church in Wales Report be useful for developing policy and practice in the Church of England?
2. Should research be commissioned to inform the debate about admissions to Church of England schools?
3. How can Anglican schools be encouraged to develop coherence between policy and practice across all of their activities?
4. How should their ethos be reflected in this search for coherence?
5. The chapter lists six expectations of the provinces service to education in the name of Christ; how far are these expectations appropriate to an English diocese?

Part Two

Current Policy and Philosophy

5

Philosophy, Theology and the Christian School

Paddy Walsh

Abstract

This chapter brings philosophy and theology together to identify and consider three matters of high priority for the Christian school.

1. It presents a philosophical case for education's essential mission being the development of persons as persons – thus also placing education at the pinnacle of social practices – from where recent theological advocacy of vocation-awareness as central to the Christian school mission can be favourably reviewed.
2. It argues that, already rationally speaking, 'love of the world' underpins and makes proper sense of other educational aims, and then draws on philosophy and theology together to bring out the deep cross-curriculum opportunities available to patient teaching for developing in students contemplative and caring attitudes appropriate to the various subjects.
3. It makes the case that faith in the mysterious inseparability of Christ's presence from his historic life, death and resurrection implies a premium on historic sensibility, the capacity to take the past to heart. The chapter considers the implications of this for history and Christian history in and across the curriculum, and it places particular emphasis on developing a working knowledge of the New Testament.

Keywords
Philosophy and theology, developing persons, vocational awareness, love of the world as first, communing and care in the curriculum, historical sensibility for the Christian, working knowledge of the New Testament

Introduction: Philosophy and theology

The chapter will propose that personhood, love, and historical awareness are fundamental concerns for the Christian school and it will put philosophy and theology to work together on each of them in turn. This anticipates the dual character of Christian education: its non-eliminable *secular* aspect, including the secular nature of the learned disciplines represented in standard curriculum subjects, and its equally non-eliminable *religious* – not just spiritual – aspect.

The standard Christian view on the relationship between philosophy and theology dates back to the birth of our universities in the thirteenth century, and the West's nearly simultaneous recovery of the long lost works of Aristotle. St Thomas Aquinas was at hand to avert a crisis. He masterminded a firmer distinction between philosophy and theology and, thereby, a firmer acceptance of sustained, scholarly enquiry based on reason alone. Henceforth, it was to be no insult to faith and theology to require them to stay out of philosophical enquiry.[1] It was also clear, however, that in mediating perspectives and motivations from Revelation that were in principle beyond philosophy, theology would continue to use philosophy as its 'handmaid', absorbing and, as often as not, transforming relevant philosophical perspectives and motivations. We will find examples of this, too, in applying philosophy and theology to education, and justification in that for resisting the temptation always to go straight to theology when considering the Christian school.

Another piece of history of enduring relevance to education is that from the fifteenth century onward, natural scientists asserted the independence of their new disciplines from Revelation and, eventually had this conceded by most mainstream churches. The benefit has been to theology and our understanding of revelation (of the creation texts in Genesis, for example) as well as to science. I will take it that the Christian school would not now wish to lose this benefit to a confused and pointless fundamentalism.

Persons, practices and vocation

One priority for the Christian school is *to show forth the dignity of the person and, relatedly, of the practice of education itself.* How can philosophy and theology work together to bring vision and energy to this decent-sounding proposal? Two recent analyses, one from philosophy and the other from the broad world of theology, are to the point.

Philosophy

Richard Pring (2000) makes the case that the core mission of education is nothing less than the development of *persons as persons.* So, activities are to be considered properly educational if and only if they bring about worthwhile learning in students that:

- far from being 'skin-deep', works towards their developing *cognitive perspectives* with the power to transform how they see the world and how they proceed in it,
- and contributes seriously to their *emergent identities*, that is, to the emergence of their identities. (Pring, 2000, pp. 14–17)

Of course, these two conditions make this an at least moderately loaded, and therefore moderately contestable, conception of education. It will have intuitive force for many and, as Pring says, it follows and combines Dewey and Peters, which is a seriously commanding philosophical lineage, but does its choice of 'person' rather than 'society' as the central focus make it 'individualist' in some suspect sense? Pring heads that suspicion off by persuasively writing key interpersonal and social capacities into the concept of a developed person. Learning to recognize others as persons, learning to relate (share a world of meaning) with other persons, even learning to collaborate with other persons in shaping the social and political environments, are all so many ingredients in becoming a person fully. And yet this conception is far from bland. It still eschews the overidentification of 'person' with 'participant' in more collectivist conceptions of education, and it has obvious bite in relation to the currently dominant technicist and managerialist perspectives on education.

Pring sees the personal and educational goal of identity as a matter, in Charles Taylor's words, of understanding what is of crucial importance to oneself – 'to know who I am is a species of knowing where I stand' (Taylor, 1989, p. 27). He evokes the dignity of young people's quest for getting a grip on 'the sort of persons they are or might become, the ideals that are worth striving for, the qualities that they wish to be respected for, the talents that need to be developed, the kind of relationship in which they will find enrichment, the style of life that is worth pursuing' (Pring, 2000, p. 19). Fostering and respecting this quest, he rightly argues, has thoroughgoing implications for what is taught – underlining, for example, the importance of the humanities – but also for how teachers teach and how they relate to students more generally. So when someone says to a roomful of teachers – as I witnessed at a recent conference – that they should go to their classrooms to *meet* their students, rather than to teach them, we get the point. The pedagogical teacher–pupils relationships have to be placed within authentic person–persons relationships if they are to realize their educational – never mind their specifically Christian – potential.

Of course, we do not think of education as coterminous with schooling nor of the young person's wrestling with identity issues as confined to school or the business only of school. However, first, the school's responsibility here must be proportionate to its major shareholding in young people's time. School is their workplace and, for most, the main context for their extra-familial experiences of friendship and betrayal, comradeship and enmity, community and loneliness, also for their experiences of adults, all of which are key general factors in their identity-building. That points up the importance of the communal life and ethos of the school and its classrooms. Second, there is the more specific school contribution to identity emergence of the transformative cognitive perspectives referred to above. (Indeed, Pring's two conditions are interconnected: developing cognitive perspectives facilitate and are facilitated by identity emergence.)

Here, too, the vocational dimension of education comes into view, for vocation enters into identity; the commitments in our lives that we would dignify as 'callings' – without necessarily identifying 'a caller' – have that combination of durability and importance that ensures we may also think of them as parts of who we are. Of course, 'vocational' has several meanings in education and the reference here is not to courses and subjects so called by virtue of an intense and/or immediate focus on a particular area of employment, but to a vital aspect of education and curriculum generally. Like Dewey a century ago, we should come clean about *all* education being vocational, while also taking his further point that this is much bigger than the delayed-action career-potency of academic curricula. 'Vocational' extends to whatever gives serious structure and direction in life, thus to marriage and stable partnerships, to parenthood and grandparenthood, and to long-term interests and hobbies, for example (Dewey, 1916, pp. 307ff.). In this properly broad sense education is, indeed, *intrinsically* vocational – even though it is *not only* vocational inasmuch as it has to be concerned with the quality of the childhood 'present', as well as, and as much as, the quality of the adult 'future' (a point on which, of course, Dewey would also insist).

Before leaving philosophy for theology, a corollary may be drawn from the argument so far. That the person is central to education and education to the person suggests a placement of education at the pinnacle of our most significant human and social practices – at any rate, as measured by the intimacy of a practice's engagement in the human. So, we might construct a table of practice categories in which this *human factor* rises steadily as the table climbs towards education:

- in the *natural sciences*, the questioning focus is on the non-human, though the *language and cultural traditions* are human (as well as the scientists)
- in *technology and engineering*, the material focus is still the non-human, but a plus factor now is an integral consultation of *human purposes* around the dispositions of this matter
- in *medicine*, the integral focus on healing humans begins to bring the human into direct focus, though with a bias towards *human bodies*
- in the *social sciences*, an integral focus on *human subjects as such* (i.e. on persons) is a new plus factor, and one that is now made quite explicit in the non-positivist, 'interpretative' tradition in social science
- in *social policy*, that focus extends further into well-meaning *interventions* in persons' lives
- finally, *educational practice* stands clear of other social policies and practices inasmuch as its interventions actually *develop* persons, *make* persons of us.[2]

Small wonder, then, that teachers in reflective mood are sometimes aghast at their own temerity!

Theology

How might reflection on the bearing of Revelation and faith on education and personal development build on, and transform, this philosophical base? The experience and concept of 'vocation' in its original religious sense, the God-given 'calling', comes quickly to mind. It relates to our personal development while raising our status to addressees of God, and – as will now emerge – it can have rather more than a terminological connection with school business.

Christopher Jamison OSB, who some years ago became known to many as the Abbot in the television documentary series *The Monastery*, is now the Catholic Bishops' of England and Wales' appointed Director of the National Office for Vocation. In this role he has been proposing, in recent addresses to Catholic headteachers in several dioceses, that 'vocation' be adopted as a new and a revitalizing centre of gravity of the Catholic school. Where vocation 'refers to the call of Christ', 'fostering a culture of vocation lies at the heart of the Catholic school'; 'it has the potential to be the heart of the curriculum'; and so:

> let's create a Catholic curriculum that has one simple vision as its core aim: *a Catholic curriculum that enables all students to respond to the call of Christ throughout their lives*. With such a vision at its heart, this would be a vocational curriculum in the profoundest meaning of the word vocation.[3]

He sees this proposal as, among other things, firming up the frequent references in Catholic school mission statements to developing God-given talents or to self-discovery in relation to Christ's teachings and values.

We should put down the reiteration of the word 'Catholic' here to office and context. I am confident that Fr Jamison would be delighted if other Christian schools were to take up his proposal, perhaps with some denominational variation of the details.

But how might it play in our Christian schools? Consider those dramatic scriptural images of vocation: the call of Abraham to leave his country for the foreign land of Canaan, of Moses to lead Israel out of Egypt, of the youngster, Samuel, to be God's prophet and judge, and later, via Samuel, of David to be King of Israel, of sometimes reluctant prophets ('Whom shall I send?' and Isaiah's awestruck 'Here I am, Lord. Send me!'), of Mary to bear the Messiah, of the apostles and disciples ('Come, follow me!'), and matching those calls of *individuals*, the constantly renewed call of the *peoples* of God, old and new, to the appropriate ways of communal and individual life. Consider, also, the calls to baptism, Eucharist and ministry, to monastic/communal life, marriage or the single state, and the more episodic calls to conversion and repentance. In all these cases the creative link with identity is maintained. When the call is answered, the called come to *identify themselves* as Israelite, prophet, king, mother, apostle, Christian, minister/priest, monk/nun/spouse/committed single person, sinner/convert/penitent. The same applies to the semi-secular extension of 'vocation' to professions involving notable elements of service, such as nurse/doctor/teacher.

Sustained use of scriptural images, balanced by similarly arresting ones from historical and contemporary Christianity, could indeed raise vocational consciousness from its present levels. Christ's 'call' comes less readily to mind and figures less in our school mission statements and discourse than His 'example', 'help', 'teaching' or 'friendship'. This may be unsurprising in institutions peopled mostly by *cradle*-Christians in *long-established* communities – in marked contrast to the Christians and churches of New Testament times – but we are the losers inasmuch as the facet of 'call' would bring something new to the table: a challenge to a self-defining and enhancing *purpose and resolve* in our communal and individual lives.

How would the roles of church and school be distinguished in an enhanced vocational culture that embraced both? That is a legitimate and important question; church must not swallow school. However, the Christian school is a finely articulated institution and there will be some overlap. Chaplaincy and liturgy have always given church a footing in Church schools and now vocation would loom larger in their services to pupils and teachers. It would also have become a prominent theme in the spiral curriculum of Religious Education, but to the direct end of really good understanding and appreciation, rather than of personal discernment. An enhanced emphasis on the ideal of service would be its outlet in citizenship projects and extra-curricular activities and, perhaps most crucially, in career guidance – and this could now be more readily contextualized within Christ's call to serve as He served. For mainstream subjects, however, we may refer once more to those varied cognitive perspectives with the power to transform how young people will come to see the world and proceed in it. As the subjects' main contributions to person formation and identity, these may also be their main contributions to vocation readiness and Christian identity (the particular elements of 'nature', themselves sanctified by the incarnation, on which 'grace builds' here). Christian subject teachers may become adept at making appropriate and graceful religious connections in their teaching, but getting their subjects and subject pedagogies right in relation to their own deep grammars is likely to remain more important for building vocation awareness.

A culture of Christian vocation will need supporting theological ideals and concepts. Christopher Jamison, to return to his address to headteachers, draws such supports from a stream of documents on the Catholic school issued by the Congregation for Catholic Education between 1977 and 2007. He takes two 'very demanding' principles from these documents. One is that, as much as is realistic, every teacher in the Catholic (Christian?) school should be held responsible for faith formation. The worked examples he sketches suggest how even teachers whose own beliefs might stop at theism may be persuaded to contribute to this. The other principle is that the Catholic (Christian) school is a school of *communion*. An arresting observation in the most recent document is cited: that education in this school 'is not given for the purpose of gaining power but as an aid towards fuller understanding of and communion with people, with events and with things', a claim which the document then connects with the young person beginning to have a sense of their place, and God's vocation for them, in this world (Congregation for Catholic Education, 2007).

'Communion with people, with events and with things' suggests a line of reflection on *curriculum* in the Christian school that is, again, part philosophical and part theological.

♦

Love in the curriculum

A second priority for the Christian school is *to be alive to the opportunities that lie deep in the curriculum for developing contemplative and caring attitudes in students*. If the equation 'contemplation + care = love' is valid, this would bring our school work close to the centre of God's revelation of Himself and of His Will for us in Christ. But since 'love' is also a vital bridging concept between religious and worldly discourses, philosophy will have its say here too. Indeed, though the general argument of this section makes a special claim on the Christian school, quite a lot of it could be proposed for schools generally.

Love of the world is first

Clearly, there are large and legitimate claims on education that conflict often and regularly in practice. Establishing some general order of priority among them would be more than useful, even if it did not provide 'read-off' solutions to every concrete policy or curriculum dilemma. A strong *philosophical* case can be offered for making 'love of the world' the fundamental aim of education and curriculum. It acknowledges the main competitor claims in turn, but allocates them to subordinate roles:

1. Education is and ought to be an *economic investment*. Learning to earn a living is obviously important, for societies and governments as well as for individuals and families. But however dominant that perspective may actually be in policy terms, it is not one that can rationally be ultimate, because the real value of 'possessions' is in their use. This point, which is at least as old as Aristotle's *Ethics*, directs us towards the next claim.
2. The *enrichment of experience* ('quality of life') – in the pupils' childhood present as well as in their adult future, it is again important to add – brings us much nearer to the beating heart of the education ideal. For the familiarity of this 'progressive' idea, we should salute Dewey as its most brilliant, measured and influential champion (Dewey, 1916). However, it begs criteria for judging the quality of curriculum experiences. Dewey himself located these exclusively in the potential *internal* relationships of our experiences, emphasizing in particular the degree of *openness* to further and ever-wider experiences that might be expected of any proposed curricular experience. For all the brilliance of his analyses around this theme, he struggled to make its exclusiveness stick. The natural assumption,

surely, is that the quality of an experience would also crucially depend on the more or less *intrinsic* interest and value of the independent 'people, events and things' that are being experienced – and of their associated contexts and worlds. A constricted theory of knowledge denied Dewey the opportunity of making that kind of ontological or 'reality' appeal, at any rate explicitly and consistently. That constriction was not particular to Dewey; he inherited it from the mainstream of modern philosophy. Furthermore, the temptation to focus on experience in isolation from reality has arguably spread out from philosophy to our culture more generally. It is all the more important to insist that, of their very nature, experiences cannot 'stand up' on their own. We need to move the argument on towards including 'the worlds' that are there to be experienced.

3. On the way, we may pause to consider the *ethical dimension and responsibility* that education also undoubtedly has. Those who would claim this is its *most* fundamental feature – perhaps citing Socrates, or Confucius, or indeed Dewey in support – would have a question to answer. *From where* does the regulative harness of ethics derive its special authority to constrain and restrain our pursuit of possessions and of experiences, and to require us to respect – if not also to cultivate and look after – persons, evidence, languages and discourses, heritages, equality, justice and democracy, and the environment? Is it not also from the *worth in themselves* of 'people, events and things'? If that acknowledgement of the independently real is not built in, the ethical harness may easily sink back into the merely prudential. Making it explicit, on the other hand, just speeds this argument on to its conclusion.

4. That conclusion is that, rationally speaking, *love of the world* underpins and makes proper sense of other educational aims. We might even risk speaking of a habitual *ecstatic* attitude to a (re-)enchanted world to be cultivated in and with students, provided we were careful to stress that this 'standing out of oneself' is no stream of 'peak experiences'. To some degree, it is spontaneously unavoidable in any sane life. At the deeper and more consistent levels where it has had to be cultivated, it is still an everyday grace and achievement. That everyday, taken-for-granted quality is, indeed, the educational goal, though sustaining it will depend on times and exercises of reflexive attention and commitment.

It remains now to work at the pedagogical and curriculum implications of prioritizing this love (this 'inward-outwardness') in its two modes of contemplative 'communing' and care, recognizing, as we go, that this quite everyday power to experience the real world – to begin to understand, know and care about it – is among nature's greatest miracles and God's greatest creations.[4]

Communing and learning

As for 'love', our uses of 'communion' and 'communing' are not confined to religion and theology. They quite generally suggest habits or episodes of shared intimate presence, attention and communication between people, and they may be extended to apostrophizing those among the absent, the dead and the historical who we feel close to, or 'in touch with'. We may 'commune', too, with animals and with personified features of the inanimate world: work-animals and pets, familiar places, favourite works of art and music, materials and artefacts on which we are working or have worked, and – of course – nature in many of its forms and moods. Companion words include 'presence', 'wonder', 'attending', 'absorbed by/in', 'dwelling', 'empathizing', 'identifying with', 'appreciating', 'participating', 'contemplating', 'enjoying' and 'delighting in'. Now how salient are such terms and attitudes to education? Don't they imply stillness and resting, while education implies constant learning, and thus continuous movement, progress from one discovery to the next discovery, non-stop accumulation and growth? Communing is for old people, it might be said; children are required to be in a hurry, especially nowadays! Despite its grain of truth, that crude contrast quickly provokes a recall of other essential aspects of learning and progress: practice, repetition, revision, consolidation, spiral learning, perspective construction and reconstruction. Again, there is always *delight* (even if often fleeting) in understanding and discovery and, I venture, not just in the achievement itself, but always also in the objective – often intrinsic – interest of *what* is discovered and, deeper down, in the general intelligibility of things. At every stage from wonder, to understanding, to competence and mastery, communing happens naturally, but its time needs protection if it is to be sustained and to become a habit. *Patient* teaching facilitates it for now and for later; impatient teaching (and policies) may steamroller it flat.

It seems significant that there is now a 'slow teaching movement', modelled on the 'slow cooking movement', reacting against the high-pressure education policy styles of many recent and current governments (Holt, 2002). It is also interesting that modern Jesuit documentation on education in their schools proposes pedagogies that 'develop affective experiences of knowing as well as conceptual experiences of knowing, that is, knowledge by a kind of empathic identification, as well as by logical analysis' (Meirose, 1994).

Communing in subjects

It is relatively easy to envisage habits of communing being developed in *the humanities*. For example, and as we shall see later, history can be approached quite properly as an exercise in a broad kind of *pietas*, a discriminating, critical, responsible, brotherly and sisterly love of past peoples and worlds. But consider, too, that *the sciences* might be taught quite deliberately in the way in which the young Einstein thought they were best conducted, namely, 'in a state of mind . . . akin to that of the lover and worshipper'.[5] Consider, as just one example, the potential in this regard of that familiar relativity equation, '$E = MC^2$'. Energy being such an enormous multiple of mass, not just for the unstable elements in which conversion is feasible but in principle for all matter, makes every pebble kicked on the road home from school an appropriate object of wonder. With the right teaching, good work in the science laboratory expands naturally into new perspectives on the world at large.

The 'making' subjects, Arts and Technologies, are as much opportunities for deep receptivity as for forceful self-expression. In *the technologies*, students learn an almost physical acceptance both of the laws that govern their materials and of the materials themselves. They should also learn appreciation of the 'given' skills and procedures they must use in their own work and the inventive tradition to which these belong, and of the human needs being served – and/or undermined ('hands-on' can lend itself very well to ecological awareness) – not to mention appreciation of the old and new 'wonders' among which they live. Especially for the Christian school that really is obliged to draw on its Jewish as well as its Greek roots and to remember its carpenter's son and its intellectual tent-maker, the case is a strong one for some technology on everyone's curriculum, keeping design and making at the centre of this curriculum, and contextualizing this design and making as much in cultural and environmental, as in commercial, terms.

We are used to the language of subjectivity around *the arts*. They are 'intensely personal', 'self-expressive', 'profoundly creative'. But they, too, are also intimate with materials, and in the representational cases with 'subjects' as well, and often bent on disinterested revelation and expression of the latent possibilities of those materials and subjects. More generally, 'subjective' here refers primarily to the personal intensity of the artist's or art-lover's involvement; it does not have to mean the opposite of 'objective'. The visions expressed are, after all, of some or other aspects of the world and the creativity may lie in deepening perceptions of what is. The arts, indeed, offer privileged forms of communion with the world-beyond-the-self, which the Christian school should prize and protect in a tepid curriculum climate.

These diverse ways by which the curriculum may connect young people to contemplative food and drink for their lifetimes can be further elevated by explicit faith considerations – without loss to their 'worldly' identity and logic. So science-based awe before the cosmos and biosphere can be contextualized within a worshipful faith in God, the Father, Word and Spirit; communion with the historical past can evoke and engage the communion of saints; and students in workshops and art-rooms may begin to see themselves as God's co-workers, in the monastic spirit of *laborare est orare*. (There is a fairly obvious mediating role here for classroom prayers.) Finally, a Simone Weil panorama opens up *cross-curricular* opportunities:

> The order of the world is the same as the beauty of the world. . . . It is one and the same thing, which with respect to God is eternal Wisdom; with respect to the universe, perfect obedience; with respect to our love, beauty; with respect to our intelligence, balance of necessary relations; with respect to our flesh, brute force. (1952, p. 281)

Care through the curriculum

Educating students in care is the other half of engaging them in love of the world. Here we are in the zone of moving practical reason towards an honest and just astuteness, and helping to form character in virtues like compassion, cooperativeness, perseverance and courage – while knowing that basic emotional development and self-confidence are, as often as not, half the battle. Care in this broad sense is the natural partner of regard, appreciation and communion, but it needs its own curriculum and pedagogical attention.

England's Citizenship Education, a statutory subject for the 11–16 age group since 2002, has provided schools, including Christian schools, with enhanced opportunity and good guidance in this area. In its terms, a curriculum for care involves the triad of *responsibility, skills (of social enquiry and participation)* and *appropriate knowledge.*[6] The expression 'subject-plus' emerged to convey that this is definitely a subject, with all the status that confers, but also definitely more. The Inspectorate chivvied schools to provide *all* of the following elements as a matter of course: dedicated citizenship classes; fully explicit interventions in teaching other subjects; suspended-timetable 'citizenship events'; and ongoing student participation in the life of both the school and the wider community. So, the school's specialist citizenship teachers have been expected to advise colleagues in other subjects on how to notice and convert their citizenship opportunities, for example, by preparing a space in a geography lesson on sustainable development for the question: 'what can we do about this?'[7] However, its perceived transformative potential has meant that student *participation* in school and community affairs is the element that has attracted the most attention. Thus, a Parliamentary Select Committee (no less!) on Citizenship Education:

> A whole-school approach implies that the democratic, participative attitude and skills which citizenship education seeks to develop are also put into practice in the school context; that is to say, young people participate in, comment on, and more importantly, change their learning environments. (House of Commons, 2007)

And another national report saw participation as creating a bridge between young people, their schools, their families and their communities (Ajegbo, 2007). Given these high aspirations, it is not surprising that this 'active citizenship' turned out to be the fence at which schools were most likely to be faltering or failing, according to the most authoritative research studies (e.g. NFER, 2006). The Select Committee declares that '[s]ome of the most inspiring approaches to citizenship education we have come across are those where young people have a real say in the running of their school, and are able to affect change on issues that matter most to them', but recognizes that this was new and difficult territory for many schools, as 'touching their essence'. Church schools, that pray daily 'Thy will be done on earth as it is in heaven', might reinterpret the challenge as *prophetic*, taking prophetic action to develop a prophetic Christian spirit in their students, while remembering that the *true* prophets never had things easy.

Actually, it is not clear that Church schools have been much to the fore in interpreting and implementing this still new and vulnerable subject, and defending it against sceptics. Yet, its declared flexibility and openness to experiment has left them at liberty, in principle, to give a gospel reading to the development of 'student voice', to place extra emphasis on peace and social justice issues at home and abroad, and to develop a conception of 'responsibility' that includes the virtues of stewardship, chastity, mercy and magnanimity.[8] (All this would still be open to the Christian school even should Citizenship Education lose its hard-earned *statutory* status in the current review of the National Curriculum.)

Taking the past to heart

A third priority for the Christian school *is to cultivate historical sensibility in its students.* This sensibility is required in historical religions that claim decisive divine interventions at particular times and places, and, I think, even more fundamentally in Christianity than in the other historical religions. It is not only that our Christian founder lived two millennia ago and His life on earth, mission and gospel had roots going back more than another millennium. Our faith essentially is that He is still with us – to the end of time and wherever we are – and that this 'here and now' presence is mysteriously *inseparable* from that life, death and resurrection at that earlier once-for-all time in that one particular part of the world. To put it mildly, this gives a whole new meaning to the saying 'the past lives on in the present'.[9]

The challenge to the Christian school is to convey to its students the meaning and the credibility of that 'lives on', to enable them – not force them, but make it really possible for them – to take it seriously. It has to do this in the teeth of youth's natural assumption that the modern present has little or nothing to learn from the past, especially the ancient past. In our globalized world, that assumption is probably reinforced by multiple forms of engagement with other parts of the contemporary world that already more or less satisfy the young person's appetite for what is different, exotic and faraway. To counteract such indifference and begin to meet the credibility challenge, the Christian school needs to attend rather more closely than is at all usual to its history education, to how its curriculum as a whole promotes both history generally and Christian history specifically. Three areas can be proposed for reflection and development, one at the semi-submerged level of orientation and two at the overt level of syllabus reconstruction.

Orientation: Three distinctions and a thesis

The *distinctions* are (1) between the proper concerns and priorities of history as a scholarly, research-based, specialist practice and those of history as informing general education and infiltrating outlooks and agencies in educated publics and educated societies (of course, the two sets overlap substantially in the middle and are not to be divorced, but each extends beyond the other); (2) between 'history for its own sake' and 'history for better understanding of the present', a standard distinction of motives and purposes that does rather provoke the question of how they might be interconnected; and (3) to resolve an ambiguity in 'history for its own sake', between love of *enquiring/learning* about the past – the love of 'the chase' – and love of the discovered, or being discovered, *human past itself.*

The *thesis* is that the last-named, the human past's own human value, is the bottom line. History is an impressive witness to the interest and recognition that people and their institutions and societies command long after they are dead and gone. They continue to engage our respect, admiration, pity, indignation, sense of justice – sense of responsibility even – both spontaneously and reflectively. They absorb us and we dwell on them. *Taking the past to heart* in this way has to be the most fundamental achievement and value of our engagement with history, whether as a professional historian or a primary school pupil, inasmuch as it is this: (1) that makes our engagement finally *serious* (however, we are finding the current topic – fascinating, entertaining, shocking, mournful, inspiring or even boring); and (2) that enables right and wise learning *from* the past, because 'using' the past without appreciating it curtails understanding of it – in the way 'using' people in the present ('for the experience', perhaps) prevents any real understanding of them – and therefore puts the validity of its proposed transfer to the present in doubt.

'Love of the human past', then, deserves pole position in history education. Some academic historians may jib at this, but the human, ethical and educational interest of history requires a reading of its methodological canons, not as prohibiting our natural responses, but as disciplining them into more reflective and measured, more impartial and just, even more generous and forgiving, modes.

This love may be considered a *virtue* specific to history, indicating that it is something good that needs to be developed and maintained by regular hard practice. We may hesitate to use the old Latin name of *pietas* for fear of associating it with stances that are exclusive and uncritical – restricted to familial and national forbears, who were also always 'basically right', at least 'in the end'. If, however, we see *pietas* as *caritas* in its retrospective aspect, a quite different logic emerges. It is cosmopolitan, like charity: it should indeed 'begin at home', but it certainly does not end there and its criteria for selecting pasts to engage with are broad and generous. Especially nowadays, could it be reasonable to find even most of one's historical interests, models and sympathies in the past of just one's own country? Second, as well as appreciative modes, it has more or less bitterly *critical modes.* We may be profoundly ashamed of things in the past history of our country, culture, profession, church or sex, without thereby disowning these sources of our being, indeed while owning them the more. Third, it is also committed neither to ethical relativism nor to a Whig assumption of the present's moral superiority; so it may judge, but it is also open to being judged, as it is to being inspired, by the past (Walsh, 1993, ch. 12).

History and Christian history in and across the curriculum

As well as 'History', the defined and timetabled subject, there are the comet-tails of their own histories that the other school subjects carry in their wake, the histories of literature (and language), art, music, also of science, maths and technology, also of crafts like furniture-making and hairdressing, also of religions and of history itself. The extent to which these histories 'live on' in the present of their subjects, and, therefore figure more or less automatically in the school curricula, varies significantly. Those for literature, art and music easily announce themselves, via disputatious 'canons' of Great Works, for example. The past is integral to the classroom present in those subjects. In science and maths, by contrast, past heroes and golden ages may be honoured for their contributions to progress, but are no longer actually needed when 'doing' or 'learning' the discipline. However, they can come into their own when discussion moves up a reflexive level – as it regularly should in education – to consider the nature, logic, values, significance or current state of the subject.

These subject histories have considerable potential, much of it perhaps unrealized, for expanding and deepening students' historical universes. For some students, indeed, they will be their most authentic encounter with the past. There is also the consideration that they can keep a limited historical education going for older (and more receptive?) students after they have dropped history. A 'ringmaster' role could be envisaged here for a school's history department vis-à-vis its colleague departments. However, there is no substitute for history as a subject in its own right to look after the great matters of wars and peace, social and political movements, rises and falls of institutions, empires, nations and civilizations – that are also the panoramic contexts for subject histories. Nowadays, as well, history aims to teach young people enough about methodology, sources and interpretation to conduct small-scale historical enquiries of their own. The stake that the Christian school has in historical sensibility means it should prize all of this and smile on it.

'History of Christianity' and 'Christianity in history' are to some extent unavoidable, the former perhaps most notably in the Religious Education programme, the latter in history and the histories of many other subjects. But, given the need and opportunity to be selective about periods and themes, it seems as natural and reasonable as giving special attention to the history of one's country that the Christian school should provide its students with a quite thorough immersion in Christianity's historic achievements, but obviously also its failures and complicities and fissures, and in great and good works of literature, art and music with Christian motifs. In part, this is a matter of building up their Christian identity and confidence, and the school need not be shy about it. On the other hand, great Christian achievements and scandalous failures alike are best presented in their interactions with the general history and more or less secular cultures to which they also belonged (like the teachers and students themselves). Beyond that is the obligation to attend to histories and cultures from further afield, and further back, that did not connect, or hardly connected, with Christianity. It may have taken globalization and the critiques of ethnocentrism and racism to bring it home to us fully, but, philosophically, all such pasts are those of human brothers and sisters, while, theologically, our times nudge our focus towards the universality of God's salvific will in Christ, so we acknowledge all peoples have been peoples of God and, pray God, are now in the communion of His saints.

The New Testament

This is a special case, history with a difference and fundamental to Christian faith and the Christian school.

A good working knowledge of the New Testament represents, both for believers and for any non-believers who acquire it, a clearly valid intellectual and cultural achievement, since the New Testament is the main source on the founder and the early life of a movement that has been massively influential. For believers, however, the much more important benefit it confers is huge facilitation in connecting up the Jesus of their devotion and the Jesus of the Church's creed with Jesus of Galilee and, therefore, in developing a faith that is more secure, accurate and ample – if not also deeper. Given this, why should this working knowledge not be a priority learning goal in the Christian school, specifically in its arrangements for religious education and worship? Or, at any rate, in some kinds of Christian school, for there are, of course, different models in terms of mission and admission to consider. Starting, however, with the relatively simple case of schools that are primarily for children of the faith and for education that, in Jeff Astley's terms, is more 'into', than 'about', Christianity (Astley, 2002) we might indeed charge them at least with providing students with a properly literary, as well as devotional, engagement with New and Old Testament texts over their primary and secondary school careers and, increasingly as they progress through school, with some serious awareness and tasting of biblical scholarship. In regard to the New Testament, our expectations might even include all the following:

- *enhanced uses* of the New Testament in both religious education and devotional contexts
- *specialist knowledge of some 'set' whole works and key texts*, to the same level as is required of the students for their set novels, plays and poems in literature classes, to be acquired over time and with some spiral revisiting: perhaps 7–8 whole works – a synoptic gospel (Mark?), John, Acts, and 4–5 letters of Paul and John – plus as many key passages from other works
- increasing *familiarity with many more individual works*, awareness of their structures, contents (themes, key passages) and contexts, indicating light but recurring study and use, perhaps a mixture of guided, shared and private engagements
- *background knowledge* of the world in which the New Testament was formed and to which it was originally addressed
- *hermeneutic awareness*, eventually of some sophistication, regarding and including such matters as: genre; forms and tools of memory-keeping and communication at the time; interaction of oral tradition and written redaction; the influence on texts of the immediate concerns of the early churches to whom the texts were addressed; dating and authorship; the formation of the canon; human and divine authorship – the meaning of 'inspiration' and 'inerrancy'; in short, knowing how the New Testament 'works' – a truly important aid to defending its credibility for oneself and others
- general knowledge of uses and abuses of, and battles over, the New Testament in Christian history.[10]

As for Christian schools with more open admission policies and more markedly multifaith religious education classes, a judicious core and elective programme through the years might be up to enabling those students who wanted it to achieve most of the above, around an ongoing New Testament core-course that would benefit everyone.

Conclusion – a job for sixth-form religious education?

Intuitively, how the three priorities of personhood/vocation, communion/care and historical sensibility overlap conceptually, and could usefully reinforce each other in practice, seems a promising area for further analysis and reflection. A more basic issue is *what else* should command a comparable level of priority for the Christian school. Perhaps, the most urgent – and difficult – item is likely to emerge from the conceptual complex of suffering, injustice, sin, evil, forgiveness and redemption – and its interaction with the three discussed in this chapter would then also become an issue.

All these matters could be seen as belonging to a Christian Theory of (Educational) Knowledge. This would be a body of theory that drew on theology as well as philosophy. It would also – as this chapter's arguments and discussions have exemplified – be at least as much concerned with knowledge-value considerations that are more or less *unifyingly* cross-curricular as with the logical and other *distinctions* between forms of knowledge. And it could profitably be explored in some depth with the students themselves at that point in their development where it is particularly important that they become more reflexively aware of the values that have been driving their education and take more responsibility for them; that is, in the sixth form. It could be an adjunct there to their main subjects and might most appropriately be led by the religious education department.[11]

Key questions

1. How may philosophy and theology interact in developing a Christian theory of (educational) knowledge?
2. How could awareness of the call of Christ become a leading edge in person and identity development at school?
3. How are educational priorities best ordered?
4. How might patient teaching promote 'communion' and 'caring' (love of the world) through the curriculum?
5. Why should historical sensibility matter to the Christian and how may it be cultivated in the curriculum?
6. What would an adequate initiation into the New Testament look like?

Notes

1 Unfortunately, in the *later* Middle Ages, philosophy lost confidence and declined into nominalism – and this balanced view of its service to, and relationship with, theology got rather mislaid for a time.

2 Of course, there is an element of (useful) exaggeration in phrases like 'becoming a person' and 'being developed' into a person, as though children were not already persons (and otherwise could never 'become' persons)!

3   Christopher Jamison OSB (2013), 'God Has Created Me to Do Him Some Definite Service (Cardinal Newman): Vocation at the Heart of the Catholic Curriculum', *International Studies in Catholic Education* 5 (1).

4   Readers with a philosophical bent will notice the epistemological position of 'realism' lurking visibly in this chapter's proposals, that is, the view that it is to aspects of the real world that our knowledge gets us when it deserves the name. For a fuller discussion, see Walsh, 1993, parts 3 and 4.

5   From a 1918 address, cited in Pirsig (1974).

6   This is used more or less interchangeably with the Crick Report's original formula of *social and moral responsibility, community involvement* and *political literacy.*

7   Geography can inspire pupils to think about their own place in the world, their values, and their rights and responsibilities to other people and the environment … inspectors see a lot of geography lessons with obvious potential for citizenship that remains unexploited. Perhaps most important of all, pupils are taught the knowledge and understanding without being given the opportunity to ask the question, 'So what can we do about this?'

8   Paras 74–92 of *Go Forth and Teach: The Characteristics of a Jesuit Education* (1986, now available online in PDF format), a handbook for all teachers in Jesuit schools internationally, offers one powerful vision for this curriculum area. See also Grace's (2011) on how Pope Benedict's social encyclical, *Caritas in Veritate*, might be adapted as a structure for social justice curriculum in Catholic secondary schools.

9   For the believer, it also relativizes, at the least, the easygoing distinction between the Jesus of history and the Jesus of faith. *Ultimately,* it is precisely the real Jesus of history who *is* the Jesus of faith.

10   All this might seem more like a curriculum proposal for a theological college than for a Christian school. It would be at a different level, however, and in any case why should theological colleges have a monopoly of serious New Testament study? Of course, religious education in the Christian school has other major strands, if none quite so fundamental, with which this proposed strand would have to share time (and integration opportunities). For the proposal to be realistic, then, secondary religious education would need the core-subject status and the broadly similar staffing and timetable allocations as English, maths and science that, in fact, it gets in many, or most, Christian schools.

11   The model here is the International Baccalaureate's well-known requirement of *Theory of Knowledge* as an adjunct to its six required main subjects in different subject categories. I am again indebted to Fr Jamison's *Address to Head Teachers,* this time for its reference to the introduction of just such an initiative, as part of introducing the IB, in a school of which he was the headmaster. I see no reason why these theologically informed explorations of knowledge could not also be associated with the more specialist A-level subject profiles.

6

Church Schools and the Church's Service for the Poor

Jeff Astley

Abstract

In the context of empirical research that reveals the advantages of Church schools to students of low socio-economic status, the ideals of religious schooling are explored with particular reference to the commodification of education, the Christian critique of status, the values and virtues of Christian spirituality, the imperative of a preferential option for the poor, and concepts of social and spiritual capital. A broader argument in support of the ministry of Church schools is then rehearsed.

Keywords
The poor, self-esteem, status, social capital, spiritual capital, virtues

Introduction

In his recent, sympathetic study of the influence of the King James Bible, *The Book of Books*, Melvyn Bragg finds space to praise Joshua Watson for his role in the Anglican Church's educational mission to the poor (Churton, 1863). Bragg writes, 'his aim was to plant Protestant Christianity in the minds of the impoverished young who would, he believed, benefit both spiritually and materially from a religious education' (2011, p. 269).

The hard-fought distinctions that educationalists recognize today between different uses of the phrases 'religious education', and 'Christian education', were not in place in Watson's time. The schools that were founded by the National Society 'for the Education of the Children of the Poor in the Principles of the Established Church' doubtless educated children about Christianity as they sought to educate them into being Christian, and did this in schools whose aim, ethos, relationships and entire curriculum was – at least in principle – 'Christian'.

Education and Christianity could both be seen, in that age of want, struggle and misery, as salvific. For Christians, schooling expressed the gospel values of service, justice and love. It embodied God's mission as physician to the sick, and exercised his 'preferential option for the poor'.[1] Charles Smyth, in his One Hundred and Fiftieth Anniversary Lecture of the foundation of the National Society, described it as 'a heroic missionary enterprise' (1961, p. 4).

It has to be admitted that in our own day it has mainly been Roman Catholics who have taken the lead in expressing this theme. As Joseph O'Keefe (2003, p. 97) has put it, 'Those who have the greatest need have the greatest claim on our resources.' Another Catholic, Gerald Grace (2000, p. 7), defends his Church's educational mission in these words:

> Catholic schools should be predominantly located in those communities in any society which are poor and powerless. In this way, the Catholic school can act as a beacon of hope (where hope is in short supply), a community resource (where resources are in short supply) and a witness to Christ (where this witness is most needed).

If this is part of the Christian ideal for the Church school, what has been called its 'inspirational ideology',[2] then it follows that church school education must necessarily be construed as a ministry – that is, a *service*. Such a theme has not always been at the forefront of thinking about Church schools. Nor has it always been central to the ideology of schooling in general.

The broad aims of education

Scholars have distinguished three eras in the development of the aims of general schooling in Britain. On these accounts, schooling in the nineteenth century and the first half of the twentieth century was primarily characterized by notions of 'class hierarchy' and 'class-cultural control', 'godliness and good learning', and associated values of authority and obedience. As a setting for moral education, this has been described as a period marked by the 'ruler and ruled code' (Bottery, 1990, 1992). It was followed by a shift in educational philosophy to the rhetoric and values of social democracy, with an accompanying stress on democratic and egalitarian values, and a concern for public service and pastoral care. This stage reached its zenith in the 1960s and early 1970s (Grace, 1995). These concerns were soon overtaken, however, by a radically different way of thinking about education dominated by a concern for the procedures and values of the culture of the market-place. For this third era of schooling, the keywords and phrases are management, targets, cost-efficient productivity, self-reliance, individual choice and competition; and there is a shying away from the perceived dangers of 'social engineering' and a 'dependency culture', thought by many to have been too closely associated with the preceding stage.

As this discourse of the market came to be applied more and more to schooling, embodied in school reforms such as open enrolment, school self-governance and the publication of results, the institutions and language of schooling became increasingly 'commodified'. Employers and parents – and now, sometimes, students – have become the 'consumers', and teachers, schools and universities the 'providers' of education. Children are often spoken of as the 'products' of a 'value-added', 'quality controlled' educational process that is best assessed through 'performance indicators' and 'league tables'. The primary aim seems to be that the school (or college) *business* should strive to keep and expand its market share in competition with others, as its accountability becomes increasingly corporatist and consumerist, rather than democratic. In such a context, single-minded toughness, even a certain brutality, is often valued as a proper part of entrepreneurial and realistic school management (Grace, 2002).

This market model of education has been much criticized, with a considerable body of opinion doubting whether it provides an appropriate language frame for education (Bridges and McLaughlin, 1994). Many argue, particularly with reference to equality of opportunity, that education as a public good cannot be left to the market. Others contend that education is essentially subversive of authority, being predicated on criticism and reflection, and that these outcomes are ultimately beyond the power of the market to deliver.

Much of this criticism is entirely secular, and depends both on a moral critique and on pragmatic and empirical arguments. The educationalist Mike Bottery (1990) offers four 'focuses of concern' for schools and society that may be put at risk by the adoption of a market paradigm in schooling. They are worth noting. The first is the fostering of the child's self-esteem, an outcome that is easily damaged by a culture of competitiveness that favours the few but results in the perception of failure in the many. (Bottery adds that the insecure and unloved are less likely to help others, and that the creation of 'a caring and supportive environment' is part of a school's moral duty.) Second, he argues that children's empathy needs strengthening so as to combat the egocentric preoccupation with the self that tends to be fostered by concentrating on one's own success. Without this, tolerance and the appreciation of the suffering of others will not easily be created. Third, cooperation between children is weakened if there is too much competition, as competition tends to breed suspicion and hostility. Finally, he too argues that the promotion of rationality is by no means guaranteed by the market. Rationality matters for many reasons, but particularly for the exercise of moral judgement: for example, in analysing the complex empirical facts that form the context of moral dilemmas and reveal the effects of human actions, and in forming an imaginative understanding of the distress of others.

More radically, Bottery also criticizes free market theory for routinely ignoring issues of moral *merit* by evaluating everything solely in terms of price and profit, bypassing both issues of social responsibility and the full needs of the child. He writes:

> A basic problem with the philosophy, then, is that it finds it hard to see people except as means to an end, the end being that of consumption. It tends to cheapen the quality of human relationships. (Bottery, 1922, p. 88)

The ever-present danger in free market thinking is that certain fundamental values will become mere second-order principles that are allowed to be overridden by the first-order principles of production, consumption and ownership. When we speak about values, however, we are not asking what the price of certain activities or outcomes actually is, or how much people are willing to pay for them, or even what people themselves in fact *desire*. We are talking about what we believe 'should exist', what is *desirable*, what 'ought to be'. Merit, like virtue, is therefore fundamentally 'without price'. But in the market-place, even outside the educational context, 'it is by no means guaranteed that virtue will be in sufficient demand so as to be rewarded'. Hence, 'not all services or initiatives can have their worth measured by profit or numbers or even popular success' (Scruton, 1998, p. 84; Solomon, 1993, p. 359; Hoggart, 1996, p. 10). Those who are most concerned about the ethical focus of educational provision therefore warn us against reducing it to the deliberately amoral notions of marketing, with their accompanying industrial or commercial styles of management.

A Christian critique?

The religious reaction to the market paradigm in schooling and educational leadership embraces many of these concerns, and agrees in commending a broader, more humane and more human vision for education. The view of the Catholic bishops is that we should resist 'the extension of market forces and market values into areas of "common good" services for all citizens, such as health and education' (Grace, 2002, p. 191). The Catholic Education Service argues that education is 'not a commodity to be offered for sale . . . [but] a service provided by society for the benefit of all' (CES, 1997, p. 13). Many other Christians have written in a similar vein of the importance for education of the dimensions of moral and spiritual responsibility, of a commitment independent of rewards or status, and of service and dedication. Protestant critiques of the commodification of education include attacks on forms of assessment that both 'erode self-esteem and the joy of learning', and condemnations of its limited vision for humanity – in Greg Forster's phrase, 'to train "cannon fodder" for the commerce of the future' (1997, p. 10).

In writing before on this topic, I have expressed my own concern that the impersonal language of much of the rhetoric of education encourages us to see it in less than fully human terms, almost as 'a production line moulding people into the right shapes to fit empty holes in the economy'. This is too ruthless and harsh – even 'macho' – a model either for education or for human maturity:

> If one of the aims of education is the person-making function, teaching me to be more fully human, then it needs to develop more than my technical skills and economically-valuable technological knowledge. . . . Something more is needed for that. It is something that is rather low-tech and difficult to quantify, and therefore embarrassing to mention in economic debates. But it is crucial to the development of mature personhood, and can only be provided by those who have attained a certain sort of maturity. It is *love*, and knowledge directed by love. (Astley, 1992, p. 319)

Recent events have shown that untrammelled markets are not necessarily the best companions for a society's economy. From the perspective of this chapter, they are especially bad news for the disadvantaged, who are rarely going to be seen as a good investment in the market-place of life, appearing instead as bad 'customers' with little economic or cultural capital to spend (Grace, 2002, p. 181). The philosophy of the market-place can easily create an option *against* the poor. If there is a battle of values to be joined in the debate over religious schooling, it must in part be fought over this issue. The Christian ideal of schooling, when construed in terms of a theology of service and ministry (Dearing, 2001, p. 50 and 91–2; Grace, 2002, pp. 136–8 and 222–3), should encourage us to recover our focus on the poor.

As a consequence – and, perhaps, partly as a cause – of their poverty, the poor rarely matter in the eyes of the world. Even their successes simply do not *count*. Our nation has a shameful history of hijacking organizations and buildings that were originally founded to help the impoverished many, and quietly turning them to the benefit of the well-endowed few. It is as if people find it hard to believe that those who created these institutions could really have intended to promote any cause as worthless and insignificant as the good of the poor. While the majority of Church of England schools have nobly resisted the temptations of this secular gospel, especially those that serve local communities in deprived urban and rural areas, *some* of our Church schools in the maintained sector may need to face this criticism of reneging on their title deeds. And it is a challenge that should also be addressed to those 'Christian educational foundations' that thrive so well in the independent sector. It is too easy in some contexts to forget the difference that Christianity should make to education, and to smooth out the radical disjunction between the wisdom of the cross and the wisdom of the world.

But Jesus proclaimed first and foremost a good news for the poor. Whatever else we claim to do 'in his name', we must share *this* mission.

Christian wealth creation

Let us revisit Melvyn Bragg's claim that Joshua Watson's aim was to benefit the impoverished young 'both spiritually and materially', by means of a Christian education. Can a Church school do *both*? In what sense does a Church school *work*, and how can it succeed both spiritually *and* materially? (I take the adverb 'materially' to be intended quite broadly, so as to cover the whole range of mundane human flourishing that can result from personal, social, moral and intellectual education.)

From a pragmatic perspective, many religious schools do appear to work. This is often put down to the fact that, however cash-poor these schools and their students may be, they are rich in what has been called *social* capital. Social capital is usually understood in terms of reciprocal social relationships and their positive effects. Here 'capital' is obviously a metaphor that is meant to label some sort of resource, and to suggest notions about its 'investment', 'acquisition', 'circulation' or 'exchange'. Writers in this area frequently adopt other figures of speech also, lauding social capital as a sort of 'connective tissue' or 'social glue' (both understood as positive things), and regretting 'the balkanization of society' as a negative factor that is capable of tearing or dissolving it.

The use of these metaphors may risk our slipping back into treating education – and even children and teachers – as impersonal commodities that require to be traded in some form of market. John Field's monograph on social capital, however, identifies at its heart the idea of 'personal connections and interpersonal interaction, together with the shared sets of values that are associated with these contacts' (2003, p. 13). As such, social capital is sometimes described as a subspecies of 'human capital', the resources that belong to people as human beings, as distinct from inanimate objects like plant and machinery. Prominent among the values and benefits that make social capital such an asset, even a 'public good', are the personal attitudes and activities of mutual trust and reciprocity.

These ideas have found a ready application in studies of schooling. James Coleman's study of US high school students in the 1980s showed that the norms of Catholic schools seem to have particularly beneficial effects on the dropout rates and academic achievement of disadvantaged groups (Coleman and Hoffer, 1987, pp. 118–48). Coleman noted the importance not only of the family, but also of an intergenerational church community, in making this fund of social capital available to the young who need it most.

This positive academic impact of religious (especially Catholic) schooling on pupils of low socio-economic status has been confirmed by later work.[3] Coleman's general claim that social capital is closely associated with educational outcomes has also been broadly supported – although to different degrees – by other studies (Dika and Singh, 2002). The latest research confirms that these positive academic effects do not reflect school selection policy. 'Indeed, in a study of Flemish secondary schools, non selective faith schools were associated with slightly larger increases in student attainment in mathematics as compared with selective ones' (Pugh and Telhaj, 2008). I shall return to some of the issues raised by these claims later.

Robert Putnam's better known work on social capital identifies shared membership of groups as being more important than kinship as a source of solidarity. Putnam introduced the distinction between *bonding* social capital, which reinforces in-group loyalty among people of similar backgrounds, and *bridging* social capital, which brings together more distant acquaintances who move in different circles – and which can therefore potentially create bridges across the divisions of a society.

In their recent book on religion in the United States, *American Grace* (2010), Putnam and David Campbell claim – perhaps surprisingly – that America has 'solved the puzzle of religious pluralism – the coexistence of religious diversity and devotion . . . by creating a web of interlocking personal relationships among people of many different faiths' (p. 550). In fact, their data show this only for Judaism and a range of Christian faith positions. The small numbers of Mormons, Buddhists and Muslims in their sample prevent them from including these groups in this analysis. Yet, their data show that 'religious bridging' modestly increases warmth towards these most unpopular religious groups as well (pp. 526–34, 542). Even here, the authors claim, 'our friends affect how we perceive the religious groups to which our friends belong' (p. 530, cf. pp. 547–8).

Are Christian schools divisive? Well, they shouldn't be. John Sullivan has argued that Catholic schools that are 'true to the logic of their own philosophy and mission' should show a concern for the common good that enables them to transcend any sectarian or parochial concerns (2001, p. 193). Ann Casson's (2011) recent study contends that such faith schools, as strong generators of religious identity and bonding capital, may also lead to the development of attitudes of tolerance and respect for others, thus generating bridging capital. (However, her ethnographic study of three English Roman Catholic schools, which showed strong bonding capital but only a *weak* religious identity, did not provide evidence for activities that could be defined as bridging capital.)

In the case of religious schools, social capital has been variously interpreted as accruing from: (1) the school's pastoral care and its attempts to create community; (2) their students' sense of belonging, cohesiveness and connection; and (3) the school's communal and liturgical imagination (Greeley, 1998, pp. 181–9). All the items on this list form part of the school's hidden curriculum: that set of experiences from which students learn but which do not come explicitly labelled as such. This hidden curriculum mainly 'teaches' *values* (Jackson, 1993). The school's pastoral care and its liturgical expressions are laden with values, as is that powerful medicine that social fellowship prescribes and which can only be dispensed to those who are members of a real community.

In a Church school, of course, we would not expect these values to be solely represented by the individualistic attitudes that flourish best in a commodified culture, such as unqualified competitiveness. We hope, instead, that they will mainly be religious, moral and spiritual values. As Richard Pring has put it:

The list of virtues associated with [the] distinctively Christian form of life do not include 'enterprise' and 'entrepreneurship' – which is not to say they are wrong, only that they have not the place in the quality of life worth living which many others would attribute to them. (1996, p. 68)

Although it is true that the entrepreneurs show a willingness to take risks and that faithful and trusting people are also involved in a risky 'going beyond', their activities are distinguished by their very different goals. Teachers make themselves vulnerable, 'putting themselves on the line each day' for the sake of their students – and, through them, for the greater good of all. The risks taken by capitalist entrepreneurs, by contrast, are primarily for their own pecuniary gain. (Gamblers are also great risk takers, of course.)

Gerald Grace and others employ the phrase *spiritual capital* to denote the 'resources of faith and values', derived from religious commitment, that provide the 'transcendent impulse' for guiding thought and action in the Christian form of life. This understanding seems to mesh with two aspects of Bradford Verter's account of spiritual capital (reflecting Pierre Bourdieu's analysis of cultural capital) in terms of (1) personal dispositions, abilities and knowledge that orient an individual's 'habitus', his 'mode of apprehending and acting in the world' (spiritual capital's 'embodied state'); and (2) symbolic commodities such as systems of values and theological beliefs, in which that habitus is grounded (part of spiritual capital's 'objectified state') (Grace, 2002, p. 236; Verter, 2003, p. 159). In short, they are represented by the attitudes, beliefs, values, and dispositions to act and experience that constitute the central, spiritual core of Christian identity.

The difference that Christianity can make

Factors that have been proposed to explain the relative academic success of students of lower socio-economic status in religious schools have included greater family involvement, better student behaviour, and the different 'culture' or 'atmosphere' of these institutions (including their greater academic demands). Some of these are constituent parts of the hidden curriculum of the school, and all of them may be described as either causes or components of the social or spiritual capital investment of religious schooling.

Could such elements arise from, and help to form students in, a *Christian* self-identity, with its attendant set of Christian beliefs, feelings and behaviours? Does the evidence show that focusing on religious faith, and on spiritual and moral values, puts the religious school at no *academic* disadvantage? More positively, may we argue that Christian beliefs and values can themselves enhance academic learning, as well as forming students in a character that is good for its own sake?

I should like to suggest two ways in which we might expect spiritual attitudes and values inherent in the ethos of Church schools to contribute to their students' 'material' – particularly their academic – success (see Astley, 2005).

(1) First of all, there may be a relatively direct link between a person's embracing certain values and his or her openness to, and willingness to continue to engage in, learning.

It has frequently been argued that student engagement and learning do not only require intellectual virtues, but also – and perhaps more fundamentally – dispositions of the self that may properly be spoken of as moral and spiritual. Although John Sullivan is writing of higher education, his list of the character strengths or virtues that are needed for the pursuit of truth are equally relevant to the school. These include self-control (for an attentive, concentrated mind), courage to persevere despite difficulties, humility before the truth and its authorities, and a sense of security that comes from belonging to a community (Sullivan, 2003).

It takes courage for a child to apply herself to study in the teeth of the contempt of her peers and the suspicions of her family, including their suspicion that in attempting to 'better herself' she is somehow demeaning them. It also takes humility: not a false humility, but the proper, *realistic* middle way of a virtue that stands between the extremes of arrogant self-aggrandizement ('I am better than anyone') and utter self-abnegation ('I am a total failure'). This last attitude is a natural response to the loss of autonomy and dignity, and of a sense of being wanted, that is frequently such a close companion of poverty. Reacting against this, children and their parents can too easily swing to the other extreme of a defensive arrogance that refuses either to listen or to learn (Barker and Anderson, 2005). Learners, however, need a realistic humility about their own work in order to succeed. Humility is also, of course, a spiritual virtue with a wider significance. It has been described (by an atheist) as 'the foundation of all the moral virtues' (Gert, 1998, p. 306) and is regarded as one of the most distinctive outcomes of a truly Christian education.

Disinterestedness is another virtue that may be required for true learning. 'The truth is not always kind. And the rewards for its pursuit may be small' (Pring, 2000, p. 151), so it may be best to engage in the search for truth for itself alone: despite the claims of those who acknowledge only the motivation of rewards and punishments, often delivered by market forces. It may even be said that the route to truth is properly 'pointless', in the sense that our pursuit of it may not have and does not require any *ulterior* point or purpose. This parallels what some have said about worship, an activity that is of great 'use' to us, in having a powerful (formative learning) effect on us, but which must be entered into for God's sake and not our own (Astley, 1996). It, too, is best done – it is most authentically done – 'for nothing'.

(2) A more circuitous, yet perhaps in the end a more sure and rewarding path from values to learning starts from what Sullivan calls a 'sense of security', and leads to a sense of self-acceptance and self-worth.

I have never been attracted to accounts of human beings that privilege our spiritual and cognitive capabilities at the expense of the material dimensions of our humanity, or which disparage or ignore the significance of the feelings that lie alongside – and always interact with – our thinking. Ask most mature adults about their schooldays and you will be told little about the curriculum they were taught or their cognitive learning, but a great deal about how they felt about others and about themselves, and particularly about their emotional attachments. They will probably also reveal something of how they learned to feel, and to be, as *situated* and *embodied* learners.

Recent work has shown the positive influence of some of the body's so-called feeling chemicals, such as dopamine and acetylcholine, on improving active learning and understanding, and on mental capacity and performance in general. There is also much evidence of the negative effect on memory and thinking of the stress hormone cortisol (LeDoux, 1999, pp. 224–66; Zull, 2002). Our feelings, or more generally our 'mood', of confidence, self-assurance, and even of being loved can have a considerable positive effect on our educational attainment. Feelings of failure, and the feelings that result from being bullied, abused or just demeaned, are likely to have a negative effect.

The psychologist Oliver James makes much of the effects of low levels of the neurotransmitter serotonin in depressing mood, and points to maladaptive social comparison (the 'death by a thousand social comparisons') as one grand cause of this phenomenon in our society. Although he recognizes the benign significance of social comparison in establishing 'where we stand in relation to others', James inveighs against its misuse in education:

> If seven- to nine-year-olds are over-pressurized to compare their performances to each other, then emotional death is a real risk. . . . Parents and politicians must ask themselves for whose benefit they are stealing their

children's childhoods. . . . There is too much pressure to succeed, in social comparison terms, too young. (1998, pp. 334–5)

Richard Wilkinson and Kate Pickett's famous (some would say notorious) overview of recent research on inequality, in *The Spirit Level*, reports what they claim to be 'striking evidence that performance and behaviour in an educational task can be profoundly affected by the way we feel we are seen and judged by others. When we expect to be viewed as inferior, our abilities seem to be diminished' (Wilkinson and Pickett, 2010, p. 113). This evidence includes results of maze-solving tasks by 11- to 12-year-old boys in India, both before and after their caste status is publicly announced. Before the announcement the low-caste boys performed slightly better than their high-caste fellows; afterwards their performances dropped significantly (by over 25%). Other data from the States show that black students perform worse in a standardized test when they are told that it is a measure of ability, whereas white students did equally well whether they are told this or not. Wilkinson and Pickett also remind us of the classic work on stereotyping by Jane Elliott in the 1960s. When she informed her students that blue eye colour was linked to superior intelligence and success, and started behaving more positively towards that group, their school performance improved whereas the marks of the brown-eyed students declined. The situation was quickly reversed, however, when Elliott told the children some days later that she had got the information the wrong way round!

In education, it matters how we feel, and how we feel we are judged. And in life too, of course. In writing about parenting, the clinical psychologist Paul Gilbert stresses the importance of the perception that one is valued as perhaps the central experience leading to self-worth. 'Those who grow with high levels of emotional support and pleasure develop a more integrated, explorative and optimistic orientation compared with those who grow in an environment with greater negative affect' (Gilbert, 1992, p. 296). This, of course, is not rocket science; if only because, unlike most physics, we know it for ourselves without needing to be told. We learned it at our mother's knee – or from her fists, but also in the affective crucible of the educational establishments we attended, where we underwent the second stage of our sentimental education through the schooling of our emotions.

One hardly needs to join the dots. I suggest that school may work for the poor as and when students are empowered and liberated by a gospel that respects them and loves them as *persons*, despite their poverty of wealth or social status; educational, cultural or family background; or any other worldly achievement.

We have seen that there is a grave risk in the market-place of commodified schooling that students will be treated as means to an end, and not as ends in themselves. And we know how that can affect self-esteem. But if students are treated as persons of supreme worth, as children of God and bearers of the image of God, there ought to be a 'value-added' sense of the significance of self: a renewed confidence that *may* result in their being more willing to put themselves on the line in their learning. After all, 'self-esteem is more the cause of academic success than its effect' (Healy, 1999). In any case, growth in self-esteem is a salvific thing. It is the inner dimension of God's *shalom*-peace: the this-worldly health, security and wholeness of divine salvation.

Sociologists often write of the 'intangible benefits' of social capital, presumably on the model of intangible – that is, not physical or precisely measurable – economic assets. 'Intangible' may be an appropriate description of societal norms and values, which are patently mental 'constructs' or abstract objects. But the human behaviour that incarnates and expresses these values is concrete enough: *it* exists in a material, physical form. Human trusting, accepting, valuing and loving relationships are not only 'real' (which is one sense of the word 'tangible'), but often also 'perceptible to touch' (which is the other sense). We may *feel* them in the most basic sense, through the physical sensation of being touched, embraced or held. But even where touching is absent – perhaps because it is forbidden or is just inappropriate, or because it is a relationship with the discarnate God – we may still speak of 'feeling' (i.e. experiencing) the *emotion* of being loved, valued, accepted or trusted. It all comes down to feeling. Somewhere along the line a social group or individual produces a felt reaction in another group or individual, changing how they think and feel. And especially changing how they think and feel about themselves. By someone's word, look, gesture or even posture, we can come to feel ourselves valued *or* slighted.

Studies of child health and criminality appear to show positive effects deriving from an increase in the child's self-worth or self-esteem, self-reliance and trustworthiness, that may ultimately be a consequence of social capital. Much of this benefit may accrue from changing people's perceived status and prestige, their 'standing' or (in Pierre Bourdieu's phrase) their 'symbolic capital'. Our human ranking often depends on 'a voluntary bestowal from others' (Gilbert, 1992, p. 151). Again, although status is an abstract concept, the experience of it and our feelings about it are real and tangible. They are visceral; they have bite. And they are capable of making us well or ill, good or bad; never mind academically successful or not. We surely know this about ourselves? And we know, too, that a *child's* sense of her standing can have an even more potent and long-lasting effect.

In his fine critique of 'status anxiety', Alain de Botton includes Christianity among the remedies that can overturn the dominant notions of success and failure that blight so many people's lives. He writes:

> Fear of the material consequences of failure is compounded by fear of the unsympathetic attitude of the world towards failure, of its haunting proclivity to refer to those who have failed as 'losers' – a word callously signifying both that people have lost and that they have at the same time forfeited any right to sympathy for having done so. (de Botton, 2004, p. 157)

But 'central to traditional Christian thought', de Botton writes, is the claim 'that one's status carried no moral connotations'. It bears no *moral* distinction. It is no sin to be poor; and social failure is not a fall from any moral high ground (where the socially superior have no right to encamp anyway).

The *snob* is defined as someone who shows 'exaggerated respect for social position or wealth and a disposition to . . . judge of merit by externals'. The political philosopher, Judith Shklar, located snobbery among her list of 'ordinary vices'. This 'habit of making inequality hurt . . . is simply a very destructive vice', (Shklar, 1984, p. 87). Historically, she noted, snobbery was viewed as an offence against Christian morality because it implied an indifference to true merit; and since Thackeray, it has become 'a direct attack against equality' (p. 101, cf. p. 137). Snobbery is close cousin to racism, and often reflects an atavistic fear of pollution and a (related?) contempt for physical labour (p. 107). Shklar's book has a nice section on academic snobbery (she did teach at Harvard, after all). She argued that this flows easily from the academy's inevitable separation from the usual interests and concerns of the majority, and its focus on an excellence that is always at risk from an anti-elitism that can hide a more worrying anti-intellectualism. Yet, paradoxically, she insisted that education has long been seen as 'the best democratic remedy for snobbery' (p. 111), and claims that 'snobbery is not built into academic work, and certainly not into learning. It just attaches itself to them' (p. 127). Which is a pity, I think, because – like the Church – places of learning work best when we really do feel that 'we are all in this together': all equally learners (or disciples) together, following a truth that is much greater than any one of us.

But many people don't really need academic, social or pecuniary snobs to look down on them; they are quite well versed in looking down on themselves. Interestingly, Oliver James claims that it is not only those who do poorly at school who may suffer harm to their self-esteem caused by the psychological power of social comparison and competition. This malady can also mark academic high-flyers, 'who feel like losers' because they find themselves in institutions where high performance is the norm. The point, of course, is that:

> If our self-esteem is contingent on external standards we run the risk of feeling like failures, because, even if we succeed in these terms, there will always be someone better than us. (James, 2004, p. 57)

But the Christian gospel proclaims that however we may be judged by others, we are already accepted by God. If Christianity is about anything relevant to life and education, it is about finding real life and embracing true values; it is not about judging and being judged by the values of this world. What the world calls success and failure – and therefore what the school or university calls success and failure – are only penultimate judgements: mere shadows of the semblance of truth. The lineaments of the Last Judgement are necessarily obscure, but I think that we can safely bet that no one will be asked then about their academic achievements. The Church school *must* acknowledge 'the Christian value and dignity of every pupil and student regardless of achievement' (Grace, 2002, p. 46).

It is, at least, a plausible claim that if an educational institution can somehow persuade its students that they are *already* of infinite value in the sight of God, they may be more willing to risk the hardships, false starts and repeated knock-backs of the educational process. For they will know that, in the end, they are not judged as persons by how clever they are, or how learned or rich or 'important' they may become. It is, therefore, to quote Richard Pring and then Robert Graham, 'a central job of the school to generate that sense of personal worth on the basis of values which do not depend upon the contingencies of life here and now'; so 'we have to recognise that schools and teachers are there, if they have any truly reputable purpose, to take people seriously, and essentially for that alone' (Pring, 1996, p. 69; Graham, 1996, p. 89). Well, perhaps not 'alone', but *first* anyway.

Everyone a winner?

And that can be good for *everyone*.

Whatever else is contentious about Church schools, most defenders of church education argue that a 'Christian ethos' in a school is a positive thing. Fundamentally, this thesis can – and should – be argued on intrinsic rather than instrumental grounds. Christian values and practices are good in and of themselves, and not just as a means to any further goods. But most would be willing to follow Newman's argument here. John Henry Newman held out for a liberal education that was not to be entered into for any ulterior social point or purpose, but was an education of the intellect 'disciplined for its own sake, for the perception of its own proper object, and for its own highest culture'. Nevertheless, he believed that 'though the useful is not always good, the good is always useful', and hence that 'if a liberal education be good, it must necessarily be useful too' (Newman, 1899, VII).

What is true of intellectual improvement is surely also true of the formation of Christian attitudes, dispositions and values. They, too, are both intrinsically *and instrumentally* good. We must esteem virtue for its own sake, I believe, and pursue and develop the virtues disinterestedly (i.e. not for *our* own sake, not for our own *interests*). Nevertheless, although the good life may not always and necessarily lead to human flourishing, Christian values and virtues are frequently psychologically good for us. We benefit from our own virtue.

And we assuredly benefit from the virtue of other people. The option for the poor is not just of benefit to the poor; it is something that matters to the rich as well. It is tempting to endorse a commodified approach to education if you have enough in the bank to buy or sell in the market-place of schooling, and can thus keep ahead of the game. But this blinkered view may result in your success turning into failure. For market forces are not the only potent resources operating in the market town.

Treating education solely as a commodity can never guarantee that it will flourish because markets can never exist in isolation. In the words of Alasdair MacIntyre, a market can only survive if it is 'embedded in . . . relationships of uncalculated giving and receiving' (1999, p. 117). And 'uncalculated' is the keyword here.

In debates about social policy it is frequently said that public services are dependent on the wealth creation of industry and commerce. That logic is unassailable. Where there is no business, there is no income and no taxes – and pretty soon no education, either. There is, however, another dependent relationship that is more easily overlooked and less easily quantified. It is not just that most businesses and their markets are themselves sustained by a group of comparatively lowly paid staff, without which no business would exist and no profits would be possible. It is not just that all businesses are supported at another level by public services for which we all pay. It is also that beyond and beneath all these, there lies the basic fabric of our society, which rests on the *wholly unpaid* devotion, love and service of human beings. This rich informal network of human support and care (and, indeed, 'production') comes from parents, other relatives, neighbours, friends and strangers. Only the intentionally short-sighted will fail to see and to value their contribution to the economy. As I have put it elsewhere:

> While we need to recognise that public services are parasitic on the 'business community', let us also acknowledge that those businesses are themselves parasitic on the 'private services' of a *real* community: a community that they did not create, do not pay for and have no moral right to control. . . .
>
> Markets are not the only 'forces' that exist. They are just the easiest places in which to negotiate a price. Some expenditures of energy, though costly, are not bought and sold there. And others cannot be, for they would be dissipated in the transaction. Love can have no price. (Astley, 1998, p. 383)

True education will always be concerned with the moral and spiritual education of *persons*, and it is they who forge the communities that keep everything else up and running. Education is to be encouraged because it bestows benefit by teaching knowledge and marketable skills. Its less visible but perhaps greater contribution, however, lies in moulding those values and dispositions of the forms of love that constitute the skeleton, as well as the connective tissues, of our *real* 'corporate life'.

Not all educational institutions and polities recognize this; or if they do, they are likely to answer the lawyer's question, 'Who is my neighbour?' (Luke 10.29), in rather too narrow a way. But 'no man is an island', nor is any family or neighbourhood or local church or school. All are set within the great continent of *society*. And however rich we and our group may be, we are all dependent on the sustaining forces of that wider society from which we cannot opt out. And much – most – of that sustenance is of a kind that simply cannot be bought. It is to our advantage, therefore, that a society is formed and sustained, and that it is formed and sustained for and in love.

Without some schools that privilege the underprivileged – without schools that are in every sense *for* the poor – I believe that this wider society will be in peril. And if society fails we shall all be in trouble, whatever our socio-economic status. The Church, and its schools, should do the right thing because it is right. But in exercising its mission and ministry to the poor, the Church may also claim to play some part – even if only on a human and this-worldly level – in saving the world.

And who can be against that?

Key questions

1. Should all Church schools be part of the Church's ministry to the poor?
2. What might be meant by 'spiritual capital' in Church schools?
3. Can Christian spirituality promote learning?
4. Is the commodification of education always a bad thing?
5. Do Church schools really 'work' for the poor?

Notes

1 The phrase 'option for the poor' was first coined in the 1960s by Jesuits in Latin America, and was later used by Catholic Bishops there as well as by a number of popes. See the *Compendium of the Social Doctrine of the Church* (2004, sections 182–4).

2 See Bryk, Lee and Holland, 1993, pp. 301–4. For these authors, the Catholic social ethic underpins the school's 'personalism' (humaneness in social interaction) and 'subsidiarity' (transcending pure bureaucratic concerns for efficiency and specialization through 'a concern for human dignity'). This ethic is expressed in the school's nurturing of both mind ('critical consciousness') and spirit (disposition to effect social justice) in all; respectful engagement in discussion within a school that models social justice; and the school's harnessing 'the power of the symbolic' images within the Christian tradition, particularly the words and life of Christ, the notion of the Kingdom of God, and the hopefulness implicit in our 'resurrection destiny'.

3 See Jeynes (2004, 2005). However, Gamarnikow and Green's analysis of Gerald Grace's own 2002 data leads them to write, 'faith-based social capital networks, organised around a school faith ethos, may result in marginally higher achievement among some downsiders, but they clearly also contribute to high achievement among the upsiders. Thus the contribution of faith ethos to equity remains an open question' (Garmarnikow and Green, 2005, p. 99).

7

Church Schools and Anglican Identity

Ian Terry

Abstract

This chapter demonstrates that Church of England schools draw from their Anglican heritage a dynamic potential for making connections. It looks at the history of the Church's involvement in educational provision in England and also at what Anglicanism is about as a church. It explores the unique position of the Church of England as a place in which a diverse range of interests meet, encounter each other, and make connections.

Keywords
Local places of encounter, worship, pastoral encounter, widely diverse, holding-together, incarnational encounter, national responsibilities and opportunities, established, Catholic, justice-seeking

---

Schooling in England

The Church in England has been involved in education from its earliest days, when Christian leaders needed education to equip them to correct heresy and to teach new converts. In England, an example of this pioneering work in education and scholarship is the Venerable Bede (673–735), whose work is still in print (Bradley, 1999, p. 257). Bede began his education at the age of 7, as a choirboy, at Wearmouth. Here he encountered learning, which enabled him to translate in several languages. In such ways, the monasteries built the foundations of Christian learning in Britain (Bradley, 1993, p. 74), and were the pioneers of the church's work in education.

Based in the parish

Meanwhile, throughout our country, 'the parish' had become well established as the 'de facto' centre of the church. It can be shown that these two historic developments, of the parish and its school were, and still are, completely intertwined, to the benefit of the British society. This natural rural focus on life as centred around 'your village' has meant that a very diverse range of people, all locally based, encounter each other at church and at school. The Church of England is not, instinctively, centralized. Local continuity, before and after the Reformation, reinforces this awareness of the *local* church as the focal point of meeting. Anything that mattered to the local community caused people to meet in their local church. The Church of England is rooted in local practices more than in centralized direction, and such is the binding force of local encounters that there is a high degree of local independence. This means that nationally there is diversity, and agreement can seem elusive. Meanwhile, at the local 'centre' of things for most people, Anglicanism works out its believing locally, in its worshipping.

Parish churches and their schools as places of encounter in worship

One of the well-established ways of defining Anglican Church membership is by 'those who worship' in its churches regularly. Similarly, children at a Church school worship daily in the 'invitational' context of collective worship. Done well, this balances the gentle offering of the Christian faith with a clear and unpatronizing respect for those who are not Christians. This has a positive 'ripple' effect. That is, when schools and churches act respectfully, and promote diversity, they help to work together for the good of the local community. Indeed, to this day, parochial membership is not decided in the Church of England primarily on grounds of belief. The Book of Common Prayer linked minimal worship obligations with every parishioner's payment of their ecclesiastical duties. This presupposed that every parishioner must automatically be a member of the Established Church of England by virtue of residing within the parish boundaries. At Rogation time, some parishes still 'beat the bounds' each year to keep alive awareness of these boundaries, and the rights that accompany them. English culture, and its legal constraints, have changed greatly between 1662 and the twenty-first century, but vestiges of the presupposition that the church serves all in its parish, remain in the legal right of all parishioners to be baptized, married, and, if a churchyard is open, buried according to the rites of the Church of England. Some people see their membership of the Church of England as resting in their option to exercise these rights which would mark with Anglican worship the significant moments of their lives.

Worship is adapted to needs

As each school forms its worship around current concerns and preoccupations, which may relate to the weather, some international disaster, or the fate of the local football team, so it is in the parish church. There is an explicit pastoral expectation that the 'encounter' with others and God which worship facilitates should be as carefully, pastorally 'fine-tuned' as is possible. The aim is to make the encounter meaningful. This aim will be achieved by bringing in-depth pastoral knowledge to each of a widely diverse range of situations. In practice, this opens the door, and always has, to a wide diversity of local autonomy.

Holding-together

The resulting diversity of liturgical practice and credal interpretation is valued as a richness rather than regretted as a weakness by the Church of England, which refers back to one of the 'founding fathers' of the Elizabethan settlement of the Reformation, Richard Hooker (Neill, 1958, p. 121), for its classical points of reference: scripture, reason and tradition. For Hooker, who had not only a great knowledge of scripture but also a deep grounding in the early Church Fathers, the schoolmen and classical antiquity, there was no question that 'tradition', understood, in a dynamic and interactive way, could be ignored. This formed a fundamental part of his advocacy of what Neill calls 'that characteristically Anglican thing, a defence of Reason' (1958, p. 123).

Digging deeper in distinctiveness

In digging deeper into the distinctiveness of this Anglican educational provision one finds a cherishing of local input. This makes for an encounter in both parish church and Church school which is fundamentally incarnationally grounded.

Beliefs, in the Church of England, are not, primarily, abstract notions, rather, they are contextually formed and continually locally negotiated.

Post-Reformation diversity

After the Reformation diversity of belief, growing with local input, was the flavour of parish churches. Questioning gradually became more widespread and this contributed to a desire for schooling. The Reformation emphasis on personal faith grounded in reading the scriptures, and the availability of the printed word, both helped considerably. When monastic foundations were suppressed, the fresh surge of enthusiasm for learning generated by Renaissance thinkers spread throughout Europe. Martin Luther, for example, wrote, in 1524, a 30-page tract, 'To the Councilmen of All Cities in Germany that they establish Christian Schools' (Kay and Francis, 1997, p. 8), arguing that public funds should establish and maintain new schools. First, these schools were to produce learned civic officials fit to lead the life of the nation, and, secondly, ministers who were competent in Greek and Hebrew, to lead the newly reformed church. This added to such enthusiasms already growing in England, and resulted directly in the foundation of 'public' schools[1] all of which had strong links with the Anglican Church, and required attendance at chapel as part of the overall education they offered their pupils. Thus, one line of Christian education, albeit for the privileged few, was established in England. But there was still no schooling available for village children. It was an underlying sense of obligation to serve all in the parish, and particularly the poor, that resulted, ultimately, in the Sunday school movement, the BFSS and, our own, National Society. This reflects a growing emphasis upon 'justice-seeking' as fundamental to the Church of England's pragmatic response to the industrial revolution, its taking seriously its national responsibilities, and post-Reformation awareness that to be 'Catholic but reformed' meant to cherish diversity.

Justice-seeking

The Anglican cherishing of diversity, of individual conscience, and of reasoned questioning, becomes impossible to separate from a concern for justice when the Church of England discovers and celebrates each local context. It is in these local contexts that each person's contribution will be valued. Therefore, that valuing must take the form of active defence of anything threatening each person's, and, by extension, each local community's well-being or self-determination. It follows from this that to value an individual, and to seek justice for him or her, necessitates an imaginative engagement with what it might be like to be that person; thus, nurture of the imagination is a necessity, and not an option, for Church of England schools and for parish churches too.

The biblical picture of God as a God of justice is so dominant as to make it unavoidable, and there are repeated instances throughout the history of the Church of England of both church leaders and individual church members taking initiatives for justice. The concern of the Oxford movement for the poor is one such example; another is Wilberforce's determination to end slavery. Other examples, of individual landowners and clergy forming school trust deeds which explicitly indicated that the schools they were founding were to benefit the poor children of the parish,[2] paved the way for the National Society adopting this vision at the heart of its standard trust deed, which applies to most Church of England schools. As with Church schools, so with the Church of England as a whole, this concern for justice can never be completely ignored. It gives a sharp edge to whatever shape the church takes. It ensures that encounters on this 'safe' ground cannot remain bland and unchallenging for long. Encounters should challenge us to find creative ways of connecting with others, while remaining loyal to our vision of faith. The 'rub' is that loyalty to the Anglican vision is not about cosy sentimentality but the discomfort of an imperative to act justly.

Urban developments

By the beginning of the nineteenth century, more concentrations of children were found in towns than in villages. The industrial revolution created towns with large numbers of children not accustomed to classroom behaviour.[3] This brought more demand for schooling to be made generally available. There was also fear that the overturning of the social order experienced in France might similarly impact in Britain if education for the masses was not forthcoming. Robert Raikes (1735–1811), a journalist and philanthropist from Gloucester, was disturbed by the uncontrolled and idle behaviour of the local children on Sundays, so, in 1780, he hired women to teach them scripture. This was the beginning of the Sunday school movement, which quickly became so popular that these schools also began to open on weekdays, to teach reading and other elementary subjects. Sunday schools spread throughout the country, so that, by

1795, there were over 250,000 children taking part, with the enrolment having risen to 900,000 by 1835 (Kay and Francis, 1997, p. 11).

Joseph Lancaster, a Quaker, and Andrew Bell, an Anglican, adopted a monitorial system in their Sunday schools which enabled one teacher to instruct the more capable pupils, who then passed on what they had learned to the younger pupils. The success of this system led, in 1808, to the founding by Lancaster of the BFSS, for 'the education of the labouring and manufacturing classes of society of every religious persuasion'. It was the popularity of the schools founded by this Society that prompted a specifically Anglican response, associated with Bell and with Joshua Watson, in the founding of the 'National Society for Promoting the Education of the Poor in the Principles of the Established Church'. The objectives of the National Society became enshrined in most Anglican school Trust Deeds:

> First, it wished to contribute to a program which would enable the children of the nation, especially the poorer classes, to become literate and numerate and to develop skills which they required for work. Second, it had a duty to provide education in the Christian religion in all its schools. (Waddington, 1984, p. 12)

The National Society took its name in 1811 because it was the first *national* society to be formed for any purpose, in this case being founded in order to promote the establishment of schools across the entire land. As has been indicated above, the schools founded by the National Society and other church bodies in the nineteenth century stand alongside other schools that had already been founded. Thus, the founding of the National Society was part of a chain of continuity in Anglican educational provision that goes back to the earliest days of Christianity in this land. Out of those early local beginnings has grown national responsibilities and opportunities for critical reflection and prophetic action, as distinctive facets of Anglicanism in English parishes and schools.

National responsibilities and opportunities

To be both socially aware and critically reflective on a national level is a serious and demanding responsibility for the Church of England. This responsibility carries with it, however, the opportunity to influence national legislation. The resilience and adaptability of the Church of England has enabled it to speak sometimes on behalf of the nation and sometimes in prophetic challenge to the nation, as Bishop George Bell of Chichester did on the issue of the saturation bombing of civilian and military locations during the Second World War (Beeson, 1999, p. 84). These opportunities cause Anglican leaders to encounter other national leaders, to engage with their views, and to relate to their concerns. The Church of England operates at a national as well as local level as a place of encounter between spiritual and political perspectives, and a wide range of stakeholder interests. It is influenced by these encounters, but the influence is two-way, so it will also have the opportunity to exercise a Christian influence in the forming of legislation. From an educational perspective this Christian influence is provided by the Church's national Board of Education and the far-reaching work of the Education Division of the Archbishops' Council. Undoubtedly, the Church of England's place as a major partner in the educational provision of the maintained sector gives an opportunity to exercise a prophetic ministry at a high level. This partnership and opportunity for prophetic ministry is also a dynamic encounter at regional and diocesan level through the work of DBEs operating through their elected members and their officers. In this way, schools and parishes are kept in touch with national debates and have the chance to influence educational legislation.

Catholic

The Anglican Church is part of the Catholic Church worldwide. The Church historian, Stephen Neill, links Catholicity with continuity:

> This special nature of the Anglican liturgical tradition is one aspect of the intense *sense of continuity* which is always the mark of the true English churchman. 'Where was your Church before Henry VIII?' is a question which simply makes no sense to him. He has never imagined that the Reformation was anything other than a Reformation. It was in no sense a new beginning. The English churchman regards himself as standing in the fullest fellowship and continuity with Augustine and Ninian and Patrick and Aidan and Cuthbert, and perhaps most of all with that most typically Anglican of all ancient saints, the Venerable Bede. (Neill, 1958, p. 419)

Not only is the Anglican Communion, with its Catholic continuity, spread throughout the world, but, also, it is in communion with a wide range of other Christian churches. In this way, members of the worldwide Anglican 'family' stay in touch with each other, at least to some extent, and although they may disagree, as family members have been known to do, they are committed to continuing to talk with each other. Inevitably, they will not all agree, so this way of being church has to be Catholic by cherishing diversity.

A place of encounter in loyalty and adventure

Where diversity is cherished there is a 'place' in which those of different cultures and beliefs can safely encounter each other. Increasingly, it is compelling and exciting to see Anglicanism as a place of such 'encounter'. It 'brings to the table' of encounter a combination of interests, passions, and potential contradictions. It is grounded spiritually, in worship, and in the particularity of each parish. No two congregations, or PCCs, are the same, nor yet the church buildings that serve them. There is no way out of getting to know each set of people and understanding the dynamics of how they relate to each other. These encounters, which are integral to being 'Church of England', cannot avoid local politics, and they should also not avoid the Catholic Church's imperative call to seek justice and peace, and to minister healing and reconciliation. The nature of some of these encounters is intimately personal, and yet they have to hold to their integrity, to an extent, in the public domain. Each encounter will be an 'adventure', where the 'thrills' and fears come from stepping into the unknown; its 'shape' is always open to determination by how the connection develops.

Anglicanism has always been about discovering new ways of 'being church'. It has to be so, because of the wide range of variables that it attempts to hold together. This essentially dynamic mixture will never remain the same for very long. What is important to Anglicanism is not the resulting form, so much as the quality of the encounter. The form is a means to the end of celebrating right relationships, with God, with each other, and with all life on earth. It is important, therefore, not to 'get stuck' in the form taken by the church of a particular place and time. One of the ways of minimizing stagnation, and resistance to change is to be open to potentially contradictory and challenging forces.

There is a clear call for engagement with the intellectual climate of our modern culture. The Church of England is well placed, in terms of its frequent connections with non-churchgoers, to sustain and nurture this essential openness of engagement. It follows that, to the extent to which Church of England schools reflect Anglicanism's openness, they are similarly well placed. These schools have the possibility of being places of unavoidable encounter between the local and the national, the parochial and the Catholic, the overall educational endeavour and the unique possibilities of each child, between the general nurture of spirituality and the specifically Christian worship of God, all within the richly diverse Anglican tradition. The dynamism unleashed by these connections is the synergy that comes from relating to others in ways that empower them. This creates a visionary group dynamic with an infectious energy of its own. It is nothing less than this which is the distinctive potential of Church of England schools.

The distinctive potential of Church of England schools

At the start of this exploration of Church schools and their Anglican identity, when almost everyone went to the local village parish church, there was schooling available for only very few. The situation has now changed radically. Now, everyone goes to school. This is very largely because of the pragmatic vision of Joshua Watson and the founders of Church schools throughout our land. Fewer attend our churches.[4] The Church school is now, de facto, the main place in which the children, young people and many of the adults of our country meet Christian beliefs. Ecclesiologically, the school is a face and form of the Church of England comparable with the local parish church. If the Church of England saw itself primarily as a collection of gathered congregations, that ecclesiology might be a problem, though not if there was a willingness to think outside of brick-and-stone ecclesiastical boxes. However, that is not the primary self-understanding of the Church of England; rather, as has been demonstrated, it is a parochial and national Church. Its mission is to serve and respectfully share faith with all in these inclusive 'catchment areas'. Therefore, for the Church of England this is an opportunity of service and mission not to be missed. Furthermore, for a nation that has a belief in the necessary development of spirituality as fundamental to the well-being of all, this is a gift that exactly meets the need. The Church of England is alive and active in its schools, in ways that are both proactive and respectful, pre-evangelistic and invitational, using, in service, its place of dynamic and all-inclusive encounter. Church and nation both need to cherish the Church of England schools heritage.

Conclusion

It has been shown that the Church of England is rooted in local practices more than in centralized direction, and such is the binding force of local encounters that there is a high degree of local independence. This means that nationally there is diversity, and agreement can seem elusive. Meanwhile, at the local 'centre' of things for most people, Anglicanism works out its believing locally, in its worshipping. This is so in schools as well as in churches. Children at a Church school worship daily in the 'invitational' context of collective worship. Done well, this balances the gentle offering of the Christian faith with a clear and unpatronizing respect for those who are not Christians. This has a positive 'ripple' effect. That is, when schools and churches act respectfully, and promote diversity, they help to work together for the good of the local community. This pragmatic partnership is characteristic of the historic approach of the Church of England. Further, pragmatic partnership is also characteristic of worldwide Anglicanism. Thus, whenever an issue is in question, for Anglicans, there should be reference to scripture, and the previous experience of the church. Both, however, are left open to the reasonable interpretation and the appeal to conscience of each individual. It has been suggested that diversity of belief, which emphasizes local input, is valued in principle throughout the Anglican Communion, not merely tolerated in practice. Equally, for Church of England schools, each local context, with its diversity of views and beliefs, is a rich field of potential collaborative partnerships. Each partnership can grow its own energy. The Church can experience the Holy Spirit working most powerfully through such synergy. The Holy Spirit is the 'go-between-God' (Taylor, 1972) who leads us to use that synergy to change things for the better. All schools value children, and, for the Anglican, to value an individual, and to seek justice for him or her, necessitates an imaginative engagement with what it might be like to be that person.

Anglicanism encourages encounter as a means to community building. There is a deep need for the building of communities, around mutual respect, in Britain. This mutual respect flows naturally from a spirituality which values diversity. Such spirituality is a further distinctive contribution to the wholistic education of the nation's children and young people. In this way, there is a continuing need for Church of England schools. There is also a need for a fuller theological and ecclesiological rationale to underpin further development of the distinctiveness of Church of England schools.

Anglican Church schools are grounded in ordinariness as Trinity is theologically grounded in incarnation. They are about 'Godly encounters', in which different persons engage with each other, taking each other's differences seriously. It has been shown that Anglican schools share those distinctive characteristics with Anglican parishes and that these characteristics are their greatest asset. If, as is suggested, Anglicanism's relationships are dynamic and open then the Trinitarian model is a fertile area for further exploration. It will be clear that there is an ongoing future, of offering significant service to the nation, in Anglican Academies and in VA and VC schools that work with their local churches to further develop 'Trinitarian' relationships.

Making Trinitarian relationships is at the heart of both good education and good spirituality. It is no coincidence that these two are, thus, linked, for this is about God's destiny for each of us, expressed, and lived, by Jesus: 'That they may have life; in all its fullness' (John 10.10).

Key questions

1. How well are Anglican schools placed to broker partnerships?
2. What could your school contribute as 'value-added' to the life of your local parish? Suggest at least three specific ways in which the faith and expertise of the school could enrich the local church.
3. It has been suggested that there is an unavoidable 'justice-seeking' connected to Anglicanism's valuing of the local church. To what extent do the values promoted in collective worship and in the curriculum explore 'education for justice'? ~ or is this seen as 'an optional extra'?
4. Can you be Anglican and say, 'There is only one right answer (mine)'? Suggest three specific ways in which your school/church could actively promote an acceptance of diversity?
5. How can churches and schools genuinely learn from youth culture? Can we balance celebrating the best of contemporary culture with also encouraging the development of robust self-criticism?

Notes

1 Such as St Paul's (founded in 1509), Shrewsbury (1552), Westminster (1560), Merchant Taylors (1561), Rugby (1567), Harrow (1571) and Charterhouse (1611) (Kay and Francis, 1997, p. 9).

2 I recognize variant interpretations of the motivation behind the land-owners and clergy forming these school trust deeds. That is, some suggest there was an element of competition between the Church of England and other Churches for 'territorial' ownership of the maximum number of schools, nationally. Nonetheless, the fact remains that, whatever the mixed motives for their formation, these schools did benefit the poor children of each parish. One will always find mixed motives so one must look to the impact of these schools to determine a national pattern that was established by their foundation. In this case, the impact, I suggest, is clearly to the benefit of the poor in each parish served by these schools.

3   People moved to where there was work, which was in the factories spawned by
    Britain's industrial revolution. In so doing they created towns, in which children
    were born, but without thought for the gainful occupation of the children's time and
    energies. Many children ran riot in these new towns.

4   'Fewer' is an oversimplification. Brierley, 2000, p. 96. Statistics gained from the
    English Church Attendance Survey of 1998 have been compared with those gained
    from the 1979 and 1989 English Church Censuses. There was a significant drop
    in those aged under 44, but a rise in those aged 45 and over, and especially those
    aged 65 and over. Similarly, Kay and Francis, 1996, particularly pp. 141–3, and
    156, does indicate, from surveys over the preceding 25 years that there is a 'drift
    from the churches' of children and adolescents, particularly since the early 1970s.
    However, there is a mixed message from the more recent statistics of Brierley, 2006,
    based upon the 2005 English Church Census, for example, there were 5.4 million
    in church, 11.7 per cent of the population, in 1979, contrasted with 3.2 million in
    church 6.3 per cent of the population, in 2005. So, undoubtedly, there are 'fewer'
    attending church, but Brierley demonstrates that the decline is 'pulling out of the
    nose dive', and the statistical prognosis for the future looks more positive than it was
    ten years ago.

8

Pupil Voice in Anglican Secondary Schools

Leslie J. Francis and Gemma Penny

Abstract

This study argues that it is the collective worldview of the pupils which is crucial in reflecting and shaping the ethos of schools. In order to generate insight into the ethos of Anglican secondary schools the collective worldview of 3,124 pupils (13–15 years of age) attending 15 Anglican schools is set alongside the collective worldview of 4,929 pupils attending 25 comparable schools with no religious character. The worldview of pupils was profiled across 10 value domains defined as Christian beliefs, church and society, non-traditional beliefs, personal aims in life, personal well-being, attitudes towards school, attitudes towards sexual morality, attitudes towards substance use, attitudes towards right and wrong, and attitudes towards the environment. Two main conclusions are drawn from the data: that the collective worldview of pupils attending Anglican secondary schools is not greatly different from the collective worldview of pupils attending comparable schools with no religious character; and that the collective worldview of pupils attending Anglican schools generates an ethos consistent with a predominantly secular host culture.

Keywords
School ethos, pupil values, quantitative research, school distinctiveness

---

Introduction

The foundation of the National Society in 1811 (Burgess, 1958) placed the Church of England (then the Established Church in both England and Wales) in a strong position to pioneer a national network of schools well before the parliament voted a budget for education in 1833 or established a mechanism for creating local school boards through the Education Act 1870 (Rich, 1970).

The ongoing history of the Church of England's involvement in schools has been recorded by a number of key commentators, including Cruickshank (1963), Murphy (1971) and Chadwick (1997). The changing political, cultural and religious climate of England during the latter part of the twentieth century led to three major discussions and reflections on the Church of England's policy in relation to Church schools as documented by *the Fourth R* (Durham Report, 1970), *A Future in Partnership* (Waddington, 1984) and *The Way Ahead* (Dearing, 2001).

Major debates concerning the Church of England's role within the state-maintained system of education through Church schools has focused on issues concerned with the theological and social rationale of Church schools and the connection between the purpose of Church schools and practical policy matters like admissions policies, school ethos, staff appointments and religious education. One of the most formative contributions to the debate was provided by the Durham Report's clarification of what it described as the Church of England's two distinct historic motives for involvement in Church schools. The report styled these motives as the Church of England's *domestic* and *general* functions in education. The domestic function characterizes the more inward-looking concern to 'equip the children of the Church to take their place in the Christian community'. The general function characterizes the more outward-looking concern to 'serve the nation through its children'. The Durham Report recognizes that historically the two roles were 'indistinguishable, for nation and church were, theoretically, one, and the domestic task was seen as including the general'. However, during the twentieth century this view of the close connection between nation and church became untenable.

While there is a great deal of point and value in debating, from theologically, sociologically and educationally informed perspectives, what Church of England schools should be, there may also be some advantage in empirical enquiry examining what is the case in practice. While such empirical enquiry cannot be employed to establish what Church schools *should be* like, there may, nonetheless, be some interest (and advantage) in establishing what Church schools actually are like. The present study belongs to this empirical genre.

Empirical studies concerned with what Church schools are actually like can take a number of different forms. Research can focus on what is said about Church schools in their policy documents, in their brochures or on their websites. Research can listen to what local clergy have to say about Church schools, to the views of church school governors (Francis and Stone, 1995), to the views of those who teach in Church schools (Francis, 1986b; Francis and Grindle, 2001) or to the views reflected in inspection reports (Lankshear, 1997; Brown, 1997). Studies of this type can be said to provide some insight into the ethos of Church of England schools from a managerial perspective. Yet, in the early 1970s Francis took the view that there were advantages in listening to the pupils who actually attended Church schools. Studies of this type can be said to provide some insight into the ethos of Church of England schools from a pragmatic perspective.

Both in England and internationally there has been a well-established history of listening to pupils attending Roman Catholic schools. For example, pioneering studies in the United States of America were reported by Quinn (1965), Neuwien (1966), Greeley and Rossi (1966), Treston et al. (1975) and Greeley et al. (1976). Pioneering studies in Australia were reported by Mol (1968), Ray and Doratis (1971), Anderson (1971), Anderson and Western (1972), Leavey (1972), Flynn (1975, 1979, 1985) and Fahy (1976, 1978, 1980a, 1980b). In England, pioneering studies among pupils in Catholic schools were reported by Brothers (1964), Lawlor (1965), Spencer (1968) and Hornsby-Smith (1978).

Considerably less is known about pupils who attend Anglican schools in England and Wales. One strand of research reported by Francis (1986a) administered a scale of attitude towards Christianity to all Years 5 and 6 pupils attending ten Church of England VA primary schools and fifteen non-denominational state-maintained schools in East Anglia in 1974, 1978, and again in 1982. After using multiple regression analysis to control for the influence of sex, age, parental church attendance, social class and IQ on pupils' attitudes towards Christianity, these data indicated that the Church of England schools exercised a small negative influence on their pupils' attitudes towards Christianity. The direction of the school influence on pupils' attitude was consistent for all three samples taken in 1974, 1978 and 1982.

Francis (1987) set out to replicate this earlier study among Year 6 pupils attending all Church of England VA, VC and non-denominational state-maintained schools in Gloucestershire. These data attributed neither positive nor negative influence to Church of England VA schools, but demonstrated a significant negative influence exercised by Church of England VC schools.

Two studies set out to compare pupils in Church of England and non-denominational state-maintained secondary schools. In the first study, Francis and Carter (1980) compared the attitude towards Christianity of Year 11 pupils attending Church of England VA secondary schools and non-denominational state-maintained secondary schools. These data provided no support for the notion that Church of England secondary schools exert either a positive or a negative influence on their pupils' attitude towards religion. In the second study, Francis and Jewell (1992) compared the attitude towards the church of Year 10 pupils attending the four non-denominational secondary schools and the one Church of England VC secondary school serving the area around the same town. The data demonstrated that the Church of England school recruited a higher proportion of pupils from churchgoing homes and that churchgoing homes tended to represent the higher social classes. After taking into account the influence of sex, social class and parental religiosity, path analysis indicated that the Church of England school exerted neither a positive nor a negative influence on its pupils' religious practice, belief or attitude.

Lankshear (2005) compared the values profiles of six groups of pupils: Anglicans in Church of England schools and Anglicans in non-denominational state-maintained schools; non-affiliates in Church of England schools and non-affiliates in non-denominational state-maintained schools; members of other Christian denominations in Church of England schools and members of other Christian denominations in non-denominational state-maintained schools. The data demonstrated that Anglicans attending Anglican schools recorded higher levels of personal dissatisfaction, higher levels of religious values and comparable levels of moral values in comparison with Anglicans attending non-denominational schools. Non-affiliates attending Anglican schools recorded higher levels of personal dissatisfaction, lower levels of moral values and comparable levels of religious values in comparison with non-affiliates attending non-denominational schools.

Drawing on John Fisher's model of spiritual health, Francis et al. (2012) compared the levels of spiritual health recorded by 13- to 15-year-old pupils attending three different types of school in England and Wales including: state-maintained schools with no religious character, Anglican schools within the state-maintained sector and independent Christian schools. Fisher (2000, 2001, 2004) developed a relational model of spiritual health, according to which he conceives good spiritual health in terms of good relationship within four domains: the personal, the communal, the environmental and the transcendental. Good spiritual health in the personal domain is reflected in good relationships with the self, in a good self-concept, and in a sense of personal meaning and purpose in life. Good spiritual health in the communal domain is reflected in good relationships with other people, and in secure standing among friends and among adults. Good spiritual health in the environmental domain is reflected in good relationships with the wider world, in a developed sense of global citizenship, and in commitment to sustainable development. Good spiritual health in the transcendent domain is reflected in good relationships with issues of ultimate concern, and with God.

Francis et al. (2012) found that the spiritual health of young people attending Anglican schools within the state-maintained sector was indistinguishable from that of young people attending schools without a religious character within the state-maintained sector, apart from two markers within the transcendental domain. Young people attending Anglican schools were more likely to believe in God and more likely to believe in life after death. Reflecting on these findings Francis et al. (2012) offer the following comments:

> On the one hand, this finding may allay fear that the Anglican Church could be abusing its privileged position within the state-maintained sector of education to influence young people differently from schools without a religious character within the same sector. On the other hand, this finding may lead to some puzzlement regarding the Anglican Church's commitment to a non-distinctive presence within education.

Research question

Against this background, the present study draws on data generated by the Teenage Religion and Values Survey, an ongoing project established to replicate the study of 34,000 adolescents reported by Francis (2001). These data are employed to compare the collective worldview of pupils attending Anglican schools within the state-maintained sector with the collective worldview of pupils attending schools with no religious character within the state-maintained sector.

The assumption on which this comparison is made is that it is the collective values of the pupils as a body that both reflects and informs the ethos of the school. For example, a school ethos statement may claim that the school provides a safe environment for all pupils, but, if a significant number of pupils were to report living under the fear of being bullied, it is the account of the pupils rather than the ethos statement that really names the pastoral ethos of the school. A school ethos statement may claim that the school is grounded in religious faith, but, if only a minority of pupils were to report belief in God, it is the account of the pupils rather than the ethos statement that really names the religious ethos of the school.

The form of analysis undertaken and presented in this chapter is not intended to identify the *source* of differences (if any) between pupils in different types of schools. It is not a study in school effectiveness. It is a study concerned with identifying and defining school ethos through listening to the pupils themselves.

Method

Procedure

A sample of 15 Anglican secondary schools within the state-maintained sector and spread across England accepted the invitation to participate in the project, together with 25 state-maintained schools with no religious character located within comparable communities. Participating schools were asked to follow a standard procedure. The questionnaires were administered in normal class groups to all Years 9 and 10 pupils throughout the school. Pupils were asked not to write their name on the booklet and to complete the inventory under examination-like conditions. Although pupils were given the choice not to participate very few declined to do so. They were assured of confidentiality and anonymity.

Sample

Within the Anglican schools the participants comprised 1,567 males and 1,557 females; and within the schools with no religious character 2,478 males and 2,451 females.

Instrument

The questionnaire contained 189 items arranged for responses on a five-point, Likert-type scale (Likert, 1932): agree strongly, agree, not certain, disagree and disagree strongly. These 189 items are designed to reflect a number of specific value domains. The 10 value domains selected for discussion in the present chapter are: Christian beliefs, church and society, non-traditional beliefs, personal aims in life, personal well-being, attitudes towards school, attitudes towards sexual morality, attitudes towards substance abuse, attitudes towards right and wrong, and attitudes towards the environment.

Analyses

In each case the statistical significance of the differences in responses between two groups has been calculated by the chi-square statistic after collapsing the scores recorded on the five-point, Likert-type scale into two categories, combining on the one hand the agree strongly and agree responses, and on the other hand the disagree strongly, disagree and not certain responses.

Results and discussion

In the following series of tables, the findings have been set out to profile the values of pupils attending Anglican schools alongside the values of pupils attending schools with no religious character. The value domains are discussed in the following sequence: Christian beliefs, church and society, non-traditional beliefs, personal aims in life, personal well-being, attitudes towards school, attitudes towards sexual morality, attitudes towards substance use, attitudes towards right and wrong, and attitudes towards the environment.

Christian beliefs

Table 8.1 displays the six items concerned with Christian beliefs. The first three items access belief in the three persons of the Trinity. The fourth item accesses commitment to an evangelical Christian perspective. The remaining two items explore the theology of religions.

These data demonstrate that around two out of every five pupils in Anglican schools hold traditional Christian beliefs in God: 38 per cent believe in God and 37 per cent believe in Jesus Christ, with the proportion falling to 27 per cent who believe in the Holy Spirit. Around one out of every five believes in Jesus as their personal Saviour. Only one in six (16%) take the view that Christianity is the only true religion, with twice that number (33%) believing that there is truth in all religions.

Compared with pupils attending schools with no religious character, pupils attending Anglican schools are more likely to believe in God (38% compared with 22%), more likely to believe in Jesus Christ (37% compared with 22%), and more likely to believe in the Holy Spirit (27% compared with 16%). They are more likely to believe in Jesus as their personal saviour (19% compared

Table 8.1 Christian beliefs

	Non-denominational	Anglican		
	%	%	χ^2	$p <$
I believe in God	22	38	238.5	.001
I believe in Jesus Christ	22	37	226.7	.001
I believe in the Holy Spirit	16	27	130.2	.001
I believe in Jesus as my personal Saviour	9	19	176.0	.001
I think Christianity is the only true religion	10	16	81.2	.001
I believe that there is truth in all religions	28	33	24.0	.001

with 9%). They are more likely to believe that there is truth in all religions (33% compared with 28%), and more likely to think that Christianity is the only true religion (16% compared with 10%).

By way of summary, the ethos of Anglican schools generated by the pupils' values is more conducive to Christian believing than is the case in schools with no religious character. Nonetheless, the majority of pupils in Anglican schools (around 60%) do not share the Christian faith.

Church and society

Table 8.2 displays the six items concerned with church and society. These items are concerned with the place of religion in schools, with the place of clergy and religious rites of passage in today's society, and with the perceived relevance of religion for today.

These data demonstrate that half of the pupils in Anglican schools (50%) agree that religious education should be taught in schools, yet only 12 per cent of these pupils agree that schools should hold a religious assembly every day. Around two in every five agree that Christian ministers do a good job (41%) or agree that they want their children baptized in church (44%). Around a third take the view that the Bible seems irrelevant to life today (35%) or that the church seems irrelevant for life today (30%).

Compared with pupils attending schools with no religious character, pupils attending Anglican schools hold a more positive view of the place of religion in school, with more supporting religious education (50% compared with 48%), and more supporting a daily religious assembly (12% compared with 5%).

Table 8.2 Church and society

	Non-denominational	Anglican		
	%	%	χ^2	$p <$
Religious education should be taught in school	48	50	3.9	.05
Schools should hold a religious assembly every day	5	12	114.0	.001
Christian ministers/vicars/ priests do a good job	32	41	60.6	.001
I want my children to be baptized/christened/ dedicated in church	32	44	104.3	.001
The Bible seems irrelevant to life today	40	35	20.5	.001
The church seems irrelevant to life today	31	30	2.4	NS

They are more inclined to consider that Christian ministers do a good job (41% compared with 32%) and want their children baptized in church (44% compared with 32%). They are less likely to feel that the Bible seems irrelevant to life today (35% compared with 40%).

By way of summary, the ethos of Anglican schools generated by pupils values is more conducive of supporting the role of the churches in society than is the case in schools with no religious character. Nonetheless, it is a minority of pupils who show commitment to their position.

Non-traditional beliefs

In the face of declining traditional belief, a number of recent studies point to the increase in alternative spiritualities and non-traditional beliefs (see Heelas and Woodhead, 2005). Table 8.3 displays the six items concerned with non-traditional beliefs, including beliefs in horoscopes, contacting spirits of the dead, magic, fortune-tellers, vampires and tarot cards.

These data demonstrate that around a quarter of pupils in Anglican schools believe in their horoscope (27%), believe magic can be used for good (26%), or that it is possible to contact the spirits of the dead (24%). A smaller number believe that fortune-tellers can tell the future (14%), believe in vampires (11%), or believe that tarot cards can tell the future (9%).

Table 8.3 Non-traditional beliefs

	Non-denominational	Anglican		
	%	%	χ^2	$p <$
I believe in my horoscope	28	27	0.3	NS
I believe magic can be used for good	25	26	0.7	NS
I believe it is possible to contact spirits of the dead	23	24	0.5	NS
I believe fortune-tellers can tell the future	14	14	0.0	NS
I believe in vampires	11	11	0.2	NS
I believe that tarot cards can tell the future	10	9	1.8	NS

In the area of non-traditional beliefs, there are no significant differences in the ethos generated by pupils attending Anglican schools and by pupils attending schools with no religious character.

Personal aims in life

Years 9 and 10 pupils are already talking confidently and clearly about their personal aims in life. Table 8.4 displays the five items selected to reflect this area, focusing on owning a home, getting married, having children, studying for a degree, and making a difference in the world.

These data demonstrate that the vast majority of pupils in Anglican schools follow a traditional trajectory of wanting to own their own home (86%), wanting to get married (83%), and wanting to have children (83%). Three quarters want

Table 8.4 Personal aims in life

	Non-denominational	Anglican		
	%	%	χ^2	$p <$
I would like to own my own home	87	86	0.1	NS
I would like to get married	84	83	1.7	NS
I would like to have children	83	83	0.0	NS
I would like to study for a degree	75	77	6.5	.01
I would like to make a difference in the world	66	68	4.8	.05

to study for a degree (77%) and two-thirds want to make a difference in the world (68%).

In the area of personal aims in life, there are few significant differences in the ethos generated by pupils attending Anglican schools and by pupils attending schools with no religious character.

Personal well-being

Table 8.5 displays the six items concerned with personal well-being. The first two items focus on the positive aspects of well-being, asking questions about joy and purpose in life. The other four items focus on the darker side of well-being, asking questions about depression, self-harm and suicidal ideation.

These data demonstrate that around two-thirds of pupils in Anglican schools find life really worth living (72%) or feel that their life has a sense of purpose (66%). This level of positive affect, however, should not be allowed to eclipse a significant presence of negative affect among these young people living through the unsettling years of adolescence. Over a quarter admit to often feeling depressed (30%) and almost a quarter have sometimes considered deliberately hurting themselves (23%), have sometimes considered taking their own life (21%), or feel that they are not worth much as a person (17%).

In the area of personal well-being, there are no significant differences in the ethos generated by pupils attending Anglican schools and by pupils attending schools with no religious character.

Table 8.5 Personal well-being

	Non-denominational	Anglican		
	%	%	χ^2	$p <$
I find life really worth living	71	72	1.4	NS
I feel my life has a sense of purpose	65	66	0.5	NS
I often feel depressed	31	30	0.3	NS
I have sometimes considered deliberately hurting myself	24	23	0.2	NS
I have sometimes considered taking my own life	20	21	0.6	NS
I feel I am not much worth as a person	17	17	0.5	NS

School

Table 8.6 displays the six items concerned with attitude towards school. The first set of three items focus on positive aspects of school life, including overall happiness at school, positive appraisal of the relevance of school for later life, and positive feelings about teachers. The second set of three items focus on the anxieties of school life, including worries about exams, worries about school work in general, and worries about being bullied.

These data demonstrate that the majority of pupils in Anglican schools are happy in their school (71%), feel that their school is preparing them for life (62%), and feel that teachers do a good gob (54%). This level of positive affect, however, should not be allowed to eclipse a significant presence of negative affect about school. High numbers of pupils are worried about their exams at school (68%) and often worry about their school work (54%). One in every five pupils is also worried about being bullied at school (19%).

In the area of attitudes towards school, there are no significant differences in the ethos generated by pupils attending Anglican schools and by pupils attending schools with no religious character.

Table 8.6 School

	Non-denominational	Anglican		
	%	%	χ^2	$p <$
I am happy in my school	71	71	0.0	NS
My school is preparing me for life	64	62	3.6	NS
Teachers do a good job	54	54	0.4	NS
I am worried about my exams at school	68	68	0.1	NS
I often worry about my school work	52	54	2.2	NS
I am worried about being bullied at school	20	19	0.1	NS

Sexual morality

Table 8.7 displays the six items concerned with attitudes towards sexual morality. These items cover many of those issues most frequently included in surveys, namely, sex under the legal age, sex before marriage, pornography, abortion, homosexuality and divorce.

Table 8.7 Sexual morality

	Non-denominational	Anglican		
	%	%	χ^2	$p <$
It is wrong to have sex under the legal age (16)	28	30	2.1	NS
It is wrong to have sex before you are married	7	11	44.3	.001
Pornography is wrong	29	34	18.6	.001
Abortion is wrong	28	32	16.8	.001
Homosexuality is wrong	23	25	3.8	.05
Divorce is wrong	15	19	18.3	.001

These data demonstrate that over two-thirds of pupils in Anglican schools generally hold liberal views on sexual morality. Just 30 per cent believe that it is wrong to have sex under the legal age of 16, and the proportion drops to 11 per cent who believe that it is wrong to have sex before you are married. A third take the view that pornography is wrong (34%) and that abortion is wrong (32%). A quarter take the view that homosexuality is wrong (25%). A fifth take the view that divorce is wrong (19%).

Compared with pupils attending schools with no religious character, pupils attending Anglican schools take a significantly more conservative view on five issues concerning sexual morality. They are more likely to believe that pornography is wrong (34% compared with 29%), that abortion is wrong (32% compared with 28%), that homosexuality is wrong (25% compared with 23%), that divorce is wrong (19% compared with 15%), and that it is wrong to have sex before you are married (11% compared with 7%).

By way of summary, the ethos of Anglican schools generated by the pupils' values is slightly (but significantly) more conducive to a conservative worldview on sexual ethics than is the case in schools with no religious character. Nonetheless, the majority of pupils in Anglican schools (around at least 70%) do not share this conservative worldview.

Substance use

Table 8.8 displays the six items concerned with attitudes towards substance use. These items cover many issues most frequently included in surveys, including alcohol, tobacco, cannabis, heroin and ecstasy.

These data demonstrate that the majority of pupils in Anglican schools hold liberal views on the use (and abuse) of alcohol, but less liberal views on the use of

Table 8.8 Substance use

	Non-denominational	Anglican		
	%	%	χ^2	$p <$
It is wrong to drink alcohol	13	16	21.0	.001
It is wrong to get drunk	19	23	18.2	.001
It is wrong to smoke cigarettes	53	53	0.3	NS
It is wrong to use cannabis (hash/pot)	59	57	3.2	NS
It is wrong to use ecstasy	63	65	1.5	NS
It is wrong to use heroin	75	75	0.6	NS

tobacco, cannabis, heroin and solvents. On the one hand, fewer than a quarter of the pupils take the view that it is wrong to drink alcohol (16%) or that is wrong to get drunk (23%). On the other hand, over half of the pupils take the view that it is wrong to smoke cigarettes (53%), that is wrong to use cannabis (57%), that it is wrong to use ecstasy (65%), or that it is wrong to use heroin (75%).

Compared with pupils attending schools with no religious character, pupils attending Anglican schools take a slightly (but significantly) more conservative view on the use of alcohol. They are more likely to take the view that it is wrong to drink alcohol (16% compared with 13%) or that it is wrong to get drunk (23% compared with 19%).

By way of summary, the ethos of Anglican schools generated by the pupils' values is slightly (but significantly) more conducive to a conservative worldview on alcohol use and abuse than is the case in schools with no religious character. Nevertheless, the majority of pupils in Anglican schools (77%) do not share the conservative worldview that getting drunk is wrong.

Right and wrong

Table 8.9 displays the five items concerned with attitudes towards right and wrong. These items explore issues concerned with cheating in exams, swearing and blasphemy, travelling without a ticket, playing truant, and shoplifting.

These data demonstrate that pupils in Anglican schools generally endorse honest and upright behaviour, although a significant minority argue for a less honest approach to life. Thus 23 per cent take the view that there is nothing wrong with travelling without a ticket; 17 per cent take the view that there is nothing wrong with playing truant from school; and 9 per cent take the view that

Table 8.9 Right and wrong

	Non-denominational	Anglican		
	%	%	χ^2	$p <$
It is wrong to cheat in exams	76	75	0.7	NS
It is wrong to swear or blaspheme	20	26	42.4	.001
There is nothing wrong with travelling without a ticket	22	23	2.5	NS
There is nothing wrong with playing truant (skiving) from school	17	17	0.1	NS
There is nothing wrong with shop-lifting	10	9	0.5	NS

there is nothing wrong with shoplifting. One in four agree that there is nothing wrong with cheating in exams (25%). Swearing and blasphemy are also not considered to be wrong by the majority of pupils in Anglican schools.

In the area of attitudes towards right and wrong, there are no significant differences in the ethos generated by pupils attending Anglican schools and by pupils attending schools with no religious character, except on the issue of swearing and blasphemy. Pupils attending Anglican schools are significantly more likely to take the view that it is wrong to swear or to blaspheme (26% compared with 20%).

The environment

Table 8.10 displays the five items concerned with attitudes towards the environment. These items focus on pollution, conserving the world's energy resources, and endangered species.

These data demonstrate that around half of the pupils in Anglican schools register concern for environmental issues. Thus, 53 per cent say that they are concerned about animals and plants becoming extinct; 49 per cent say that they are concerned that people use too much of the Earth's resources; and 52 per cent say that they are concerned about the risk of pollution to the environment. While half of the pupils' express concern about environmental issues, the proportion falls to under two-fifths who seem prepared to do anything about this concern. Thus, just 38 per cent say that they make a special effort to recycle, and 34 per cent say that they make a special effort to help save the world's energy resources.

Table 8.10 The environment

	Non-denominational	Anglican		
	%	%	χ^2	$p <$
I am concerned about animals and plants becoming extinct	53	53	0.3	NS
I am concerned about the risk of pollution to the environment	48	52	10.4	.001
I am concerned that we use too much of the Earth's resources	49	49	0.2	NS
I make a special effort to recycle	33	38	22.2	.001
I make a special effort to help save the world's energy resources	29	34	18.9	.001

Compared with pupils attending schools with no religious character, pupils attending Anglican schools are more likely to display environmentally friendly behaviours. More pupils in Anglican schools make a special effort to recycle (38% compared with 33%) and make a special effort to help save the world's energy resource (34% compared with 29%).

By way of summary, the ethos of Anglican schools generated by the pupils' values is more conducive to supporting environmentally friendly behaviour than is the case in schools with no religious character. Nonetheless, the majority of pupils in Anglican schools (over 60%) do not make special effort to help the environment.

Conclusion

This chapter set out to profile the collective worldview of Years 9 and 10 pupils attending Anglican secondary schools across ten value domains defined as: Christian beliefs, church and society, non-traditional beliefs, personal aims in life, personal well-being, attitudes towards substance use, attitudes towards right and wrong, and attitudes towards the environment. The collective worldview of these pupils attending Anglican secondary schools was then set alongside the collective worldview of their peers attending comparable schools with no religious character.

The key argument on which this investigation was based is that it is the collective worldview of the pupils which is crucial in both reflecting and informing the school ethos. According to this argument, it is the collective worldview of the pupils (rather than the school ethos statement, the views of the governors, or the attitudes of individual teachers) that may be dominant in influencing and shaping other pupils. For example, pupils attending schools where the majority of their peers believe in God are living in an environment in which belief in God is accepted as normal. Pupils attending schools where the majority of their peers believe that it is acceptable to get drunk are living in an environment in which drunkenness is accepted as normal. The present chapter has been concerned to map the ethos of Anglican schools on the basis of this argument. From this basis two main conclusions emerge from the data.

The first conclusion is that the collective worldview of pupils attending Anglican schools is not greatly different from the collective worldview of pupils attending comparable schools with no religious character. It is true that there are some statistically significant differences, but even the largest of these differences is just 16 percentage points in respect of belief in God. The two value domains in which there are differences of at least 10 percentage points concern Christian belief (three items) and church and society (one item). The four value domains in which there are differences of at least 4 percentage points concern sexual morality (four items), attitudes towards substance use (one item), attitudes towards right and wrong (one item), and attitudes towards the environment (three items). In the other four value domains there are no items showing differences of more than 3 percentage points: non-traditional beliefs, personal aims in life, personal well-being, and attitudes towards school. These differences may not be large enough to support the view that Anglican secondary schools provide an alternative ethos distinctive from schools with no religious character.

The second conclusion is that the collective worldview of pupils attending Anglican schools generates an ethos that is consistent with a predominantly secular host culture. In Anglican secondary schools it is a minority of pupils who hold traditional Christian beliefs, support traditional Christian teaching on sex and drugs, or who promote a radical commitment to care for God's creation.

These conclusions are, of themselves, neither evidence to justify or grounds to criticize the Church of England's engagement with education. They are, however, conclusions worth taking into account when formulating policy or implementing practice in the field of Church schools. According to the gospel tradition, when people asked Jesus to reflect theologically on the Kingdom of God, he advised them to go to collect the evidence: to observe the sower in the field, to observe the cook in the kitchen, or to observe the master of ceremonies at the wedding feast. Today empirical theology stands in that gospel tradition.

The present analysis is inadequate and incomplete in a number of ways. Only 15 Anglican schools are included in the study; but the Teenage Religion and Values Survey is on target to double that number. Only Anglican schools have been studied; but comparable data are already becoming available on Roman Catholic schools, independent Christian schools and independent Muslim schools. Only one research question has been addressed to the data; but subsequent analyses can be undertaken to explore further questions concerning school influence and school effectiveness.

Key questions

1. How valid are pupil attitudes as indicators of school ethos?
2. Would we expect pupil attitudes to be different in Anglican schools?
3. How useful is research listening to pupils for developing Church schools in the future?
4. If you were designing the survey, what would you want to know about the pupils?
5. Would qualitative research be a better method than quantitative research?

Part Three

Reflection on Current Practice

9

The Church Schools as 'Safe' School

Alan Brown

Abstract

The primary aim of this chapter is to consider the way in which an Anglican school should offer a dynamic and creative challenge to all those involved with the school in order to promote harmony and inclusion. Church schools will, like all schools, be schools where children are safe but will need to move on to explore how radicalism in religion should be endemic to the understanding of what a safe place means in the context of an Anglican school. The energy and dynamism of the Christian message suggests a challenge to Anglican schools in the midst of the growing secularism of the twenty-first century rather than the erection of a fortress where children may be corralled against the demands of contemporary society. Christian character is then considered in the school context, followed by ways in which Religious Education enable this. These both contribute to how the Anglican school can be both a 'safe space' and a 'safe place'. The importance of allowing children, in the context of an Anglican educational community, to develop their own narrative and understandings is examined.

Keywords
Dialogue, change, ethos, commitment

Introduction

All schools are, or should be, safe schools. It is one of the few non-controversial aspects of the system of education in the United Kingdom. Of course, there are times when the press reveal schools as being less 'safe' than they should be but the growing importance of safeguarding has made schools so much more aware of these responsibilities (*Every Child Matters*) (DfES, 2003). It is not this form of a 'safe' school, however, with which this article is concerned. In 1984, Robert

Waddington, the then General Secretary of the National Society and the Church of England's Board of Education, wrote a book called *A Future in Partnership* (1984). It was not the view of the National Society (Pilkington, 2001, p. 54) but Waddington's personal view of the present and future state of Church and State relations in education. The partnership to which Waddington referred was the partnership between the State and the Anglican and Roman Catholic churches. It was a partnership formulated in the Education Act 1944 but Waddington's book was the presage of a fundamental change in 'partnership' leading to the 1988 Education Reform Act and further subsequent changes in government legislation. Waddington's 'partnership' would look very different today in the light of the 2011 Academies Act which appears to be introducing the biggest changes to education since 1870.

In his book, Waddington listed 10 key characteristics of a church (Anglican) school, which might well stand the test of time, and one of these was that a Church school should be a safe school. They are listed here in brief as they have a direct focus for the direction of this chapter.

A Church school should be:

(i) *a safe place* where there is no ideological pressure and yet Christian inferences are built into the ethos and teaching as signals for children to detect; (ii) *an ecumenical nursery* which builds from children's fundamental unity a sensitivity to difference, and the faiths of others; (iii) a *place of distinctive excellence* which is not tied to what is academic but linked to all aspects of the life of the school including the manual, technical, aesthetic and non-verbal; (iv) *stepping stones to and from the local community*, for children, staff, parents and local interests. The school learns to be part of a local community, to share its concern and to be open to those who seek help, support and resources; (v) *a house of the Gospel* in which, starting at governor and staff level, there is a deliberate attempt to link the concerns of Christ's gospel with the life of the school, and to do this in educational terms; (vi) *a place of revelation and disclosure* in which the rigour of learning and the art of acquiring skill are seen as parables of the revelation of God and his continuous involvement in His Creation; (vii) *a foster home of enduring values and relationships*, in which the selfless care and unlimited love of the Suffering Servant is the model for the life of the community; (viii) *a beacon signalling the transcendent* by the development of awe, mystery and wonder through the curriculum, exemplified in acts of corporate worship including contact with the Christian calendar and sacraments; (ix) *a place where you can see the wood for the trees*, for there are attempts to develop an integrated view of knowledge alongside sensitivity to the interests of others, as well as to cross traditional subject boundaries and carry out integrated projects in learning; (x) *a creative workshop* which facilitates a thorough induction into cultural tradition and skills yet allows pupils to practise initiative, change and new direction as they shape their future. (Waddington, 1984, p. 71; see also Duncan, 1990, pp. 5–6; Francis and Grindle, 2001, p. 4)

It is clear from 'Waddington's list' that virtually all of his ten characteristics could relate to the aspirations of a Church school today. Waddington's understanding was that an Anglican school should be a place where pupils and staff were free to debate and discuss religious and non-religious questions and affiliations without feeling they were in any way 'odd' or separate from the normal intercourse of human life.

In one VA secondary school a fourteen year old boy, a Baptist, talked with classmates about his adult [sic] Baptism during the previous weekend. The class listened in an empathic respectful silence while he described the importance of the event to him. It was a powerful moment and an excellent example of a safe place.

To one reading Waddington's aspirations over 25 years later it may appear surprising that he should feel the need to express this characteristic of a Church school as being so important but society has evolved and moved on in many ways over the past 25 years: falling church attendances, the influence of the internet, changes in distribution of wealth, and so on. It may also be the case that attitudes to Church schools have changed both inside and outside the church. Issues of separation and division are still raised with regard to 'faith schools' but the tentative attitude to Church of England schools that existed in the General Synod of the 1980s (Marks, 2001, pp. xii–xiii) has been dispelled through the work of the Board of Education/National Society over the past 15 years – really since the Labour Party came to power in 1997 (but see DfEE, 1997, p. 67). The then Secretary of State for Education, David Blunkett, expressed his regard for the ethos of Church schools (*Independent*, 24 February 2001).

What is a 'safe' school in the sense that Waddington meant? Does it have any relevance for Anglican schools today? This article will consider ways in which Anglican schools may well be 'safer' than they were a quarter of a century ago. Waddington was a liberal thinker in both educational and Christian terms and his liberalism would not (and maybe will not) be appreciated by all (Thompson, 2001). In conversation with the author he once described himself as a 'liberal – but a hard-line liberal' and for a number of years after he left London for

Manchester to become Dean of the Cathedral and then on to York he reminded the author of the need for hard line liberals to hold the 'line' – whatever that line was and wherever it was to be drawn.

One of the most fluent and coherent articles on a defence of liberalism and faith schools remains that of Andrew Wright (2003). Wright (2011) developed his thoughtful and challenging theme in address given to a symposium in 2004 and further still to the Watson Symposium in 2011. He offers five thoughts covering on Christian engagement in an essentially pagan, post-Christian world and post-Christian education system. He concludes:

> Is there such a thing as an alternative Christian liberalism? Yes but not if you mean recasting the gospel according to the latest fashion. If you mean tolerance, reason, openness, lack of arrogance – these are Christian virtues that were hijacked by liberal humanism, Christians have the right to demand them back or at least share them. Christian liberalism can't ever be a matter of revising the gospel. My view is that the more orthodox you are doctrinally, then the more radical your ethics ought to be. . . . Education in a secular liberal context can't replace Christian education. Christian education can come from Church schools – although some Church schools need to think about how they embody the faith – but if they're not available, there are alternatives, e.g. withdrawing – see how the Muslim community respond to this – Muslims in Britain have invested a lot of energy in developing their 'out-of-school programmes' for young people. (Wright, 2004)

The Fourth R: Some implications for contemporary society

The most influential of all National Society reports in the twentieth century was *The Fourth R* (Ramsey, 1970), often referred to as the Durham Report. The primary aim of the Durham Commission was to inquire into religious education but it did identify two motives as the Church's domestic and general function in education with the emphasis being on the general function (Francis and Grindle, 2001). In other words VA schools were to be provided by the Church for the service of the nation rather than something provided for the Church. This chapter is not primarily concerned with this debate although the consequences lasted for some decades (Pilkington, 2001, p. 55). What is more relevant is the omission from the Durham Report of almost all reference to the multifaith nature of society and the consequences for VA or VC Anglican schools. Francis is a measured and respected researcher on

Church schools and his observations are that partnership, as expressed by Waddington, should be emphasized in preference to the dual system and the voluntary aspects of Church schools in preference to denominationalism (Francis and Grindle, 2001). Francis highlights Waddington's characteristics but not the 'safe place'; he is more concerned with Waddington's statements on ethos and teaching as 'signals for children to detect' and Francis makes cogent points in the following pages regarding the changes in emphasis in National Society publications on schools in succeeding years (Francis and Grindle, 2001, pp. 4ff.). Indeed the National Society found it difficult to come to terms with the changing environments and constituencies of its schools. The search for a theology was expressed on *The Multi-Faith Church School* (Brown, 1992) but this has been built on and surpassed by *Everyfaithmatters* (Worcester Division of Education, 2007) and publications from a number of dioceses (dioceses of London, Birmingham and Manchester among others). The point at issue is that in the years from *The Fourth R* (Ramsey, 1970) to *The Multi-Faith Church School*, Anglican schools were facing new challenges to which publications like *Faith in the City* (Archbishop's Council, 1985) drew sharp attention. Were these inner city schools 'safe places'? Were Anglican clergy and headteachers up to the challenge of *Faith in the City* not just in terms of resources but by the manner in which schools could become places and spaces of safety for children living in inner cities regardless of whether they had a faith or not?

> *One governor of a voluntary controlled school, a Somali refugee, expressed her initial concern that her daughter would attend the local school, a church school, in Birmingham. During an inspection she talked about her anxiety and concern for her daughter. She came to love the school and the education her daughter and subsequent children received together with the respect offered to Muslim children and parents with regard to their spiritual and religious education. She and another Somali parent became governors.*

The nature of religion and religious education in a Church school must always have a challenging edge. On the one hand there will be children in Church schools who come from Christian homes with all the diversity that entails; but there will also be children from homes where no faith is either followed or even referred to and the Christian faith is summarily marked only by school holidays; again in many schools there will be children from homes where their religion is not Christian at all: Muslim, Sikh, Hindu, Rastafarian and a significant number of others. How can a Church school handle these two key aspects? To be true to the school foundation there must be an overt celebration and acknowledgement of the importance of the Christian religion in its Anglican form (again acknowledging the diversity of Anglicanism) but the presence of all children and the willingness of the school to accept the children and their families into the broad family of Anglicanism places a responsibility on the school itself to respond to these concerns. (The reports made under SIAS inspections pay attention to diversity.)

The challenge of having children from diverse faith backgrounds provides the essential context for what a safe place (or a safe space) can mean for children.

On one inspection in a West Midlands secondary school a year nine student, when asked what she felt about the school replied: 'You see all this fighting and bombing on the television, then you come into school and just get on with your mates. It is you adults that mess everything up'. (SIAS archives)

The safe place for that child and that parent, and others too in other schools, as found in other SIAS reports, indicates that the diversity of the school is a mirror of the diversity of society. These multifaith concerns which are both a challenge and an opportunity for some Anglican schools will not be the focus for other schools, but they will have their own challenges and opportunities. Schools function at the interface of society.

The following are brief extracts from *Everyfaithmatters* (Worcester Division of Education, 2007) based on what SIAS inspectors might expect to see in Anglican schools which relate to the belief in the Church school as a safe place:

- Christian values are demonstrated in relationships between staff and all learners;
- Evidence that every learner is equal in the eyes of God. Respected by all for who they are . . . . Inclusion is at the heart of the work of the school.
- When talking to learners of all faiths do they feel happy, secure and confident in school? Are their gifts used, do they feel encouraged, valued and special for who they are?
- Quiet area or memorial garden/space for reflection containing multi-faith symbols and/or quotations from writings of faith and faith leaders. (p. 9)

The need for theology

The Anglican concern for all children can never just be an educational response – though there will certainly need to be one – there has to be a theological response.

This is, it appears, the essential difference between a good Church school and a good community school. The community school may explore religious responses to the religious and non-religious diversity in the school but it will not have the Christian foundation underpinning its response which one would expect in an Anglican school. Waddington's 'safe' school means that religious and theological issues cannot be set to one side; this becomes clear as one works through his ten characteristics. All state schools, in their diversity, are at the interface of society and Anglican schools may well be full of church attending Anglican children or they may have a majority of mixed race Muslim children or even a headteacher who claims not to be a Christian, but whatever the situation, religion has to be taken seriously. It must be seen to be playing a full and influential part in the life of the school as well as in the individual lives of pupils and staff.

> *When inspecting an Anglican/Roman Catholic Joint Secondary School in the north of England some years ago, the Anglican inspector asked the (Roman Catholic) headteacher what his theology of his school was. He later wrote to the inspector saying he kept waking up in the night trying to 'get his head round an answer'!*

He might have found some support in the words of John Hull:

> In 1984 the National Society published a Green Paper on education which outlined a Trinitarian basis for the Church of England schools. Amongst other things it was suggested that the Trinitarian faith should lead to an education which recognises mystery (God the Father), fosters identification with the suffering and marginalised (God the Son as suffering servant and Messiah) and encourages creativity (God the Holy Spirit as Lord and Giver of Life). . . . The present study would argue that by following a Trinitarian model in their self-understanding, church schools would be more open to the social and educational needs of children from deprived backgrounds while the Church of England secondary comprehensive school would draw strength from the social aspects of the Trinity. (Hull, 1995, pp. 21–2)

Hull's words are a continuous challenge to the Church of England's Board of Education and the National Society to express its educational mission in clear theological terms and to present headteachers with a clear and accessible theology. It may not be possible for all teachers or headteachers to explore theology in the way Hull suggests but SIAS inspection reports indicate that Hull's points are being met in practical terms in many Anglican schools (SIAS Reports, 2010). There is, in many schools, a recognition of the mysterious nature of God present in collective worship, in the school Eucharist and in the importance for the school of the spiritual life of its children.

> *In a voluntary controlled primary school in Nechells in Birmingham, the headteacher, an African-Caribbean member of a Pentecostal church, when asked what her aims were for the children in her school had no doubts. 'I want my children to leave here with hope. Hope in a better life and a recognition they don't have to carry a knife or run drugs or be in a gang. There is life for them and hope is what the Gospel offers.'*

Christian character

If an Anglican school is a safe school how can its Christian character be maintained? The word 'ethos' is slippery as an eel, but 'character', now accepted as a significant word in the inspection of Anglican schools, is no less difficult to grasp (National Society, 2010). What is the Anglican ethos of a school and if that is too obscure a question, how about: 'What is the Anglican character of a school?' How do Anglicans characterize themselves? Is the PCC a good model? Or the General Synod? Could it be that the characterization of a safe school in Waddington's terms is where the hurley-burley of debate, difference and dispute is in the open, which is where debate, discussion and practice of religion should be? The religious affiliation and conviction of the school cannot be hidden or compartmentalized in religious education lessons or in collective (or corporate) worship or behind the demands of a syllabus; it has to play a prominent part in the daily interaction between pupils, between staff, and between pupils and staff. And then, of course, there are the parents and the religious (and non-religious) communities the school serves. It is a cauldron the contents of which are mindful of the witches' cauldron in 'the Scottish play' (*Macbeth*), but it represents the place of religion in society in contemporary England and Wales. Could it be that in these terms no Anglican school can be 'safe' as it will be an organic institution as policies on religious education and Christian character change to reflect the evolving nature of the school population? Dare one say that one hopes so? Why? Because religion itself is dynamic and organic; it is in a state of constant flux. One only needs to think of the continuing debate in the Church of England over women priests and women bishops. What happens to religion when it fails to manage change? Now one needs to be careful – this is not an argument for Anglican schools to change with the societal wind; it is the need for the theology that underpins Christian faith and practice to be in a condition to reflect not only what is happening now but also to be prophetic about the future (Wright, 2004).

Trevor Cooling, educator and theologian, pays an all too brief visit to the possibilities for 'faith' schools in the threateningly titled book, *Doing God in Education* (2010b). He argues coherently for 'faith' schools to prove themselves. Towards the end of this excellent book he uses the model of St Ethelburga's in the City of London blown up by the IRA in 1993. He writes that in the vision of its rebuilding it has become a place for people to meet to share their own opinions and insights into scripture.

> This is not a neutral space, being in the grounds of a Christian church. But it is an inclusive space where Christian hospitality aspires to be as fair as possible. Maybe the 'tent of meeting' is an appropriate metaphor for the distinctive ethos of a faith school. (2010c, p. 66)

Should this not form a model for the 'safe place' in an Anglican school, where fears of the views of others are set to one side and the safety of the 'tent' offers children the freedom to explore and engage with religion? Debate and difference are very much the pattern of the Anglican Church but it continuously struggles to be an inclusive church and it finds its very being in the energy of debate and the will to remain inclusive. Is this not the safe place Robert Waddington writes of as being a true resurrection of the Christian spirit?

Character education

James Arthur has written much about character education. He is most readable; an excellent scholar and researcher although much of what he writes cannot be addressed here. By writing about Christian character, however, he draws attention to the difference between Roman Catholic education and other forms of Christian education. 'For the Christian, character formation is not independent of religious faith. . . . The Christian who is concerned with moral development cannot remain long with Piaget or Kohlberg. . . . Storytelling is a powerful way to display virtues and vices and the Bible presents numerous examples of moral success and failure' (Arthur, 2003, pp. 56–7). Arthur's perspective on Christian character is very much rooted in Roman Catholicism and is surely none the worse for that. While Arthur's approach to character formation is seductive to all Christian educators he does come down on the content side of education.

He is critical of Bishop David Konstant, the bishop responsible for Roman Catholic education in most of the 1980s and 1990s, for appearing to encourage a secularization of Roman Catholic schools giving weight to methodology over Christian content (see Bailey, 2002, pp. 29–30; Pilkington, 2001, pp. 51–6).

> Education must pay regard to the formation of the whole person, so that all may attain their eternal destiny and at the same time promote the common good of society. *Children and young persons are therefore to be cared for in such a way that their physical, moral and intellectual talents may develop in a harmonious manner, so that they may attain a greater sense of responsibility and a right use of freedom, and be formed to take an active part in social life.*
> (Canon 795 quoted in Arthur, 2003, p. 57; author's italics)

There may be a few things in canon 795 to which some Anglicans may take exception but in the main this is a comprehensive statement with which most Christian educators would have some sympathy. The aim is to create a safe environment in which growth and development may take place. Some Christians may choose to accept the canon but interpret it more liberally, perhaps omitting the word 'formed' as if Anglican schools could be seen to be manipulating the education of children in some way! Language is so important. The crux remains that Catholic schools were built for Catholic children ideally taught by Catholic teachers under the control of the Catholic authorities. That ideal may not be the case in all Catholic schools but, generally, they would be very different from most Anglican schools where the number of practising Anglican children is probably in the minority across the nation and there are certainly Anglican schools without Anglican headteachers and few Anglican staff. This should not be regarded as a weakness. Anglican dioceses have had Catholic Diocesan Directors of Education and at the time of writing one of the senior education officers in the Church of England Board of Education is a Roman Catholic. So ecumenism is alive, struggling but alive.

A fortress mentality?

The Church of England has schools which were built 200 years ago for the communities and parishes of the time. Now 200 years later, those communities will have changed. Some will have become urban schools, having been rural schools in the 1800s; some will have children for whom Christianity, never mind Anglicanism, is a new and bewildering phenomenon; some will have high percentages of children of other faiths – sometimes many other faiths and sometimes largely from one non-Christian faith; and others will be full of Christian children but still racially mixed. The rationale for schools built so long ago may have changed but so will the theology. There have been arguments that the Church should give up schools where Anglican (or Christians) were in a small minority, but communities move and shift, ebb and flow. Mixed religious and mixed race areas change – so the school changes and with it the challenge to Christian educators is to maintain the school as a safe school. It will remain the heartbeat of the communities it serves. Change is the lifeblood of a safe place as it ensures that dialogue has to take place continuously. Is the alternative to stagnate?

There is an ambiguity about the notion of a safe place in an Anglican school if interpreted in this manner as it may be that 'safe' is a place which is secure and protected against those who may seek to be a threat. Is a Church school a 'Camp Bastion' against those who are clamouring at the gate? Do those inside look out and see the parents, friends, carers and relatives waiting at the school gate for their children as symbols of a world that threatens the peace and harmony of the inner sanctum of the school? In some cases the answer will be 'Yes'. This is where most Anglican schools would be very different from the Roman Catholic ideal as represented by Arthur, for his rationale for the Roman Catholic school is very different from the Anglican vision for education. Anglicans rarely expected their schools to be built only for Anglican children and taught by Anglican staff (and that would be true today); that is not the rationale on which Anglican schools were originally founded. Children live busy noisy lives and they leave the carefully constructed harmony of the school to rush into a culture of computer games, clubs, madrassas, family life and a world apart from the pace and relationships they forge in the classroom. School is a safe place in that sense but it is also the place where the values of the home and society may be challenged – but in a protected and safe environment.

The Self-Evaluation Toolkit for Church Schools produced by the National Society for the purpose of preparing schools for the SIAS inspection is probably the most effective way of discerning what expectations the Anglican Church currently has of its schools (SIAS Toolkit) (2009). Here the inspector is required to evaluate the school based on four areas. The first is *How well does the school, through its distinctive Christian character, meet the needs of all its learners?* There are subheadings relating to Christian values, spiritual, moral, social and cultural development, responsible citizens and relationship within the community. It is a demanding set of questions for the school to respond to and for the SIAS inspector to comment on. Under Prompt 1e *How well is the spiritual development of learners enhanced by the school environment?* (National Society, 2009). There are some pertinent areas to consider: focus for reflection, use of outside space, use of common space, quiet areas, prayer corners and respect for creation. Are these some of those important aspects of Anglican education that Waddington wrote 25 years earlier? They certainly capture something of his understanding of a safe place.

If a Church school is to be a safe school then it has to create a platform for a vigorous and adventurous religious education and experimental forms of worship. The rationale is that if the school is a strong Christian school with clear evidence of a Christian character then there will be a natural springboard to explore new and exciting ways of teaching religious education and engaging in worship. The irony of being a secure and safe school is that it does not just allow for innovation and initiative, it demands it. All of us know that if we feel secure we are more ready to move into challenging areas whether they are of belief or educational practice.

Religious education

John Bailey (2002) writing of Church of England VA schools, says

> [they] are usually community schools in the sense that they draw all children from a particular neighbourhood, parish or village. This is particularly true of primary schools. . . . There can be no assumption made that the children themselves are committed to Christianity, and by and large the Religious Education provision in such schools makes no such assumption. The Christian nurture, if such there be, is much more to do with the context in which the Religious Education is offered, rather than the actual content of Religious Education. (p. 34)

This observation, whether one accepts or not, provides the basis for further reflections on the Church school as a safe place. Bailey's general point is that the Church school draws from a particular neighbourhood or parish. Some secondary schools may draw from many schools over a wide area which makes the notion of 'community' an interesting one as children will be bussed into and out of schools. The community the students understand will be the strength of community forged within the school gates. There can be many aspects of a Church school which bond children together and some of these would be shared with community schools. There should be, however, in all Anglican schools a fundamental understanding of the Christian character of the school. This emphasis on ethos or character has been a focus for SIAS inspections for nearly 20 years (Brown and Lankshear, 1995; National Society, 2010). The question with regard to this chapter is whether the firm Christian foundation of the school allows for a radical exploration of religious education, worship and a deeper awareness of the spiritual life of the children than would be possible in a community school.

Church schools have the chance to be more radical in religious education than community schools because they (should) provide a framework where religious belief and practice can be understood in the context of everyday life. The work of the Errickers has much to contribute to the importance of listening to children, though the notion of listening to children is not new but appears to have to be reinvented in each generation. Mary Ellison and Christopher Herbert, later Bishop of St Alban's, published an extraordinary book in the early 1980s analysing the quality of children's religious and spiritual conversations. It made one wonder whether teachers should teach what interests children not what adults think they should know (Ellison and Herbert, 1983). Erricker, however, moves the argument on:

> Teachings about religious traditions are most obviously reflections on experience, but theologies are meta-narratives that systematise such teachings to construct knowledge. This marginalises the learner in the classroom in so far as his or her narratives are concerned. . . . It is by releasing the grip religion has on faith that the subject can achieve its pedagogical potential. (2010, p. 203)

It is the experience of the author that in inspecting over 500 Church of England schools, from first schools through to secondary schools, the creative forces locked up in religious education can find a true place in the children's imagination where and when risks are taken. Let us be clear. There are no risks to the safety of the child: the risks are those risks taken in collective or corporate worship or religious education so that the children are allowed to construct their own narratives, to enable them to make sense of what they see and hear and relate them to their own experience. Of course, we want, in Church schools, all children to be aware of Christian teaching, Christian exemplars and experience the creative ways in which Christians worship, but for many, if not most, children what they experience of worship or any form of religious belief and practice will be in their Church school. In some perverse way, the school is the church for many pupils. The school becomes the bridge between the religion and the child. In simple terms, the Bible was not written for children so when we use it with them can we remember that and allow the children's narratives to explore their own understanding at a level appropriate to them? (Wright, A., 2010; Worcestershire Agreed Syllabus, 2010).

> *An example of the above was given some years ago by Ronald Goldman (1965). He was researching into Religious Education and at a lecture given following the publication of his book he told this story. He related the story of Moses and the Burning Bush to a class of 9-year-olds. The story is not related here but can be accessed in Exodus 3.1–21. After telling the story he asked a few questions of the children until one boy asked, 'Was Moses' mother cross with him when he got home?' As told by Goldman, this was gob-stopping moment! Why should Moses' mother be cross? What has that to do with the story? It is, of course, simple. Moses takes his shoes off for he is told that the ground on which he is standing is holy but he never puts them on again and the child knew that if he went home without his shoes his mother would be cross or worse. The wrath of God is one thing but the wrath of your mother quite another! The point is that the story only made sense to the child in terms of his experience. The great theophany was lost on him; his interest in the story had stopped with Moses' shoes being removed and the pupil was waiting for them to be put on again. (One may wish to suggest that Goldman's style of questioning could have left something to be desired!)*

This story had a great effect on someone starting out on a teaching career for when teaching from the Bible or from other religious sources, what are the teachers' expectations of the pupil? If the same story were retold to the child in several years time there may be a quite different response as the child would have moved on from the age and aptitude of a 9-year-old (Brown, 1987, pp. 53–4). Do teachers assume too much? Should they not build on the child's experience? Do children climb a ladder of learning? Are they struggling all the time to understand 'religion' in the context of their lives?

The Welsh Anglican priest and poet, R. S. Thomas (1996) takes up the import of an understanding of scripture that offers an insight into what Anglican schools might provide for their children. It could be a risk, but a risk worth taking as the experience of Anglican education and the creativity of religious education allows children to turn aside when their spiritual awareness is charged:

The Bright Field

I have seen the sun break through

to illuminate a small field

for a while, and gone my way

and forgotten it. But that was the pearl

of great price, the one field that had

the treasure in it. I realize now

that I must give all that I have

to possess it. Life is not hurrying

on to a receding future, nor hankering after

an imagined past. It is the turning

aside like Moses to the miracle

of the lit bush, to a brightness

that seemed as transitory as your youth

once, but is the eternity that awaits you.

(Thomas, 1996, p. 302)

Thomas links scripture with the experience of living. He does not ask us not to look back to an imagined past (where everything was so much better than it is now) nor worry about the distant future which accelerates away from us the more we think about it, but we should respond to the moment of revelation and imagination. Surely, the role of a Church school, an Anglican school, is to aim to provide opportunities such as this for all children regardless of their religion or worldview. Thomas' poem is a beacon call to schools to recognize the miracle of the lit bush and offer children the time to turn aside and reflect on their experience.

Conclusion

The Bright Field could be the paradigm for the aims of this chapter for the poem places the imagination and experience of personal insight within the context of a Christian vision. If Anglican schools are to be 'safe schools' in the sense Waddington intended they have to allow and even encourage the pupil to turn aside to the miracle of the lit bush to the brightness offered by faith in Christ. The struggle of Anglican schools to represent the gospel is caught up within the communities they serve. They need to be inclusive and find safety not in the 'Camp Bastion' interpretation of scripture and tradition but in the challenge they both offer to the world in which the child searches for meaning. There will always be differences regarding Christian ethos or Christian character but the organic and dynamic nature of Anglican schools has to be represented in the spiritual vision they can offer to children and staff. They are required through the eternal relevance of the gospel for each generation to offer children and staff the opportunity to find and explore the brightness of the lit bush in the safety of their school.

Key questions

1. Is it still possible, if it ever was, to use 'safe schools' in this context?
2. Are Church schools committed to dialogue?
3. Has the perception of what a Church school offers changed in the past 25 years?
4. Has the acceptance of Church schools changed in the Church of England/Church in Wales in the past 25 years?
5. Is dialogue always an 'unsafe' activity?

10

The Distinctiveness of Christian Learning in Church of England Schools

Trevor Cooling

Abstract

Current research indicates that understanding of how to implement the aspiration that a Church of England schools should be distinctively Christian is not as good as it should be. This is particularly so in relation to the nature of learning, where there has been minimal discussion. This chapter will explore a model of distinctively Christian learning appropriate for Church of England schools inspired by the theological work of Bishop Tom Wright. It will begin with a discussion of what it might mean for such schools to claim to be distinctively Christian given that most serve a religiously diverse community. It will then describe the model being developed by the Kuyer's Institute at Calvin College and the *Transforming Lives* project in partnership with Canterbury Christ Church University. Finally, practical examples of the planning of distinctively Christian learning will be described.

Keywords
Distinctively Christian learning, Kingdom of God, virtue, character education, church

Introduction

It is claimed that Church of England schools are a 'distinctively Christian' brand of state education. The problem is that it is not at all clear what this means and, therefore, whether it is a justified claim. In particular, the research evidence suggests that there is little comprehension of what this designation might mean in relation to teaching and learning, which are, surely, the essence of what education is all about. In this chapter, a distinctively Christian approach to pedagogy is proposed, which interprets it in terms of faithfulness to a Christian vision of life.

Church of England schools: The brand?

The publication of the Dearing report *The Way Ahead* in 2001 marked a watershed in the history of Church of England schools. The writing group had been charged with reviewing the nature and purpose of the Church's schools on the eve of a new millennium. The context they addressed was the dual system, the legacy of the 1944 Education Act settlement between Church and State, wherein approximately a third of all government-maintained schools in England were designated as voluntary schools because they had a foundation link with the Church. Many pupils came from families that were not churchgoing, particularly where the Church school was the only school in the area, as was often the case in villages.

A significant factor in the context addressed by the report was the growing opinion in the education profession that 'confessional', church school education was no longer appropriate. This view was exemplified in the writings of Paul Hirst when he was Professor of Education at Cambridge. Hirst's criticisms were twofold. On the one hand, he charged Church schools with being educationally illegitimate, dubbing Christian education 'a contradiction in terms' and 'a kind of nonsense'. He also described them as 'primitive' in contrast to 'sophisticated' secular schools. On the other hand, he charged them with irrelevance, arguing that there was nothing distinctive that theological reflection could bring to the educational table (Hirst, 1971, 1974). The charge of 'confessionalism' has tarnished Church schools ever since and is undoubtedly a factor in the diffidence demonstrated by headteachers in enunciating a distinctive Christian rationale for them (Green and Cooling, 2009). It was the task of *The Way Ahead* to give a clear lead in the light of this challenge to the legitimacy of Church schools.

As it turned out, *The Way Ahead* re-energized the Church in its thinking about education. Its starting point was the earlier General Synod motion of 1998, which asserted that Church schools stand 'at the centre of the Church's mission to the nation' (p. 1). To fulfil this mission, the Report argued that Church schools must be *distinctively* Christian in order to justify their continued links with the Church (p. 3). Another seminal report published 3 years after

The Way Ahead argued that the transformation of society was central to the concept of the Church's mission (Archbishops' Council, 2004). This led the Association of Anglican Diocesan Directors of Education (the people charged with responsibility for implementing church policy on education in the 43 dioceses) to explore the synergy between these two influential publications and thereby was stimulated a whole newly invigorated discussion about the Christian mission of Church schools that was to characterize the first decade of the new millennium (Worsley, 2006; Elbourne, 2009). Centrally, the Church has invested heavily in supporting schools to achieve this by providing a framework for the Statutory Inspection of Anglican Schools (SIAS) and by developing a Christian values website. In the latter, the emphasis is on the theological underpinning to the values with a view to highlighting a distinctively Christian understanding of each. The intention has been to challenge the notion that values education should be founded on a set of neutral shared values which are 'entirely independent of religious beliefs' (Norman, R., 2004, p. 114). Alongside these initiatives, the Church has significantly increased the number of its secondary schools since *The Way Ahead* was published and is now seeking to be a major player in the current coalition government's drive to set up academies.

However, although *The Way Ahead* has created much greater awareness of the need for identifiable Christian distinctiveness and has stimulated the setting up of many new Church schools, the available evidence is that, ten years on, the impact on the education that actually takes place in Church schools is not as great as was desired. A recent book from an experienced Church of England Diocesan Director of Education laments the fact that it is hard to find headteachers who can articulate a clear understanding of the distinctiveness of a Church school (Cox, 2011). This anecdotal evidence is supported by a review of the research evidence published in the past decade, which concluded that a fundamental problem is that headteachers lacked clarity in their understanding of the distinctiveness of Church schools (Green and Cooling, 2009). In particular, two Ph.D. studies on Church of England schools completed since the publication of *The Way Ahead*, both found that generally headteachers were unable to distinguish the mission of their schools from the dominant secular educational discourse (Jelfs, 2008; Street, 2005). Given that the National College for School Leadership (2011) views the role of the headteacher in a Church school as 'the interpreter of faith for the community', the fear is that the Report's aspiration for distinctiveness is in danger of being unrealized. Since the Church of England has a 200-year history of involvement in schools, this lack of impact is perhaps surprising. However, it seems that the problem may be wider than just schools.

In particular, the Church of England colleges, initially set up to train teachers but now functioning as general universities, appear to struggle even more with the challenge of distinctiveness (Thatcher, 2004; Arthur, 2006; Glanzer, 2008a).

Ten years on from the publication of *The Way Ahead*, the Church of England presides over ever increasing numbers of schools and promotes its brand on the basis of their Christian distinctiveness. However, the evidence is that there is a long way to go in converting this brand rhetoric into reality.

The concept of distinctiveness

At the outset, it is important to clarify what is meant by 'distinctively Christian' because one understanding creates a particular barrier to using the concept (Astley, 1994, pp. 141–2). For many people, the notion of distinctiveness is interpreted as a claim to uniqueness. For this reason, the British Humanist Association (BHA) has criticized the distinctively Christian approach that will be developed later in this chapter on the grounds that the 'conclusions are accessible to, and can be utilized by, Christians and non-Christians alike' (Copson and Norman, 2011). The implication is that this pedagogy cannot legitimately be described as distinctively Christian because it does not generate *uniquely* Christian classroom outcomes. To be distinctively Christian, it appears that the resulting classroom practices must, by definition, be unattractive to those who do not hold the Christian faith.

It may be that many Church school headteachers also understand the word in this way and therefore struggle with seeing how classroom approaches to teaching and learning across the curriculum can be distinctively Christian without hijacking the subject disciplines so that they become vehicles for teaching Christian theology. A published example which illustrates such hijacking is where point-by-point analogies are drawn between a physics lesson on magnetic attraction and a theological lesson on the loving heart of God. The physics is in effect functioning as an allegorical illustration of the theological teaching (White, 2009). Headteachers, rightly, have concerns at the appropriateness of this approach for Church of England schools since it collapses all knowledge into theology. Another source of concern might be the danger of trivializing the notion of Christian distinctiveness by treating it as the addition of blessed thoughts or Bible quotations to lessons which are otherwise indistinguishable from a secular approach in an attempt to make them uniquely Christian. In this case, the Christian contribution can justifiably be called a gloss.[1]

However, the phrase 'distinctively Christian' need not be understood in this widely assumed sense of *uniquely distinguishing difference*. Rather, it can legitimately be taken to mean *characteristic* of the Christian tradition. Stephen Williams developed this understanding in a discussion of Christian epistemology where he highlighted the danger of dissonance between stated aspiration and practice which can result when people's thinking is shaped by other worldviews (Williams, 2011). It was such dissonance that Helen Jelfs observed among Church primary school headteachers in their 'unwitting compliance with values and principles that may compromise those that they seek to promote' (2008, p. 2). Williams, therefore, emphasized the idea of thinking *faithfully* as Christians, which is to emphasize 'staying true' to the Christian tradition as the defining characteristic of distinctiveness rather than 'being different'. In this chapter, it is this notion of faithfulness that will underpin the use of the term distinctively Christian.[2]

The other barrier to clear understanding of the concept of Christian distinctiveness is the lack of clarity that surrounds the nature and purpose of Church of England schools. 'The Way Ahead Report' recognized two basic aspirations in what it called the nurture and service models. The former reflects the desire to 'pass on the faith', which the philosopher Michael Hand (2003) identifies as the defining feature of Church schools. In contrast, the service model embodies the desire to make a contribution to the wider community and to affirm the fact that there are many people who feel a kinship with the Church, but who do not see themselves as religiously committed. The desire to affirm both these aspirations is reflected in the 'distinctive and inclusive' mantra that emerged from the report and was subsequently widely trumpeted in Church of England circles (see also Sullivan, 2001).

This ambiguity as to the function of Church of England schools came to prominence on Good Friday, 2011 when the media was alive with reports that the Bishop of Oxford, then the Church's spokesperson on education, had made a statement recommending that only 10 per cent of places in Church of England schools ought to be reserved for church families. A furore resulted. The Bishop's comments were not intended to focus on percentages as such, but rather to provoke consideration of what is the mission of a Church school. In his view, it was not to collect 'nice Christians into safe places', but to serve the wider community (Marley, 2011). Others disagree profoundly (Shepherd, 2004). The persisting ambiguity is perhaps reflected in Rowan Williams' comment that a Church school is a 'kind of church'. Jeff Astley's (2002) suggestion that the Church school functions as a threshold to the church resonates with the Archbishop's 'kind of' notion. The Church school is then a place where everyone can, so to speak, put their toe in the water of church without having to regard themselves as belonging to the real thing. However, there is an implied reticence in this language about the legitimacy of the Church's mission being 'fully' implemented through a school and possibly this fuelled headteachers' anxieties about achieving an appropriate balance between inclusiveness and distinctiveness and their difficulties with the 'distinctively Christian' aspiration.

Perry Glanzer's (2008b) reflections on higher education offer a faith-based model that indicates how the aspiration to remain faithful to the Christian tradition can still be inclusive and open to diversity. His main concern is with elucidating the task of the Christian scholar, but his article has considerable significance for Church schools. His central thesis is that the Christian scholar's primary task is 'the creation and redemption of scholarship', which language, he maintains, communicates that Christian learning entails interpreting 'all of life within the Biblical drama of creation, fall, redemption and restoration' (Glanzer, 2008b, p. 43). This then is the faithfulness to the tradition which makes Christian scholarship distinctive in that scholarly work is filtered through the interpretative lens of these four theological themes.

However, Glanzer also affirms partnership in learning with scholars from other traditions, because his model is 'Christ-like redemptive scholarship' (2008b, p. 46), in which hospitality in debate rather than victory in argument is the scholarly mind-set that is faithful to being 'Christ-like'. Furthermore, and very importantly, his way of thinking 'allows for the recognition that through common grace, anyone can be and is involved in both the creation of scholarship and what I would call redemptive forms of scholarship that free aspects of God's creation from some effects of the fall' (2008b, p. 47). Creation and redemption of scholarship is therefore, for Glanzer, inclusive by inviting participation from all, by being of service to the whole community and by being conducted according to an ethic of hospitality.[3] At the same time, it offers a distinctively Christian way of seeing the world through the lens of creation, fall, redemption and restoration. The rest of this chapter will assume Glanzer's model and reapply it to the task of learning in Church of England schools, viewing them as places where the creation and redemption of learning takes place.[4]

What if learning

The Way Ahead Report stated that 'Church schools are places where a particular vision of humanity is offered' (Dearing, 2001, p. 11) and where 'we can begin to discover who we are, why we are here and – perhaps most importantly – what we might be' (p. 15). The vision laid out in the report was that schools participate in the mission of the Church by promoting the formation of their pupils as image bearers of God (p. 18). But what might this mean for a distinctive approach to teaching and learning?

The Norwegian journalist, Åsne Seierstad, offers a pointer to answering this question in her description of her time spent living with the family of a bookseller in Kabul just after the invasion of Afghanistan in 2001(Seierstad, 2004). She describes how he sees an opportunity for supplying textbooks to schools in the new term now that those used previously by the Taliban were useless. The inadequacy of a Taliban approach is captured in her evocative account of teaching calculation skills. These, she says, are not approached through counting apples and cakes (an exercise familiar to Westerners of a certain age) but bullets and Kalashnikovs. Pupils are required to calculate how many 'infidels' are killed per bullet by 'little Omar' given that they know the number of bullets in a magazine, the number of magazines that he had, the percentage of the bullets he fired and the number of infidels killed. This is clearly an extreme and shocking example, but it illustrates, rather starkly, that, in order to teach like this, teachers would have to believe certain things about their pupils. These would include that the world is divided into two types of people, the true believer and the infidel, and that the desired destiny for their pupils is to kill the infidel in holy war.

The question of what teachers would have to believe about pupils in order to adopt any given approach to teaching and learning is the focus of a collaborative project called *What If Learning*.[5] This draws on the work of David Smith, the Director of the Kuyers Institute for Christian Teaching and Learning at Calvin College in Grand Rapids (Smith and Carvill, 2000). Smith began his career as a secondary foreign languages teacher in Derbyshire and his early experience led him to ponder the question of why languages are taught in schools. His conclusion was that, to a large degree, the teaching and learning approaches that he was required to use were based on the belief that pupils were being prepared to be effective tourists; hence, the preponderance of exercises which seemed to assume that achieving successful commercial transactions while on holiday was the motivation for learning a language. In order to teach in this way, one has to believe, for example, that the core relationship between the language learner and the native language speaker is one of consumer and provider.

Smith and Carvill (2000) identified other views of the nature of the learner that were products of different teaching and learning approaches and would lead to distinctive conceptions of the relationship between language learner and native language speaker. These included the entrepreneur (to grasp new economic opportunities), the persuader (to gain advantage in a foreign culture), the connoisseur (self-improvement through cross-cultural experience) and the escapologist (to escape the strictures of one's own cultural shaping). In each case, the underpinning approach requires certain beliefs about pupils. Smith's distinctively Christian alternative is an approach where the teaching and learning is based on the belief that pupils learn a language in order to equip them for building hospitable relationships with native language speakers. This was derived from asking the question as to what type of relationships Christians should seek to build with foreigners if they are to be faithful to biblical teaching.

What If Learning extends and applies these insights from languages teaching into other disciplines. In doing this, the approach draws on Etienne Wenger's (1998) influential work on 'communities of practice'. Wenger's classic text starts with an extensive ethnographic study of a medical claims processing centre in America, which then frames the social theory of learning he elaborates in the rest of the book. By a community of practice, Wenger means a group that works together to fulfil a shared enterprise. In order to be a member one has to share the vision of what that community is 'all about' and participate in common practices that fulfil that vision. Teachers and students in classrooms can be such a community. Part of what makes them a community of practice is ongoing negotiation of the shared imagination of what it is that they are about when engaged in learning in the context of a church school classroom.

In explaining his concept of imagination, Wenger offers this example of two stonecutters who are asked to say what they are doing.

> One responds: 'I am cutting this stone in a perfectly square shape.' The other responds: 'I am building a cathedral.' Both answers are correct and meaningful, but they reflect different relations to the world. . . . The difference between these answers does not imply that one is a better stonecutter than the other, as far as holding the chisel is concerned. . . . But it does suggest that their experiences of what they are doing and their sense of self in doing it are rather different. This difference is a function of imagination. As a result, they may be learning very different things from the same activity. (1998, p. 176)

In respect of classrooms, the significant implication of Wenger's analysis is that teachers hold responsibility for the shared imagination of their class. Do their pupils think they are cutting square blocks or building a cathedral? Do they, for example, think they are learning a language to be a tourist or to offer hospitably to strangers? And how do the activities of the classroom build or undermine this shared imagination? It is the exercise of this responsibility in a distinctively Christian manner that eludes many involved in Church of England schools.

What If Learning has two dimensions that together enable teachers to develop a distinctively Christian pedagogy. The first, called 'seeing anew', is where the teacher identifies the shift in imagination that is the basis of the claim that any pedagogy is 'distinctively Christian'. It essentially involves an act of imagination on the part of teachers where they ask themselves 'what if I taught this topic to support a Christian understanding of what it means to be human?' In the example above, the shift involves the realization that the current pedagogy reinforced a taken-for-granted anthropological vision that learning a language is undertaken primarily to further one's own interests. To identify a prevailing assumption like this involves a process of 'defamiliarization', or enhancing one's perception of that which is familiar, so as to be able to critique it. Then it entails the identification of an alternative anthropological vision which is faithful to Christianity. In our example, this was derived by interrogating the Bible in order to discern the sort of person that Christian educators might aspire to emerge from a Christian experience of learning a foreign language. This resulted in the decision to focus on developing a desire to offer hospitality to the stranger.

Talking about using a Christian-based anthropological vision to shape classroom pedagogy will alarm the critics of Christian education. They usually favour an anthropological vision that is based on shared human values or some other supposedly neutral specification. Stanley Hauerwas (1983) is one of many scholars who challenge this concern. He argues that the idea that there is a 'mid-air' or neutral ethical stance that someone can take, unqualified by any particular worldview perspective, is an illusion. His counter-argument is that every ethic is qualified by the narrative of the community with which a person identifies because it inevitably has a shared *telos* or sense of direction. This is what is meant by an anthropological vision. Applying Hauerwas' comments on ethics we can see that schools are such communities, with a telos or anthropological vision that is shaped by the narrative that underpins their work. In the Western world, the narrative is most often provided by politicians and is framed in terms of economic performance and academic excellence, closely followed by education professionals propounding various theories. None of these offers a neutral position that can be assumed to be unproblematic for all pupils. In arguing for the importance of a distinctively Christian approach to teaching and learning, *What If Learning* accepts Hauerwas' insights about the epistemological significance of belonging to a community shaped by a Christian narrative and offers that narrative as an alternative to the prevailing narrative (Cooling, 2010c and 2011).

The second dimension of *What If Learning* is implementation of this distinctively Christian imagination in the classroom through what teachers and pupils actually do. In elaborating his social theory of learning, Wenger introduces two key concepts: participation and reification. By participation, he means the ways in which members of a community learn how to engage appropriately with the activities of that community, for example, the activity of writing up an experiment in the required format in a science class. By reification, he means the way in which these forms of participation are turned into concrete things, for example, the template that every student has to use in writing up their science experiments. Together these patterns of participation and the different forms of reification make up the repertoire that becomes characteristic of the community of practice in each classroom. The repertoire of the classroom serves to build the shared imagination of what 'we are about'.

David Smith describes in some detail how Wenger's analysis can be applied to classroom pedagogy such that it is shaped by a distinctively Christian imagination (Smith, 2011). For example, he makes the distinction between teaching approaches to texts which encourage students to 'use' texts and those which encourage students to 'receive' texts. The latter is a charitable use which seeks 'personal transformation through attentive encounter' (p. 44). The former is satisfied with a shallow encounter valuing 'speed and efficiency' and seeks mainly instrumental benefits from the encounter with the text, for example, as material for exam essays or personal gratification through reading for pleasure. It is described as 'consumerist reading'. Smith's aspiration is that a distinctively Christian practice of reading texts should flow from an attitude which displays humility before, listens charitably to and looks for transformation through reading a text.

Here the foundational question is: 'What if we approached the Christian literature classroom not only in terms of what interpretations change hands, but also in terms of what kinds of practices are shared?' (Smith, 2011, p. 47). Smith's detailed description of his attempt to answer this question in relation to the teaching of an undergraduate level survey of the literature of German speaking countries since 1945 is worthy of detailed attention. Unfortunately, there is only space here to give a taste of his approach. His concern was that in earlier offerings of this course, the practices generated by the pedagogy associated with a survey approach resulted in students reading 'superficially and once only, gaining enough acquaintance with the text to avoid embarrassment in class. They then blithely offered evaluative opinions about complex texts barely mastered' (p. 48). Smith's conclusion was that this was not the students' fault, but was down to the nature of the pedagogical practices that he, and other teachers, employed. For example, by running discussions where offering a briskly stated evaluative opinion was more important than owning up to bafflement at what the text might be about, the adopted practice was already shaping the imagination of the students. Through experiencing practices that were reified in reward systems (like the teacher's smile in acknowledgement of a contribution), students were implicitly encouraged to believe that they were in literature classes, so to speak, to carve square blocks rather than build a cathedral.

Smith made a number of changes to his course which were designed to 'begin to generate a repertoire consistent with charitable reading' (Smith, 2011, p. 51), and which prompted students to 'read with humility'. For example, he reduced the number of texts studied and designed practices that emphasized the importance of reading texts charitably. Three examples are given below:

1. One story was read twice, the first time in a circle and the second with chairs clustered tightly in the centre of the classroom which physically hunched students around the text and embodied close, intimate attentiveness.
2. Different assessment tasks were set instead of an exam. For example, students were sent to an undisturbed spot with a notebook and required to meditate in silence on a text for at least 1 hour. Then they met with two other students to discuss the insights gained. The assessable product was a summary of their conversation.
3. One day on entering class he sat quietly among his students absorbed in a book. After a couple of minutes, he commented to the bemused students that he had often read this text and yet still he found the sudden change of topic on page 40 strange. This is in contrast to how he had started a lesson at other times, marching to the front of the students and announcing the page number to be read and asking for immediate feedback from homework. These contrasting practices embody different conceptions of the relationship between readers and authors of texts.

An important element in the programme was the inclusion of 'explicit reference' to why particular strategies to teaching and learning were being utilized. This included conversations with students about different reading practices and study of a short text on what reading might have to do with Christian charity. This element was essential if a shared imagination was to be created which shifted students from thinking that they were, metaphorically, carving square blocks to building a cathedral.

I have lingered with Smith's work on teaching languages with undergraduate students because of the significance of his ideas in *What If Learning*. However, that the approach is easily applicable to schools as well as higher education and to subjects other than languages is indicated by this summary of one example that is available in more detail, alongside many more, online:

> An art teacher wished to introduce pupils to a painting by an African artist. Because his pupils are like most people when confronted by something they find 'strange', he is concerned that they might react unhelpfully. He wanted to promote a new shared imagination around the experience of encountering unfamiliar artistic styles. His question is 'what if my pupils were taught to react as if the painting were a visitor from overseas?' In doing this he wished to promote humility as the appropriate response to encountering a culture that we find strange. He therefore introduced the lesson with a discussion on how to make an overseas visitor feel welcome. The class conclusions included, for example, agreeing not to make a judgement until they had listened carefully to what the person had to say. Then, much to the pupils' surprise, the teacher 'introduced' the painting as though it was the visitor. The seeing anew here is recognising the potential of art for developing humility and hospitality in the encounter with the unfamiliar. The reshaping of the classroom experience lies in the unexpected interactions with a new painting. The distinctively Christian foundation lies in a Biblical notion of respect which leads to generosity of spirit.

What If Learning seeks to be distinctively Christian by drawing on an anthropological vision that is faithful to the Christian tradition and then applying that to classroom pedagogy across the curriculum. This means that every teacher, whatever their subject, is involved in fulfilling the school's anthropological vision. This may be a very new way of thinking for some teachers. For example, science teachers may object on the grounds that their responsibility is only to teach science understood as a body of facts, concepts and procedures. But the objection ignores the professional responsibility that science teachers have for the sort of scientists their students become. Science indeed is pretty well the same in a concentration camp laboratory and a hospital laboratory. But teachers *should* care whether their pupils end up using their scientific knowledge in a hospital or a concentration camp. As *teachers* their discipline is not, therefore, just science, but science education, which means paying attention to the religious, moral and spiritual framework within which their pupils think about and practice science.[6]

What If Learning therefore offers Church of England schools a practical, classroom-friendly approach to being distinctively Christian. It entails implementing two key actions:

1. Clearly defining the school's shared imagination for the sort of person that it aspires will emerge from it, as the means of expressing its distinctively Christian worldview. A key leadership responsibility for heads and principals is therefore to negotiate and then articulate that vision for the school community. This will require a critique of the contemporary vision that is assumed in received educational thinking and practices and the offering of a vision that is consciously faithful to the Christian tradition. The former requires educational expertise; the latter requires theological understanding and is where Glanzer's four themes will be drawn upon. This is what we call seeing anew.

2. Embedding this vision in the day-to-day work of teachers through careful examination of the pedagogical practices that are employed in the classroom, of how they are reified into artefacts (written procedures, classroom layout, etc.) and of the repertoire of expected ways of belonging in that classroom that develop. This process requires pedagogical expertise. The vision will need to be made explicit to ensure that pupils know why they are 'doing things the way they are' so that a shared imagination grows as a community of practice develops. In this way meaning is negotiated which contributes to the identity that pupils develop so that how they see themselves reflects their participation in a Church of England school community.

These two actions create pedagogical practice that results in the *formation* of people in a distinctively Christian way rather than simply achieving the effective communication of *information*. We are, therefore, talking about a pedagogy which focuses on character development.

A theology for What If Learning

The question still has to be answered as to the sense in which this approach can claim to be distinctively Christian, rather than an affirmation of shared values with a Christian gloss. It needs to be demonstrated that it is indeed an explicit attempt to be faithful to the Christian faith. This final section describes one such attempt.

A body of recent research literature on Christian faith and character education recognizes the significance of formation and expresses dissatisfaction with an approach to moral education which is overly concerned with providing pupils with information and then leaving them 'free' to make their own autonomous choices (Arthur, 2003, 2006, 2010a, 2010b; Glanzer, 2000, 2003, 2005; Pike, 2010; Hunter, 2000). The problem is this makes moral education a largely cognitive enterprise where pupils mainly learn how to think about and debate values. The challenge is to find an approach to moral education that pupils and teachers can connect with their classroom work (Crick, 2002). In this respect, virtue ethics with its focus on character has a lot to offer as a corrective to an overly cognitive approach (Hursthouse, 1999).

The Anglican scholar and former Bishop of Durham Tom Wright, has published two influential books that are, in this respect, of significance for Church of England schools (2007 and 2010). In the first, he tackles the subject of eschatology (i.e. Christian beliefs about the last things – perhaps initially seeming to be an unlikely source of insight for Church schools). His hypothesis is that too many Christians have read their Bibles incorrectly by believing that life after death is about 'going to heaven'. Rather, Wright argues that the heart of this doctrine is the future establishment by Jesus Christ of the new heaven *and the new earth*. This means that 'going to heaven' is not to be understood as the escape from material life on earth to a disembodied existence in some ethereal 'other' place, but is, rather, the restoration of life on earth in the form that God originally intended through a bodily resurrection. The guarantee of this is the Resurrection of Jesus himself. In the words of Wright: 'With Jesus the future hope has come forwards into the present' (2007, p. 163). Jesus' incarnation has inaugurated the Kingdom of God on earth. The significance of this for the here and now is that, by their lives as followers of Christ and through their relationship with God in Jesus, people can participate in signalling to others God's intended purpose (telos) for human life.

Why is this important? Because, Wright says, what we believe about the last things fundamentally impacts our practical theology, which he describes as 'Christian reflection on the nature of the task we face as we seek to bring God's kingdom to bear on the real and painful world in which we live' (2007, p. xiii). In other words our eschatology fundamentally affects how we think and how we act in the world now. As Wright explains it:

The point of the resurrection . . . *is that the present bodily life is not valueless just because it will die*. God will raise it to new life. What you do with your body in the present matters because God has a great future in store for it. . . . What you do in the present – by painting, preaching, singing, sewing, praying, teaching, building hospitals, digging wells, campaigning for justice, writing poems, caring for the needy, loving your neighbour as yourself – all these things *will last into God's future*. They are not simply ways of making the present life a little less beastly, a little more bearable. . . . They are part of what we may call *building for God's kingdom*. (2007, p. 205)

Wright's eschatology, therefore, leads him to the conclusion that the mission of the Church includes building for the Kingdom as co-workers with God through action that improves the lives of others. The important implication this has for Church of England schools is that it shapes their approach to character education through adopting what Wright describes as 'an eschatologically driven virtue ethic' (Wright, T., 2010, p. 149). This provides their anthropological vision, drawing particularly on Glanzer's theme of restoration.

In *Virtue Reborn*, Wright considers the doctrine of sanctification, which he describes elsewhere as answering the perception on the part of many Christians that there is a vacant slot between people having 'prayed the prayer' to become Christians and experiencing salvation after their death (Wax, 2010). The question he tackles in *Virtue Reborn* is what happens 'after you believe'? For Wright, the answer lies not *in what you do, but in the person that you are becoming*: in other words in your character. This development of virtue is not primarily to do with individual flourishing, but is rather about God's people together exemplifying the eschatologically future Kingdom of God by being a signpost community for it in the here and now. It is not primarily concerned with keeping rules; rather it is about being God's people, about exemplifying wise rule of God's world, about living appropriately in anticipation of Christ's coming. In other words, the development of Christian virtue is the way in which we build for the Kingdom of God by being a 'character formed by God's promised future' (Wright, T., 2010, p. 51). As Wright describes it in discussing the Pauline epistles: 'Virtue, for Paul, is part of inaugurated eschatology, part of the life of the future breaking into the present' (2010, p. 163). The follower of God already has a foretaste of what is to come (2010, p. 118).

Wright maintains that Christian character develops through thousands of small choices made day by day in the context of belonging to a formational Christian community. 'Virtue is what happens when wise and courageous choices have become "second nature"' (2010, p. 9). Christian communities where this is happening are acting as signposts to the Kingdom of God; they are embodiments of the telos of life as understood in the Christian faith. For Wright, this telos is embodied through developing the three great Christian virtues of faith, hope and love.

What If Learning resonates with this 'eschatologically driven virtue ethic' in the following ways:

1. it aims at the development of Christian character in the context of a Christian community, namely a Church school
2. its anthropological vision (or its shared imagination in Wenger's terms) is shaped by the biblical vision of the human future in the Kingdom of God
3. it is distinctively Christian in its attempt to be faithful to Christian teaching about the Kingdom of God, which is a central motif in Jesus' teaching
4. it interprets the mission of a Church school as 'building for the Kingdom of God'
5. it views the development of Christian virtues as integral to a pedagogy which promotes the school's vision for the sort of people its pupils are becoming
6. it frames the first part of the pedagogical process of 'seeing anew' in terms of the telos or anthropological vision of the new heaven and the new earth
7. it utilizes pedagogical practices, reifications and repertoires that are designed to reinforce habits that develop Christian virtues in the formation of character.

Three concluding comments are necessary.

First, a list of definitive Christian virtues is not offered on the *What If Learning* website: only the three broad categories of faith, hope and love are provided. Each school will need to develop their own aspirations, taking into account the context in which they operate and the characteristics of the anthropological vision that they find embedded in their current curriculum and the degree to which it is felt that it needs 'seeing anew'. Furthermore, the virtues developed should not just be moral, although these are obviously important, but also spiritual and intellectual.

For example, given that one of the major criticisms made by opponents of Church of England schools is that they are a threat to community cohesion, and given the plural nature of English society, it would seem that an appropriate virtue that ought to be promoted is Christian openness to diversity.[7] In this case the work of Miroslav Volf (1996), a Professor of Theology at Yale who cut his teeth as a theologian in his home country of Croatia during the Yugoslavian civil war, might offer the resources of academically credible, Christian reflection to support schools. In particular, his vision that theology should foster 'the kinds of social agents capable of creating just, truthful and peaceful societies' (1996, p. 21) is clearly applicable for *What If Learning*.

Secondly, it needs to be remembered that *What If Learning* is not delivering all the components of a distinctively Christian education. Rather its purpose is to support teachers in designing teaching and learning experiences for the classroom that are consistent with, faithful to and supportive of the school's Christian character. There will need to be other elements in place as well which will include worship, high standards of personal relationships, service programmes, demonstrable Christian integrity on the part of staff and specific curriculum content. In particular, pupils will need to be taught the Christian beliefs and practices that underpin the pedagogical experiences that they are having. A specific subject where Christianity and other religions are studied will therefore be essential to give a doctrinal context for the distinctively Christian pedagogy in the other subjects.

Thirdly, we have noted earlier the challenge of defining the nature of a Church school. What does it mean to be 'kind of' church? The argument of this chapter leads to the conclusion that a Church school is a community that is shaped by a Christian eschatological vision. Perhaps, we should call Church schools 'signpost communities', offering the wider community associated with them a vision of God's intended way of being human in his Kingdom?

Conclusion

What really matters in the work of education? Probably what gives teachers most satisfaction is a clue to answering that question. No doubt, the success of their pupils in academia and career is up near the top of the scale. But I suspect what gives teachers the greatest satisfaction is to see strength of character emerging, particularly if they can identify how they have contributed to that. Of course, each person has their own view as to what constitutes strength of character indeed, one person's virtue may well be another's vice. What is surely true, however, is that there are distinctively Christian understandings of it. If that is the case, then it makes sense for schools that claim to be distinctively Christian to imagine a future where their pupils manifest distinctively Christian strength of character and for the school to seek to develop that in all that it undertakes, particularly, teaching and learning which is the core activity for education. That makes developing a distinctively Christian pedagogy a priority for Church of England schools.

Key questions

1. Is there a model of being distinctively Christian that is appropriate for Church of England schools?
2. Is the suggested link between distinctively Christian learning and character education convincing?
3. To what degree can the work of a Church of England school be described as 'building for the Kingdom'?
4. In what way might it be appropriate to think of pupils at Church of England schools as part of the church?
5. Can learning be appropriately thought of as a Christian practice?

Notes

1 The word used by Andrew Copson, Chief Executive of the BHA, in a public debate at the Royal Society of Arts. See www.thersa.org/events/audio-and-past-events/2011/ is-there-a-place-for-god-in-education. See also Smith, 2005, pp. 71–4.

2 This raises the huge hermeneutical question of how actually one remains faithful to the Christian tradition and biblical teaching. This is too extensive a subject to tackle in this chapter, but it should not be thought that a literalist or slavish following is being suggested. Rather the concept of faithful living in the light of the Christian narrative is implied. For discussion of this see Cooling, 2005 and 2010a.

3 Hospitality is a well-developed idea as a Christian response to difference. See, for example, Bretherton (2009) and Cooling (2010c) where I explore similar ideas using the work of St Ethelburga's Church in London as a metaphor for Church Schools.

4 The question of whether non-Christian pupils and staff can engage in creative and redemptive learning, or, as I shall describe it later, learning that is 'building for the Kingdom of God' is theologically controversial. In this section, a position has been taken on the basis of the briefest of discussions. That is not to imply that further detailed consideration is not necessary, it is, but simply to establish the starting point for the approach to learning that underpins the rest of this chapter.

5 The *What If Learning* project has three partners; the *Transforming Lives* Programme based at The Stapleford Centre, Nottingham, the Kuyers Institute for Christian Teaching and Learning at Calvin College, Grand Rapids, Michigan, USA and the

Anglican Education Commission in the Diocese of Sydney, Australia. The project has published a website for schools that can be consulted at www.whatiflearning. co.uk. *What If Learning* has drawn extensively on another project, the *Valparaiso Project on the Education and Formation of People in Faith*, also based at Calvin College. An edited volume of essays arising from this project is available in Smith and Smith (2011).

6　This paragraph should not to be interpreted as a claim that only Christians think ethically about the use of science. It is simply arguing that science education can be legitimately described as distinctively Christian when Christians seek to be faithful to their tradition in undertaking it. Likewise, other belief communities can also seek to remain faithful to their own traditions in their approach to science education. The notion of distinctively humanist or distinctively Islamic science education makes as much sense as does distinctively Christian science education.

7　In my view, this criticism is mostly unjustified and is a stereotype that feeds on some extreme examples of Christian schools, which are usually the ones featured in the media, for example, in *Faith Schools Menace*, a programme made by Richard Dawkins for Channel 4 screened on 18 August 2010.

11

Church School Ministry as Contextual Theology

Andrew Wright

Abstract

All theology is necessarily contextual theology, because Christian theologians cannot establish a god-like view from nowhere, but rather must work from within their given and limited cultural contexts. This means that the theory and practise of church school ministry must be contingent upon specific cultural contexts. However, it must at the same time be bound to the ultimate authority of God's revelation within, and mediated by, human culture. The path of faith walked by teachers, school leaders and theological educators must preclude both a docetic affirmation of an idealized Christianity dislocated from the contingencies of culture, and an ebionite affirmation of a nominal Christianity identified with the contingencies of culture. Just as the incarnate Christ was truly God and truly man, so church school ministry must strive to be truly grounded in contemporary culture and simultaneously truly transformative of it. Anglican Church schools in the United Kingdom are generally good at grounding themselves in local culture, but less good at transforming them in the light of the divine economy of salvation.

Keywords
Church schools, Christian theology of education, incarnation, contextual theology

The National Society for the Promotion of the Education of the Poor in the Principles of the Established Church, responsible for founding the system of Anglican Church schools in England and Wales, was founded 200 years ago in 1811. This chapter offers a theological assessment of the achievements, challenges and future prospects of Church of England schools. Though the practice of theology is unavoidably grounded in particular cultural contexts, this does not require the theologian to embrace a cultural relativism that precludes any possibility of a theologically driven critique and transformation of the culture within which she is working. The ontological actuality of the incarnation requires the Church, as the Body of Christ and Spirit empowered mediator of Christ's continuing presence on earth, to be both fully engaged with and prophetically transcendent of culture, in a manner that precludes any ebionite accommodation with, or docetic separation from, the world. The doctrine of the incarnation provides an explanatory framework through which we can better understand the nature and task of Church schools in a cultural context dominated by the hegemony of secular liberalism.

Two types of contextual theology

Stephen Bevans (1992) defines contextual theology as 'the attempt to understand Christian faith in terms of a particular context', so that the contextual theologian seeks to relate the Christian tradition and gospel message to the culture in which she is theologizing and to social changes within that culture. On this definition it is difficult to conceive of any form of theology that is not, at least implicitly, contextual. How can a theologian possibly avoid being, however minimally, engaged with and responsive to the received cultural heritage in which she works? The notion of a radically decontextualized theology assumes that theologians generate timeless, objective and universally valid doctrinal truths that transcend all cultural contexts. Such a view is largely the product of the legacy of the Enlightenment, predicated on Descartes' equation of knowledge with epistemic certainty, Locke's binary distinction between objective fact and subjective opinion, and Lessing's dictum that 'accidental truths of history can never become the proof of necessary truths of reason' (Lessing, 1957, p. 53). Together they support the modern myth of universal reason, which claims access to a neutral decontextualized vantage point: a god's-eye 'view from nowhere' (Nagel, 1986). One of the achievements of post-modern philosophy has been to show that the dream of universal reason is itself a culturally bound product of the European Enlightenment, to expose the incoherence of this 'myth of neutrality', and to demonstrate that all knowledge is necessarily relative to specific cultural contexts. Theology cannot extricate itself from historical events, intellectual currents, cultural shifts and political forces: just as the first theologians did their theology in the context of Jewish and Hellenistic culture, so most contemporary theologians operate in the cultural context of our post-Enlightenment world (Bevans, 1992, pp. 5ff.). The suggestion that theology is unavoidably contextual is reinforced by the material substance and inner logic of Christian doctrine, which identifies the incarnation as a historical event rather than an eternal ideal, and affirms a sacramental understanding of reality in which God is encountered in concrete objects and events. If it is clear that all theology is inevitably contextual, the implications of this fact are less transparent. At the risk of oversimplifying a complex situation, I will outline two contrasting forms of contextual theology: relativistic and realistic.

Relativistic contextual theology

Bevans suggests that contemporary theologians cannot avoid the Enlightenment's 'subjective turn' (1992, p. 2). He appears to be referring here to the post-modern romantic strain of post-Enlightenment thought, which abandoned the Enlightenment's concern for objective knowledge grounded in universal reason in favour of the recognition of the subjectivity and relativity of all knowledge claims. According to Bevans, whereas pre-modern classical theology functioned as a science concerned with objective propositional truth, contemporary theology cannot avoid the subjectivity of all truth claims. Because we do not experience reality as objectively meaningful in itself, our only option is to project our own subjective meanings onto the world. As a result, reality is mediated by the 'meaning we give it in the context of our culture or our historical period', so that our cultural context 'plays a part in the construction of the reality in which we live' (Bevans, 1992, p. 2). According to this constructivist position (Fosnot, 2005), since we can never be sure that our constructions connect truthfully with the external world, we must accept both that knowledge of the world is necessarily subjective and relative to the perspective of the individual theologian, and that it is exceedingly difficult to privilege one theologian's perspective over another and assert its greater truth. For many theologians, this means abandoning the classical *cognitive–propositional* model of theology – most clearly visible in the Christian creeds – which seeks to develop realistic descriptions of God and the divine economy of salvation, and replacing it with either an *experiential–expressive* model that views theological statements as subjective constructs that express the spiritual experiences and perspectives of individual theologians, or a *cultural–linguistic model* that views doctrines as contextually grounded communal rules for Christian living (Lindbeck, 1984, pp. 30ff.). Having accepted a broadly constructivist epistemology, Bevans goes on to present a series of 'models of engagement' which suggest different ways of bringing the transcendent God into contact with immanent human culture. At one end of the spectrum, the *translation model* seeks to reconfigure the language of faith into contemporary language with maximal fidelity to scripture and tradition and minimal theological revisionism and reductionism. At the other end the *anthropological model* gives contemporary culture priority over scripture and tradition, and allows the theologian to assimilating the latter within the former regardless of any theological revisionism or reductionism that might occur. Although the translation model might appear conservative, both have an inbuilt liberal bias that reflects Leslie Houlden's assertion that, as theologians, 'we must accept our lot, bequeathed to us by the Enlightenment, and make the most of it' (Houlden in Hick, 1977). Because the Enlightenment's subjective turn tells us that all knowledge is contextually relative, the conservative theologian can do no more than translate Christian doctrine into contemporary language, while the more radical liberal theologian is free to abandon the creeds and construct an entirely new theological perspective. Since God's self-revelation to humanity is deemed to be unavoidably filtered through the subjectivity of the theologian and conditioned by the cultural context in which she operates, there is little place in relativistic contextual theology for a prophetic model of resistance and transformation, in which the Christian gospel challenges both the presuppositions of the theologian and the established norms of post-Enlightenment culture.

Realistic contextual theology

Bevans associates classical theology with the affirmation 'of one right, unchanging theology, a *theologia perennis*'. However, this is to read the past through the eyes of the objective–subjective polarity generated by the Enlightenment. Following St Paul's recognition that 'for now we see through a glass, darkly' (1 Corinthians 13.12), the vast majority of classical Christian theologians accepted that their doctrinal formulations were generated by fallible human beings and, as such, were neither fixed nor timeless. Anglican theologians were no exception: 'Councils . . . forasmuch as they be an assembly of men, whereof all be not governed with the Spirit and word of God . . . may err, and sometimes have erred, even in things pertaining unto God' (*Thirty-Nine Articles*). However, the fact that theological statements are human constructs generated within specific cultural contexts does not necessarily mean that they are irretrievably subjective. This is the case for all knowledge claims, not just theological ones. Though it is true that palaeontologists construct accounts of the dinosaurs, we have good reason to suppose that such constructs, though never complete and always open to revision, are in the main broadly accurate, and that in the case of contested accounts – for example, the ongoing dispute about the causes of their extinction – it is possible over time, through the careful scrutiny of the available evidence by a community of scholars, to identify some as possessing greater explanatory power than others. If this were not the case there could be no progress in the pursuit of knowledge, and we would be unable to distinguish between alchemy and chemistry or astrology and astronomy. In the same vein, though it is true that Christian theologians construct accounts of the distinctively Trinitarian God of Christian faith, we as Christians have good reason to suppose that such accounts, though never complete and always open to revision, are in the main broadly accurate and possess greater explanatory power than alternative religious and secular accounts of the ultimate order-of-things. In philosophical terms, critical realists argue that despite the fact that knowledge claims are generated in particular cultural contexts (epistemic relativism), this does not preclude the possibility that they provide truthful accounts of reality (ontological realism), and that it is possible to make informed judgements between conflicting truth claims (judgmental rationality) (Archer et al., 2004). Since 'human intellectual enterprises are necessarily fallible, but not for that matter, necessarily mistaken' (Gunton, 1983), contextual theology need not embrace a thoroughgoing relativism. In responding to the life and person of Jesus of Nazareth, the early Christian theologians sought to generate a more powerful and comprehensive explanation of the acts and being of God than alternative religious and philosophical explanations current within Hellenistic culture. Colin Gunton (1998), following Charles Cochrane, suggests that in doing so they 'out-thought the decaying classical civilisation in which [they] lived by providing answers to certain questions that pagan antiquity was unable to answer'. This opens up the possibility of a realistic contextual theology capable of challenging and transforming the norms and assumptions of our prevailing post-Enlightenment culture.

Anglican theology: Context and transformation

The Anglican Communion embraces a rich diversity of theological positions (Markham, 2011). Viewed from the perspective of relativistic contextual theology, since 'Anglican theology' is a nominal construct that identifies a loosely connected set of incommensurable theological positions, there is no such thing as a single coherent Anglican theology. This is reflected in Edward Norman's counter-complaint that Anglicanism's lack of an adequate theological understanding of ecclesiastical authority has resulted in the reduction of the Body of Christ to a nebulous religious society and generated a crisis of Anglican identity and mission (2004). According to Stephen Ross White (1996), attempts to secure a clear Anglican identity risk separating the Church from the world and establishing an enclave of holiness that would effectively occlude Anglicanism's distinctive capacity for moderation and openness. Such arguments and counter-arguments imply the necessity of a binary choice between nominalism and essentialism: between a range of relativistic theologies and a single perennial theology. However, such polarization does a disservice to the distinctiveness of the Anglican position, which follows the *via media* of a realistic contextual theology that affirms the basic truth of Anglican doctrine while refusing to place any premature closure on its ongoing theological investigations. On this reading, Anglican theology cannot be reduced to a plurality of relativistic constructs generated by individual theologians. Just as it is impossible to play chess without the collective intentionality to obey the rules of chess, or play in a symphony orchestra with the collective intentionality to perform a particular symphonic composition, so it is impossible to participate *truthfully* and *honestly* in the Anglican Communion without the collective intentionality to subscribe to a set of relatively stable core beliefs and practices, as articulated in the Communion's shared creedal statements and liturgical formulations (Searle, 1996). Of course, many lay and ordained Anglicans no longer subscribe to the Communion's received beliefs and evolving practices; however, in failing to do so they adopt heterodox positions that depart from the historical continuity of the established collective intentionality of the Anglican Communion – an intentionality that cannot be altered or eradicated by any *individual* opinion or act of will. To affirm a relatively stable set of core beliefs and practices in this way is not to suggest that Anglican doctrine is fixed, rigid and brittle; on the contrary, the affirmation of the threefold authority of scripture, tradition and reason created space for evangelical, Catholic and liberal forms of Anglicanism within a common set of formative beliefs and practices (Nichols, 1993). 'Paradoxically, at first sight, the basis of Anglican self-understanding is the assertion that there is no such thing as the Anglican faith. There is only "the faith once for all delivered", taught, proclaimed and (through grace) lived, by Anglicans' (McAdoo, 1997).

Despite the reductive efforts of some theologians (e.g. Hick, 1977), Anglicans collectively subscribe to an orthodox incarnational Christology which they share with other orthodox Christian traditions: 'God was in Christ reconciling the world to Himself' (2 Corinthians 5.19). At the very heart of the Christian gospel stands the belief that the triune Creator and his creation are ontologically reconciled in the person of Jesus Christ: 'Jesus Christ is the incarnation within our alienated being and perishing existence of the eternal Son of the eternal Father' (Torrance, 1996, p. 142). Because the full and perfect humanity of Jesus is fundamental to Christian faith, the Church opposes all forms of the docetic heresy that denies or qualifies Christ's human nature: 'He worked with human hands, he thought with a human mind. He acted with a human will, and with a human heart he loved' (Pope Paul VI, 1996). Because the full and perfect divinity of Jesus is fundamental to Christian faith, the Church also opposes all forms of the ebionite heresy that denies or qualifies Christ's divine nature: 'God from God, light from light, true God from true God . . . of one substance with the Father.' Where Greek philosophy viewed the essential identity of an omnipotent and omniscient God and a limited human being as a logical contradiction, Judaism regarded the notion that God would subject his holiness to contamination by the created order as anathema (1 Corinthians 1.23). The two basic Christological heresies sought to overcome this philosophical and theological conundrum by denying the incarnation: docetism by proclaiming a divine being devoid of humanity; ebionism by proclaiming a human being devoid of divinity. Though the Anglican Communion collectively asserts the authority of the doctrine of incarnation, it does not subscribe to any single fixed formulation of the doctrine, and recognizes that the formulations that do exist are open to ongoing interpretation – on the understanding that any reformulation or clarification of the doctrine must penetrate more deeply into the truth of the incarnation, rather than deconstruct and undermine it, if it is to remain a valid expression of the collective faith of the Anglican Communion. Some conservative Anglicans flirt with docetism by generating interpretations of Christian theology that appear to be fixed, timeless and dislocated from all cultural contexts, while some liberal Anglicans flirt with ebionism by generating interpretations of Christian theology that appear to be ephemeral, time bound and dislocated from the objective reality of God. Both risk departing, whether deliberately or inadvertently, from the collective intentionality of the Anglican Communion, which asserts that the transcendent God was incarnate in immanent culture, and that the Christian creeds, despite being time-bound human constructs, nevertheless provide epistemic access to the ontological reality of the Trinitarian God.

We have seen how relativistic contextual theology seeks to bind theological statements to the cultural context in which they are expressed, and suggested the alternative possibility that the statements of realistic contextual theology are able to transcend, and thereby critique and transform, the cultural context in which they are generated. The doctrine of the incarnation offers a framework for unpacking this latter suggestion and thereby developing a richer notion of contextual theology. According to Mike Higton, Rowan Williams holds that theology and Christian praxis is only 'useful and honest' when 'the particularities of experience are brought slowly into connection with the communally-confessed truth of God's nature and activity' (Higton, 2004). In doing so he affirms both the unavoidable contextuality of all theological endeavours ('the particularities of experience') and the transformative potential of the gospel message ('the communally-confessed truth of God's nature and activity'). On this reading the Anglican Communion is called to be fully engaged with the world, and thereby necessarily vulnerable to the contingencies of history and culture, while at the same time striving, in the power of the Holy Spirit, to hold fast in thought, word and deed to the truths of Christian doctrine. In such a context there can be no docetic retreat from, or ebionite accommodation with, the world. Ben Quash calls Anglicans towards a polity of presence – if Christ is God's transformative presence in creation, then the mission of the Church as the Body of Christ is to actualize the transformative presence of God in the world: 'Thus God is made present in the community of truth and love; in the body of the Church. God's action makes possible true human community; true human community makes possible God's presence' (2003, p. 9). The ontological reality of the incarnation thus reveals the manner in which the Church should engage with the world: contra docetism, fully involved and engaged rather than withdrawn; contra ebionism, holy and distinctive rather than compromised. The collective intentionality of Anglicanism demands of the various Anglican groups not the schismatic mind-set of the docetic reactionary, nor the accommodatory mind-set of the ebionite liberal, but the orthodox incarnational mind-set of communal participation in the Body of Christ on which true mission and service depends. Theology must be contextual not because we cannot look beyond our limited horizons of meaning, but because Christ was fully human and because the incarnation took place within a concrete cultural context; at the same time, theology must be transformational, not because humanity can engineer its own salvation in acts of self-transcendence, but because Christ was fully God and because the incarnation justified fallen humanity before God and made possible our future sanctification. It is only by being unashamedly orthodox in this way that the Anglican Church can fulfil its contextual–transformative mission to – in Dan

Hardy's (2001) formulation – 'place the intensity of the gospel in the closest affinity to those lives and societies to which it is addressed'.

Church school ministry in context

The National Society for the Promotion of the Education of the Poor in the Principles of the Established Church was founded in 1811, in a particular political, economic and cultural context. The industrial revolution was driven by technological advances that engineered fundamental changes in the agricultural, mining, manufacturing and transportation industries that had profound socio-economic and cultural consequences. The rapid increase in middle-class entrepreneurial wealth was dependent on child labour to provide the economic foundation of the new factories, mills and mines. The resulting economic polarization had an educational impact: whereas the middles classes could afford to provide for the education of their children, no such provision was open to the working children of the poor. At the risk of being over schematic, we can categorize the initial aims of the National Society under four headings: (1) to lend support to the poor in a society devoid of any system of social benefit beyond that of ad hoc personal and institutional charity; (2) to provide a nationwide system of education for the poor by raising money to provide for schools and teachers; (3) to offer children the basic skills of literacy and numeracy; (4) to provide for their personal, social, moral and spiritual development and well-being by nurturing them in the principles of the formal Christian faith of the nation, as constituted and upheld by the Established Church of England.

Two hundred years on the system of Church schools continues to flourish: the Church of England is a major provider of statutory education, the National Society promotes and resources about 4,700 Church of England and about 170 Church in Wales schools, and there are established plans for extension (Dearing, 2001). However, the political, economic and cultural context is now very different.

1. Despite an ever increasing wealth gap between rich and poor, there is now a statutory system of social security in place that seeks to provide support for those in situations of economic need.
2. There is now a statutory system of mass public education in place: state sponsored provision for schools open to all and free at the point of access was introduced in 1870 and consolidated in 1944, and Church schools are now fully integrated into this system and work in partnership with the state.

3. The 1988 Education Reform Act introduced a National Curriculum that extends the scope of compulsory education far beyond the acquisition of the basic skills of literacy and numeracy.
4. Though the Church of England retains its formal established status, the nation has been transformed into a religiously diverse multifaith society, and the 1988 Education Reform Act makes provision for the spiritual development and religious education of all pupils in a manner that recognizes the Christian roots of society while taking into account a range of other religious and secular worldviews.

In such an appreciably changed context, one would expect to see significant revisions in the Church of England's approach to education, as well as in the aims and rationale of the National Society. The current Church of England policy is that Church Schools should be both (1) 'distinctively Christian . . . providing nurture in their faith for children from Christian families', and (2) 'inclusive communities . . . serving the whole local community in which they are situated'. The nature of this division becomes clear in the light of the current debate surrounding the admissions policies of Church schools. In the minority of primary schools and majority of secondary schools in which demand for places outstrips availability, the task of achieving an appropriate balance between places offered to church families and places offered to members of the local community is now a major challenge. Following the lead of the Dearing Report, the National Society distinguishes between 'foundation' and 'open' places: '*Foundation places* are those offered to children whose parent(s) or carers are faithful and regular worshippers in an Anglican or other Christian Church'; '*Open places* are those available for children from the local neighbourhood or community surrounding the school, irrespective of religious affiliation'. Our primary concern here is not with the substance of the question of how to balance foundation and open places, but rather with the fact that the distinction has become an established feature of National Society advice to DBEs.

The National Society, in affirming the twin aims of Christian nurture and social service alongside the distinction between foundation and open places, identifies them as a restatement of the Church of England's traditional educational policy: the 'lesson from the history of Church schools is that they have both served the local community as an expression of service and also provided for the Church family an education within an explicitly Anglican Christian ethos and framework'. There is, perhaps, something slightly disingenuous in the suggestion that the original aims of the National Society remain firmly in place, and that the 'twin objects' of nurturing children of Christian families and serving the broader society 'remain valid today'. Of the four original aims of the National Society outlined above, the first three – (1) to lend support for the poor, (2) to establishing a nationwide system of mass education, and (3) to offer access to the basic skills of literacy and numeracy – are now largely redundant and no longer drive the agenda of the National Society. The fact that the state has assumed responsibility for provision in all three areas is, in part at least, a direct result of the work of the National Society, and constitutes one of its major achievements. This leaves only the last aim: (4) to provide for the personal, social, moral and spiritual development and well-being of children by nurturing them in the principles of Anglican Christianity. Though this aim has been retained, it has been subject to significant revision, so that the National Society now draws a distinction between nurturing children from Christian families and serving the broader society. Such a distinction was unimaginable in 1811: the prevailing assumption was that all (or, at the very least, the vast majority) of children came from Christian families, and that consequently Church schools should serve the local community by nurturing *all* enrolled children in the Christian faith. Though the revised understanding of the task of Church schools, with its distinction between children from Christian and non-Christian families, seems to me to be an entirely appropriate response to a new cultural context, it does constitute a shift from the traditional understanding, and as such raises at least two fundamental questions. First, if service of the broader society is no longer concerned with the provision of mass schooling designed to provide the poor with basic literacy and numeracy skills, and if the broader society is no longer essentially Christian, what exactly does 'serving the broader society' now entail, especially given the recognition that 'accompanying children and young people of all faiths and none, in their search for self and identity' entails an acceptance 'that this search will not always result in following the Christian way'? (Archbishop's Council, 2010). Second, if nurturing children from Christian families in the Christian faith remains one of the primary aims of Church schools, what form should such nurture now take, given the fact that, between 1811 and 2011, we have moved 'from a society where belief in God is unchallenged and, indeed, unproblematic, to one in which it is understood to be one option among others, and frequently not the easiest to embrace'? (Taylor, 2007, p. 3).

Theology of mission and the distinctiveness of Church school

In 2001, *The Way Ahead* offered an embryonic theology of mission with respect to children and young people, in the general context of a recovery of an understanding of the importance of children (National Society, 1988), evangelism (National Society, 1991) and youth work in the Church (National Society, 1996), and in the specific context of General Synod's location of Church schools at the centre of the Church's mission to the nation (Dearing, 2001). This mission is to proclaim the gospel, nourish Christians in their faith, bring others into the faith, and maintain the dignity of all human beings by speaking out on issues such as social justice. In 2010, the Archbishop's Council Report *Going for Growth* offered a more expansive theological statement, grounded in three core principles.

1. The absolute value of each individual child and young person, created in the image of God and called to be transformed and grow into God's likeness: Christians are called to model and teach what it means to be a Christian and to accompany children and young people of all faiths and none in their search for self and identity, while recognizing that this search will not always result in following the Christian way.
2. The importance of relationship with God, other persons and the created order, rooted in and mirroring the relationship of divine love that constitutes the mystery of the Trinity: Christians are called to bring about relational encounters with God and other persons in the midst of the created order that make possible, through the redemptive power of the cross, the transformation of fractured relationships grounded in fear, shame and mistrust – such encounters must be open and honest, and recognize the freedom of the individual to choose whether or not to engage with them.
3. The task of establishing the Kingdom of God on earth: Christians are called to be active citizens, engaging with the world in the light of Christian values, challenging oppression and injustice, and caring for the environment. These three principles underpin five distinctive marks of Christian mission: to proclaim the good news of the kingdom; to teach, baptize and nurture new believers; to respond to human need by loving service; to transform unjust structures of society; and to strive to safeguard the integrity of creation and sustain and renew the life of the earth.

Pulling these strands together, it appears that this emergent theology is grounded in the proclamation of a gospel rooted in the ontological reality of the Trinitarian God, who in the power of his Word and Spirit creates the world and, in an economy of salvation driven by love for the whole of humanity, overcomes the fractured relationships between Creator and creation, between human persons, and between humanity and the created order. With specific regard to those in the sphere beyond the Church, the missionary task is twofold: first, to bring persons into an encounter with God – in a manner that is open, honest and respects their freedom – and teach, baptize and nurture Christian converts; second, to work for the common good by responding to human need, challenging oppression and injustice, and caring for the environment. *Going for Growth* (2010) makes it clear that these twin tasks are interdependent: authentic proclamation of the gospel means that the task of bringing people to an encounter with Christ cannot be separated from the pursuit of the common good, and the pursuit of the common good cannot be separated from the task of bringing people to an encounter with Christ. This constitutes a genuinely (if embryonic) incarnational theology of mission: to reduce mission to the task of bringing people to an encounter with Christ without regard to the common good is intrinsically docetic insofar as it threatens to dislocate Christianity from the wider culture; to reduce mission to the pursuit of the common good without seeking to bring people to an encounter with Christ is intrinsically ebionite insofar as it threatens to subsume Christianity within the wider culture.

Earlier this year, the Board of Education applied this emergent theology to the mission of Church schools: they 'are called to bring fullness of life to their pupils, whatever the beliefs of the children and young people or their families'. Since they are equally loved by God, all children – and especially 'those who often remain invisible, through ethnic or cultural disadvantage, or through disability or poverty' – are worthy of 'the highest possible standards of education and care and the closest attention to what will enable them to flourish'. With regard to non-Christian pupils, this commitment to inclusivity means that the Church school will embrace the twin tasks: (1) of enabling every pupil to 'engage at a profound level with faith in general and the Christian experience and way of life in particular' and have 'a life enhancing encounter with the Christian faith'; (2) seeking the common good of justice and freedom from oppression by working *with* and *for* pupils as 'agents of change and transformation for themselves and for their communities'. The key test of this vision, I suggest, lies in the ability of Church schools to combine these twin tasks into an incarnational unity by rejecting both docetic sectarian schools concerned exclusively with the conversion and formation of pupils, and ebionite nominally Christian schools concerned only with questions of social justice.

According to *The Way Ahead*, since the task of providing mass education for the poor has been achieved, 'the justification for the Church's presence in education must be to offer an approach to education that is distinctively Christian'. Indeed, unless a school is distinctively Christian, it cannot be considered as part of the Church's mission. It is here that problems begin to emerge, in the form of an incipient ebionite tendency in the Report. Many of the distinctive features of Church schools it identifies are indistinguishable from those one would expect to find in any good school, religious or secular: 'an explicit commitment to honesty and openness; a celebration of the identity and nature of culturally and ethnically diverse groups; a readiness to seek and offer forgiveness . . . and an awareness of the challenge of the spiritual life within everyday experience.' Other features are indistinguishable from those one would expect to find in any good faith school, Christian or non-Christian: 'values of loving God and one's neighbour', 'a sense of the presence of God and of the numinous', and 'knowledge of how to pray'. This leaves understanding of the Christian liturgy, especially the Eucharist, as the only distinctively Christian mark of the Church school.

This ebionite tendency is carried over into *The Way Ahead*'s account of religious education. The previously quoted claim that 'the justification for the Church's presence in education must be to offer an approach to education that is distinctively Christian' implies a distinctively Christian religious education. This implication is reinforced by the welcome given to 'the work of those engaged in developing methodologies for a distinctively Christian approach to the curriculum and materials for the theory and practice of Christian education'. However, such work is not elaborated on, and there is no account of a distinctively *Christian* religious education grounded in theological principles, one capable of challenging the hegemony of the relativistic and secularized liberal religious education currently being delivered in most local community schools.

(1) With regard to *policy*, it is suggested that the subject should be a particular concern of the headteacher and foundation governors, who should ensure the presence of 'clear, coherent and professionally competent policies', and of DBEs, who should establish 'agreed objectives with schools to raise the standards of teaching, learning and achievement'.

(2) With regard to *delivery*, it is recommended that the subject be given at least 5 per cent of curriculum time, that all pupils take at least the short course GCSE and preferably the full course, and that schools with sixth forms should offer A and AS Level courses and encourage students to take them.

(3) With regard to *quality*, schools should strive to achieve a 'good' inspection rating in the subject.

(4) With regard to the *curriculum*, Church schools 'whilst covering other faiths' should 'give particular weight to the Christian faith' – thereby replicating the stipulations of the 1988 Education Reform Act with regard to religious education in local community schools without a faith foundation. There is

nothing here, with regard to either policy, delivery, quality or the curriculum, which is in anyway distinctively Christian: any non-Christian school, whether of a secular or religious foundation, that takes its legal responsibility to teach religious education seriously could adopt these strategies without any risk whatsoever of their being mistaken as distinctively Christian. There is no vision here of a *qualitatively* distinct approach to Christian religious education, only of a religious education that is *quantitatively* better than the religious education delivered in non-Church schools.

Towards incarnational distinctiveness

Despite the concerns of some secular humanists, there is relatively little prospect of the Church of England following the docetic option of remodelling its schools as exclusive sectarian ghettos, withdrawn from society at large and concerned only to serve the educational needs and aspirations of Christian families. While acknowledging the potentially negative impact of faith schools on social inclusion, the Cantle Report on *Community Cohesion* recognized 'the desire of church leaders to promote religious tolerance and understanding' and identified its own position as consistent with the vision of social cohesion and inclusion outlined in *The Way Ahead*. There is, however, a significant danger of the Church of England following the ebionite route of seeking an accommodation with the prevailing post-Enlightenment culture to the detriment of the distinctively Christian identify of its schools. Positively, the Church is committed to pursuing the common good by affirming, celebrating and upholding 'whatsoever things are true, whatsoever things are honest, whatsoever things are just, whatsoever things are pure, whatsoever things are lovely, [and] whatsoever things are of good report' (Philippians 4.8). This fits with Bevans' translation model of contextual theology, in which the core values of the Christian faith are translated and applied to the host culture within which the Christian theologian operates. Negatively, however, the Church is equally committed to actively resisting all that is untrue, dishonest, unjust, impure and unlovely in contemporary society. The core danger here is that, in the wake of the concern to affirm the positive values of society, the Church will make the fundamental error of allowing post-Enlightenment culture to define its own ills (and, indeed, goods), rather than draw on its theological resources to serve society by providing a distinctive prophetic and potentially transformative critique of that culture's normative beliefs, values and practices.

Take, for example, the twin values of freedom and tolerance that dominate the value system of secular liberalism. (1) The value of freedom is significantly underdetermined, since many elect to exercise their freedom in ways detrimental to the flourishing of themselves and others, for example, through self-harm or self-aggrandizement. Christian theology insists that true freedom lies not in freedom *from* all forms of external coercion and *for* autonomous self-affirmation and self-determination, but in emancipation *from* all forms of sinful relationship and *for* proper, divinely ordained relationships with self, others, creation and the Creator: 'But now that you have been freed from sin and enslaved to God, the advantage you get is sanctification' (Romans 6.22). Theologically, Descartes' displacement of God and relocation of the autonomous individual at the ontological centre of reality (*cogito ergo sum*), together with Kant's call to individuals to have the courage to trust their own reason (*sapere aude*), constitute a repetition of Adam's primal sin. Since we are made in the image of God and our restless hearts can find no peace until they rest in our Creator, we cannot possibly find any lasting contentment in the hubris of autonomous self-assertion (St Augustine, 1976). This Christian vision does not imply a coercive God, nor does it undermine 'the freedom of the individual to choose whether or not to engage with' Christian teaching. However, such personal responsibility cannot be exercised unless pupils have prior access to an understanding of the gospel and of its implications for their lives, including an understanding of the Christian rejection of personal autonomy as an intrinsic good. (2) The value of tolerance is similarly underdetermined, since there is much in the world that demands proactive resistance. School policies that seek, in the name of tolerance, to promote anti-racist, anti-sexist and anti-homophobic attitudes systematically induct pupils into an economy of intolerance – racism, sexism and homophobia are not to be tolerated under any circumstances. We come face-to-face here with Karl Popper's 'paradox of tolerance', which claims 'in the name of tolerance, the right not to tolerate the intolerant' (1966, p. 265). I am not questioning the virtues of anti-racism, anti-sexism and anti-homophobia; on the contrary, these are virtues the gospel requires Christians to cultivate and uphold. Rather, I am questioning the limitations of the blanket valorization of tolerance, which is not a positive virtue, but rather a morally neutral one. Both Nazi Germany and apartheid South Africa desperately needed schools with the courage to teach and cultivate the virtue of intolerance. Within a liberal economy we must be intolerant of anything that serves to undermine personal autonomy and self-determination; within a Christian economy we must be intolerant of anything that undermines proper, divinely ordained, relationships between oneself, others-in-communion, the created order and the Triune God. Hence, the task of the Church school is not to cultivate a blanket, indiscriminate and relativistic tolerance, but rather to empower pupils to discern, in the light of the demands of the gospel, the difference between that which is, and that which is not, worthy of tolerance.

Recognition of the underdetermined nature of the liberal values of freedom and tolerance opens up the possibility of discerning a deeper, ontologically grounded, appreciation of the differences between the worldviews of Christianity and secular liberalism. The latter places the isolated and dislocated individual at the centre of reality and seeks to maximize their personal freedom, in the belief that self-determination is the highest possible good to which human beings can aspire. Because the exercise of autonomy inevitably generates clashes of interest, liberalism employs tolerance as a means of policing them: thus, in a liberal polity we are free to do whatever we like, provided that we avoid harming others by exercising tolerance. As John Milbank points out, this liberal model of society is predicated on an ontology of violence: if the ontological basis of society is a nebulous collection of atomistic individuals each pursuing their private visions of the good life, then the default relationship between human beings is that of violent conflict. Secular liberalism is thus committed to 'a reading of the world which assumes the priority of force and tells how this force is best managed and confined by counter-force' (Milbank, 1990, p. 4). The Christian worldview, on the other hand, is predicated on an ontology of love grounded in the reciprocal loving relationships between Father, Son and Spirit in the unity of the Holy Trinity. Since we are created in God's image, our ultimate end is to enter into reciprocally loving relationships with self, others-in-community, the created order and our Creator. There is no place in this Christian economy for the exercise of either unrestricted personal autonomy of an indiscriminate blanket tolerance. Our true freedom lies in allowing ourselves to be embraced by God, and this requires us to work positively for the good of all God's creatures, rather than merely avoiding doing them harm. Here, I suggest, we arrive at the theological basis for a prophetic and transformational engagement with the dominant culture of secular liberalism. Just as the incarnate Christ was fully human and fully divine, so we must be immanently engaged with liberal culture yet simultaneously set apart and transcendent of it: seeking to identify and uphold all that is good, and negate and transform all that is evil, not by translating Christian values into liberal values and seeking accommodation with a liberal ontology, but by subscribing to Christian values and holding fast to Christian ontology.

Contemporary liberal religious education operates with two well-established aims: pupils should both 'learn about' and 'learn from' religion: learning *about* religion tends to operate on the relatively superficial level of phenomenological and/or ethnographical surface descriptions of religious culture, beliefs and practices; learning *from* religion tends to encourage pupils to express their own spiritual attitudes, experiences and feelings in response to the phenomenon of religion.[4] These twin trajectories function to cultivate the twin liberal values of tolerance and freedom: learning about religion seeks to encourage pupils to become more tolerant of different religious traditions and cultures; learning from religion seeks to encourage pupils to become spiritually autonomous by expressing their own personal beliefs and values. Any suggestion that religious education should explore the conflicting truth claims of different religious and secular traditions is looked on with suspicion, since such a move might undermine the promotion of tolerance. Similarly, any suggestion that religious education should explore the truthfulness of the spiritual outlooks of individual pupils is looked on with suspicion, since such a move might undermine their freedom of belief and expression. The exclusion of a vigorous pursuit of truth and truthfulness in contemporary liberal religious education has at least three major consequences. (1) Despite being significantly underdetermined, the liberal values of freedom and autonomy provide a default value system for the subject, to the extent that pupils are effectively inducted into a closed liberal worldview: as a result, and not without irony, liberal religious education embraces the traditional confessional religious education it so ardently rejects – pupils are no longer taught to confess the truths of Christianity, but rather to confess the truths of secular liberalism. (2) The eclipse of the pursuit of truth and truthfulness undermines any attempt to cultivate the capacity of pupils to make informed judgements between conflicting religious and secular worldviews, and thereby tends to undermine religious, spiritual and theological literacy. (3) The distinctiveness of the truth claims of Christianity are effectively submerged in an implicit universal theology in which, in the name of freedom and tolerance, all religious and secular worldviews (apart, that is, from the worldview of secular liberalism) are deemed equally true and equally valid.

This being the case, the religious education provided by Church schools needs to be distinctively Christian, not merely a more effective version of secular liberal religious education. This requires the adoption of a theological agenda in which religious education, operating within an explicitly Christian framework, is driven by the pursuit of ultimate truth and truthful living from. Historically, such an overtly theological approach to Christian education took the form of catechetical instruction in the core scriptural, doctrinal, experiential and practical elements of Christian faith, and was designed to contribute to the faith formation of pupils by opening up an intellectually robust and spiritually rich understanding of the nature of Christianity, as opposed to the mere surface description of Christian phenomena ('learning about' Christianity) and expression of attitude towards Christianity ('learning from' Christianity). Such a process requires the tools and methodologies developed in the academy by the discipline of Christian theology, rather than those developed under the secular umbrella of 'religious studies' (D'Costa, 2005). For the liberal, such an approach can appear deeply offensive: intrinsically indoctrinatory (in the sense of being restrictive of freedom) and inherently intolerant. However, Christian catechesis is not inevitably indoctrinatory: to open pupils up to a deep understanding of the Christian faith is not the same as forcing them to accept it as true, and not to make the Christian vision available to pupils is *both* to restrict their freedom of choice *and* to risk imposing by default an implied relativistic universal theology that holds the truth claims of all religious traditions are equally true (Thiessen, 2011). Further, since it is impossible to appreciate the distinctiveness of Christianity without contrasting it with alternative religious and secular worldviews, Christian catechesis cannot avoid addressing the truth claims of non-Christian religious and secular traditions. To advocate the recovery of Christian catechesis is not to advocate a one-way process in which the learner's legitimate concerns and questions are systematically excluded from the learning process: an authentic catechetical programme will offer answers to the questions asked by the catechist, an inauthentic catechesis will require the catechist to learn both question and answer by rote. Similarly, there is nothing intrinsically intolerant in Christians, Muslims and secular humanists engaging in the pursuit of ultimate truth in a manner that recognizes the incompatibility of their respective positions; there is, however, something intrinsically intolerant in attempts to curtail that shared enterprise on the false grounds (1) that since we are free to believe whatever we like all three positions must be deemed to be equally valid, and (2) that to continue the shared enterprise will only serve to generate intolerant attitudes among the protagonists.

Conclusion

I have argued: (1) that the unavoidably contextual nature of theology does not mean that we must resign ourselves to a thoroughgoing theological relativism; (2) that the doctrine of the perfect humanity and perfect divinity of the incarnate Christ, as affirmed by the collective intentionality of the Anglican Communion, provides the ontological ground for a model of the Church as simultaneously fully engaged with yet prophetically transcendent of human culture; (3) that the National Society emerged in response to educational challenges in a specific cultural context, and while it has met the challenge of providing mass education for children from poor families by entering into partnership with the state, it has fallen short of meeting the challenge of teaching and nurturing the nation's children in the Christian faith; (4) that during the last decade it has made positive moves to address this failure by affirming the central place of Church schools in the life of the Church and its mission to the nation, and developing an emergent incarnational theology of education grounded in the twin principles of serving the local community and providing for the Church family; (5) that, unless the Church finds the courage and will to fully explore, embrace and act on the implications of this emergent incarnational theology, it risks continuing along its current trajectory: a trajectory that, in replicating the ebionite heresy that denies the divinity of Christ, risks embracing by default the explicit values and implicit ontology of secular liberalism, and thereby abandoning any hope that the Church can, in the power of the Holy Spirit, genuinely transform the nation through a holistic mission of social service and evangelism – while continuing to give lip-service to that ideal.

Key questions

1. Do Church schools tend to reproduce culture or transform it?
2. Are Church schools fearful of proclaiming the gospel?
3. Are Church schools truly distinctive?
4. Which Christian theology is most operative in Church schools?
5. Which Christian theology of education is most dominant in Church schools?

Part Four

Instrumental in Shaping the Future (Blue-Sky Thinking)

12

Can Church Schools Promote Tolerance in the Twenty-First Century?

Helen Everett

Abstract

In the ongoing debate over the place of faith schools in our society, one of the concerns expressed is that faith schools make their students less tolerant of diversity. Church schools would defend themselves by stressing Christianity's emphasis on tolerance. Drawing on Ph.D. research conducted in a variety of English faith schools which concluded that there was no overall faith school effect, this chapter uses these insights from the research, together with more general research relating to how education may impact on tolerance, in order to suggest ways in which Church schools could work effectively to increase the tolerance of their students.

Keywords
Church schools, tolerance, diversity, student attitudes

Introduction

Even from the inception of the dual system, faith schools were controversial (Murphy, 1971). Concern over faith schools are quite wide-ranging, including admissions (Allen and West, 2009; Schagen and Schagen, 2001), autonomy (Callan, 1985; MacMullen, 2007; McLaughlin, 1985) and segregation (Pring, 2005). Increasingly though questions have been raised about faith schools' ability to promote community cohesion (Berkeley, 2008; Ofsted, 2009). Concerns about faith schools in this area were being expressed before the riots in the north of England and the attack on the World Trade Centre, both of which were in 2001. These events which pushed forward the community cohesion agenda in general can also be seen to have intensified debates over faith schools. One aspect of Community Cohesion which has come under scrutiny is the ability of faith schools to promote tolerance, with the assumption being made that faith schools are inherently bad at doing this (MacEoin, 2009; National Secular Society, 2011).

Despite the vociferous condemnation of faith schools from some quarters, such as the National Secular Society (2011), for not promoting tolerance there is very little empirical evidence to support this view with several studies finding no significant difference between various faith schools and their community counterparts (Dronker, 2004; Short and Lenga, 2002). While on the whole some of these studies found little variation between faith and non-faith schools they have also highlighted some differences in attitudes which can be seen to be related to tolerance in particular circumstances (Francis, 2005; Peshkin, 1986).

Recent research which has compared faith and non-faith schools students' attitudes of tolerance of diversity concluded that, when taken as a dichotomous category, no difference is evident between faith and non-faith schools in this regard. However, as this chapter will discuss in more detail, differences could be detected between the schools, and aspects of the schools, in the case of both faith and non-faith schools, and could be seen to be impacting on the students' attitudes of tolerance. Rather than focusing on the research and the reasons for these differences, though, this chapter will draw on the insight gained from that research (Everett, 2011) and will discuss how faith schools can be proactive in promoting tolerance. Christianity, along with all the major world religions, would claim that an important aspect of its understanding and teaching is about tolerance. Therefore, this chapter aims to challenge Church schools to not just play the defensive game, but actually become beacons of excellence in terms of promoting tolerance in their students.

After a discussion about the meaning of tolerance this chapter will briefly describe the findings from the research before using these findings to highlight ways in which aspects of the school can actively be used to develop tolerance, ways in which the faith aspect of the school can actually be an asset rather than a hindrance as many critics of faith schools would assert.

What is tolerance?

The first question to ask is what we mean by tolerance? The criticisms of faith schools in this area are particularly difficult to counteract particularly because tolerance is very ill-defined on not just one but on two axes.

The first axis is the object of tolerance – what are the students meant to be intolerant or less tolerant of? Some critics of faith schools do not give an object of tolerance, the implication being that there is a generic attitude of tolerance. Others though would be more precise suggesting that faith schools are bad at promoting tolerance of other faiths and thus refer to a particular group. Social Identity Theory (SIT) (Herriot, 2007; Tajfel and Turner, 1986) relates identification with a particular group (the in-group) to discrimination and potential conflict towards another group (the out-group) in order for the in-group to maintain its collective self-esteem, which in turn is related to the self-esteem of an individual group member. Certainly one could consider that another faith group would be a relevant out-group for members of a faith group and therefore a group that discrimination and intolerance might be directed towards. But, as SIT also argues, a number of other conditions need to be met before there is necessarily a problem and that the presence of an out-group alone is not sufficient to instigate lower tolerance (Tajfel and Turner, 1986).

In the speech David Bell made in 2005, when he was Chief Inspector of Schools, he raised concerns about faith schools and tolerance and suggested a slightly different object of tolerance. In that speech he said that schools should help students 'to acquire an appreciation of and a respect for other cultures in a way that promotes tolerance and harmony' and that 'pupils should know the positives of a diverse community and its importance in a world where too many communities are fractured' (Bell, 2005). Again this could refer to particular groups or markers of identity, but it also could apply to a difference in ideas and beliefs and, possibly, behaviours. Much tolerance research, and this is certainly the case with the large cross national studies such as the IEA Citizenship and Civic Education Study (Torney-Purta, 2001), tends to concern itself with specific groups. As the criticisms of faith schools and tolerance are imprecise and inconsistent regarding the object of tolerance the research discussed in this chapter takes a broad approach, looking at both diversity and various specific groups. These groups themselves were chosen as being the six defined identity markers in the English KS3 and KS4 Citizenship Curriculum (gender, disability, ethnicity, religion, socio-economic status and sexual orientation) (QCA, 2008a; 2008b).

The second axis considers how tolerance is defined. At the most basic level tolerance can be considered to be about allowing someone to exist despite dislike or disapproval or some element of discomfort (Creppell, 2003; Walzer, 1997). Locke, in the eighteenth century, is considered to be an early employer of the concept of tolerance as it is broadly conceived today (Creppell, 2003).

He saw tolerance as a gospel value (Locke and Gough, 1966). Maintaining that faith could not be enforced he concluded therefore that it was 'irrational not to endure limited diversity' (Quillen, 2005, p. 5). The nature of this tolerance though merely advocated restraint from harm (Locke and Gough, 1966). Some though would see this type of tolerance as 'mere tolerance' and not something that is worthy of promotion, instead arguing for something which involves respect or a reaching out towards the group to help them live their understanding of a 'good life' yet still despite some element of disapproval or disagreement (Scanlon, 1996; Walzer, 1997). As Christians, despite the breadth of our Muslim friends and despite the similarities we perceive between Christianity and Islam, we do have a fundamental difference of belief with the Muslim. At some level we disagree, but this does not necessarily need to stop the Christians, for example, supporting the Muslim community in their campaign to build a Mosque because that Mosque is important for the Muslim person in order to live their concept of the good life.

There are those who would consider tolerance as a relativistic licence meaning that anything goes and more perniciously perhaps that everything has to be approved of (Walzer, 1997; Weissberg, 2008). This is not tolerance, although traces of this can be detected masquerading as tolerance within English education policies and certainly can be seen within particular interventions in the United States such as the 'Teaching Tolerance Project' (Weissberg, 2008).

Walzer (1997) takes a slightly different, but I feel helpful approach. He does not see tolerance as having a fixed definition, but rather considers that it can have a range of meanings which can be seen to exist on a continuum which runs between the mere tolerance, which allows something to exist but nothing more, at one end and stops short of the relativistic understanding at the other.

Those who criticize faith schools for not promoting tolerance rarely define what they understand by the term. Even government policies such as those relating to community and social cohesion fail to define the term. Thus in order that it be able to respond to the criticisms at various understandings of tolerance the research drawn upon in this chapter has used Walzer's notion of a continuum rather than one particular definition of tolerance. But as this continuum was impractical to implement, not existing in discrete stages, two broad levels of tolerance were employed which were termed passive and active tolerance.

Passive tolerance involves non action. A person displaying passive tolerance is not required to do anything, merely to allow something to happen or at least not stop it happening. At a higher level passive tolerance can be seen to be connected to the application of human rights. In contrast active tolerance requires the person doing the tolerating to actually do something, to engage and emotionally connect in some way with another. At a low level of active tolerance this could be as simple as showing an interest in another's life, perhaps just an active attempt to know more, and at a higher level some form of active engagement as I have described above.

Faith schools and tolerance?

The basis of the discussion in this chapter is the research carried out in six English secondary schools. However, the research only serves as the starting point for discussion rather than the empirical findings themselves being the subject. Therefore beyond naming the schools and categorizing them, a detailed methodology is not included here.

The six schools in the research were St Joseph's (Roman Catholic Independent), St Mary's (Roman Catholic State), the Well (Evangelical Christian Independent), Al Medina (Muslim Independent), Queen Victoria's College (Non-faith Independent) and the Forrest School (Non-faith State). The main findings from the research will now be briefly introduced in order to highlight the ways in which Church schools can promote tolerance.

There was no difference between faith schools and community schools (non-faith schools) if this dichotomous classification was used. However, Two differences in tolerance were found which could be seen to arise in part from an aspect of the school.

The first was that the students in *all* the schools, including non-faith schools, showed lower active tolerance towards other religious groups than they did towards certain other groups (immigrants and those on the margins of society such as ex youth offenders, ex-drug addicts and gypsy or traveller children). This finding emerged from the analysis of a set of interview questions which asked about the students' responses to various groups. In one question the students were asked about their responses to faiths celebrating their own festivals, but the majority of the responses came from a pair of questions. In the first the students were asked what their response would be if a local place of worship belonging to another faith was being forced to shut down; in the second a similar scenario was posed but this time relating to a centre for immigrants or the establishment of an outward bound centre for those on the margins of society. It should be emphasized that this was only at the active level of tolerance with the students almost universally showing themselves to be tolerant at the passive level.

In the faith schools the impact of the school was related to the fact that none of the faith schools provided any opportunity for the students to interact with those of other faiths and in addition there was limited teaching about other faiths. In the non-faith school the impact of the school was seen to result from the school not helping the students to effectively develop an emotional connection with members of other religious groups. Although these two aspects are not precisely the same they can be seen to be connected around the broad notion of contact. In the faith school this difference can be seen to be connected to a faith aspect of the school in that one of the schools' primary aims was faith nurture.

The second difference only related to Al Medina school. In this school lower tolerance and sometimes intolerance was shown towards those whose behaviour contravened religious teachings. In this question the students were asked to name something which they believed as prohibited within their faith and then asked how they would respond to a friend not of their faith doing this thing and a friend of the faith doing this thing. The least tolerance was shown towards members of their own faith who dissented, but low tolerance was also shown towards non-Muslims. The school was seen to impact in this situation in two ways, through ineffective development of cognitive sophistication and through the reinforcement of a religious identity. Both of these were related to faith aspects of the school.

So the research has highlighted three aspects of schools whereby schools negatively affected their students' attitudes of tolerance. These were

- through ineffective contact
- through ineffective development of cognitive skills
- through the formation of a religious identity.

Contact

The first of the school aspects related to tolerance is contact. Gordon Allport (1954) in his book *The Nature of Prejudice* ascribed the origin of prejudice to a thinking error based on 'faulty or inflexible generalisation' (Weatherell, 2004, p. 190). These generalizations can be described as stereotypes in which traits or attributes are associated with certain groups of people, preventing people being seen for their unique characteristics (Weatherell, 2004). Allport's (1954) work led him to propose the 'Contact Hypothesis' as a way of correcting these thinking errors thus reducing prejudice and by extension increasing tolerance.

In its original form any contact between groups was considered beneficial in this regard with the basic idea behind the theory being that contact between antagonistic social groups would 'undermine negative stereotypes' as well as reduce mutual antipathies (Donnelly and Hughes, 2006, p. 496). The theory was subsequently refined to include criteria, which should govern the nature of the contact with contact only being considered to yield positive results if these are satisfied (Vogt, 1997). These criteria are as follows:

1. it must be introduced swiftly, firmly and enforced by an authority
2. the contact must be meaningful and be sustained over a period of time
3. the groups must have equal status within the contact situation
4. the contact must be in a cooperative, not competitive setting.

A significant difference between the Contact Hypothesis and more traditional work on intergroup relations is the former's emphasis on emotions rather than attitudinal change being solely based on increasing knowledge (Davies, 2008), which is encompassed under the understanding of contact being meaningful.

The Contact Hypothesis has been very influential in education policy and thought. The Cantle Report into the ethnoreligious riots in Northern England in 2001 highlights the segregated nature of the schools as a contributing factor to the unrest, a conclusion which was clearly influenced by the Contact Hypothesis, but for which there was no empirical evidence (Cantle, 2001). This hypothesis can also be seen to underpin a major criticism of faith schools (Barker and Anderson, 2005). Segregation through restrictive admission policies results in the students in the faith school not encountering people of another faith or no faith, a situation which is exacerbated by the schools' concentration on teaching about one particular faith interpretation. The consequence of this is that the faith school students must necessarily be less tolerant than their counterparts in community schools (Barker and Anderson, 2005). Similar reasoning can also be seen to be applied to Community Cohesion and thus faith schools again are regarded as suspect in this area (Berkeley, 2008).

Although much research has supported the link between a more varied school mix and increased tolerance, or at least outcome indicators associated with tolerance, there is a growing body of research which is beginning to indicate that the situation is more complex and that mixing alone does not always yield positive results and, in fact, can produce a negative effect (Janmaat, 2010).

The results from my research showed that all the students, those in the faith and non-faith schools, were less tolerant of other religious groups in comparison to their responses towards immigrants and those on the margins of society such as ex youth offenders and ex-drug addicts, but only when active level tolerance was considered. In addition the students saw other religious groups as separate and bounded groups and thus did not feel able, or want, to interact with the group. As can be seen from Amina's response, which is typical of responses from students from all the schools, she does not see the need to act because their faith, in this case the question referred to the closing of a Sikh Gurdwara, was seen as separate and private.

> *I'm not against it being closed down, but I wouldn't take action with them because it's their religion, their faith, their temple . . .' [Amina, Al Medina]*

Almost certainly this view of other religious groups will have been formed from a variety of sources such as family, media and friends to name but a few. This discussion therefore is not about the origin of the view of the religious other which the students' may have, so much as about the *schools' role* in creating or not modifying that view. Based on the Contact Hypothesis the analysis of the schools had suggested that in the faith schools in the research this difference in response towards the other religious groups was related to the schools providing little opportunity for the students to mix with members of another faith and limited amounts of teaching about other faith groups, meaning that the students had little knowledge and understanding of the Religious Other. All the faith schools in this research had at least 80 per cent of their students from their faith. In the Roman Catholic schools the non-Catholic students were almost all from practicing Christian families with a handful of students from other faiths. In the Well all the students were not merely from the same faith, but the same church and in Al Medina all the students were Sunni Muslim, although attending various Mosques. Apart from the Well[1] all the schools were ethnically mixed.

The two non-faith schools were ethnically and, more importantly in this case, religiously mixed populations. Analysis of the school data from these schools suggested that the response towards (other) religious groups was related to the school not providing sufficient opportunities to enable the students to understand the significance that religion might have in a person's life or seeing religion as a lived reality.

Both these findings are in line with the Contact Hypothesis, but they highlight some very important aspects.

The first is that teaching about other faiths is beneficial for increasing tolerance as is opening up possibilities for contact. But as the results from the non-faith schools indicate religiously mixed school populations and teaching about other faiths is in itself not enough, what is important is the quality of the contact and what that contact involves. Thus faith schools merely opening themselves up to other faiths and teaching more about other faiths will not in itself seemingly be enough to affect the tolerance outcome.

The contact that is necessary is a deep form of contact (Dixon et al., 2005). Studies have suggested that this deeper form of contact should help students to consider the significance that some 'thing' has in someone's life and promote the idea of a shared humanity (Donnelly and Hughes, 2006; Rutter, 2005; Yablon, 2011), but also ensure that underlying tensions are tackled and explored. The importance of the latter can be seen in Donnelly and Hughes' (2006) research which contrasts integrated schools in Northern Ireland and their similar counterparts in Israel, highlighting the effectiveness of the Israeli school's approach. In the Israeli schools disagreements were confronted and discussed in a way which allowed students to emotionally engage with each other (see also Yablon, 2011). This contrasted to the situation in Northern Ireland where schools were considered to take a 'detached and aloof' (Donnelly and Hughes, 2006, p. 508) approach and where information was presented in what was perceived by the participating teachers as a position of neutrality. Symbols and celebrations of the Other's life were rejected by the school and the teachers were reluctant to go into dangerous and contentious places, a point also highlighted by Vogt (1997) when he discussed the ineffectiveness of much citizenship teaching for changing attitudes.

For the faith school it may be that actually this deeper contact is in some ways easier to access in that religious significance, and the importance of and meaning associated with religious objects and practice, is something which is familiar to these students through their own experience of faith. Even if the students are not themselves practicing members of the faith nevertheless still within their daily experience of school they are interacting and associating with people for whom faith is a lived reality. This situation can be very different in community schools where faith and religion are assigned to the private sphere and thus even where staff and students hold a religious faith it is not explicitly encountered within the daily life of the school.

The problem which arises for the faith schools is to what extent they feel comfortable engaging with other faiths in the way which seems to be a requirement of this form of contact. The emphasis on shared humanity fits very comfortably within a Christian framework, but requires that schools do not underplay these religious aspects. As has been discussed merely opening up the school to students of other faiths is unlikely to be enough to have a positive impact on tolerance. The Muslim student at an Anglican school will hopefully begin to see Christianity as a lived reality, but to what extent is that reciprocated and does the school enable the Christian students to begin to gain access to Islam as a lived reality rather than something that has to be accommodated?

The second aspect of the deep contact is that underlying tensions are discussed and tackled (Dixon et al., 2005). In situations such as Israel and Palestine and Northern Ireland those tensions are obvious. In England these tensions are much less explicit. Research into Islamophobia (Driel, 2004) certainly indicates that this is one underlying tension and there are likely to be others which only emerge when they erupt into violence, much of which is only in isolated local incidents which rarely enter the national consciousness. This type of contact is seen to require trust to be built up over an extended period (Yablon, 2011) and thus this may be problematic in schools which are segregated on religious grounds. Projects such as The Three Faiths Forum do provide input and advice for schools wishing to develop such dialogues (Three Faiths Forum, 2011).

Cognitive sophistication

Among those that study the relationship between education and tolerance many would wish to emphasize the importance of higher cognitive sophistication for the exercise of tolerance (Bobo and Licari, 1989; Vogt, 1997). The term cognitive sophistication is just one of many which is used to describe the ability to 'process large amounts of information and to differentiate' between competing truth claims (de Witte, 1999). Other terms which are also used to describe this ability include reasoning skills, critical thinking, intellectual flexibility, reflective judgement and cognitive complexity (de Witte, 1999; Pascarella and Terenzini, 2005; Vogt, 1997) quite like how increased cognitive sophistication relates to increased tolerance is complex and uncertain with very few studies linking the three aspects, education, cognitive sophistication and tolerance, in the same study (Bobo and Licari, 1989). With specific reference to racism research de Witte (1999) describes this unresearched space in the middle as being akin to a 'black box' (p. 60) of this type of research. Nevertheless many would see that increased cognitive sophistication is beneficial and leads to higher levels of tolerance.

Although much research studying the link between cognitive sophistication and tolerance is concentrated on racism and inter-ethnic relations this issue is also relevant to faith schools. In one school in the research, Al Medina, the students showed lower tolerance in a particular circumstance. This was seen to be linked to the school's ineffectiveness at developing higher-level cognitive skills in its students, which was primarily related to a faith aspect of the school. This section will look at the results from this particular school before going on to suggest how faith schools can in fact use their faith to improve this situation.

The particular question in the student interviews which showed the difference in tolerance was when the students were asked to name a religious prohibition which they saw applying to them and which was related to their faith. A range of prohibitions emerged including abortion, drinking alcohol and sex before marriage. The students were then asked how they would react if their friend who was not of their faith did this and subsequently their response if their friend who was of their faith did so.

The responses from the Al Medina students were markedly different from those given by the students in the other faith schools,[2] all of whom were Christian. The Al Medina student responses were almost all less tolerant than those from the students in the other faith schools with some being considered intolerant. In St Joseph's, St Mary's and the Well the students sometimes made a distinction between their faith and non-faith friends in that they would be more inclined to offer advice and discuss the matter with their faith friend. This difference in approach is illustrated in Ruth's response below. In the first she is referring to her non-faith friend and in the second to her faith friend.

> *I think it's her choice and unless she's underage I probably wouldn't talk about it* [Ruth, the Well]

> *I probably would talk to them because they're not being true to their own faith or if they declared that they're a Christian. I wouldn't be that really patronising judgemental but just say to them you know you said one thing and I mean their views might have changed on the whole faith* [Ruth, the Well]

But the overriding element of all the responses was that the friend, faith or non-faith, could exercise personal autonomy and thus ultimately it was the friend's choice as to how they should behave, as can be seen in Sarah's response to her friend's decision to have an abortion.

> *it's not my place to try and change what they want to be. If they want to have an abortion I'd probably say think about it first* [Sarah, St Mary's]

In all cases the friendship remained intact and Ruth's response is typical when she says

> *'I'd still treat them as the same person.' . . . 'because they're my friend I don't want them to get hurt'* [Ruth, the Well]

The Muslim school responses varied. In some cases a distinction was made between the faith and non-faith friend with the prohibition not being seen to apply in the same way in the case of the latter. In other responses the prohibition was seen to apply universally. References to personal autonomy were absent from most of the responses, particularly in the case of the faith friend. The starkest contrast with the other faith school responses was the way in which the Al Medina students either removed themselves from the person who was contravening the religious prohibition or required that the offending action be stopped. In many cases friendship was withdrawn as is illustrated by Zainab's response in which she is talking about a faith friend who is drinking alcohol

> not that I would say anything to them but I wouldn't be friends with them for any longer [*Zainab, Al Medina*]

Within the Al Medina student responses there was little understanding of shades of grey in these situations, neither was there a wide appreciation of the concept of personal autonomy. Here though the lower tolerance was shown not towards a particular or easily defined group in society, but towards those whose behaviour contravened religious teachings. Reactions towards those of the faith who dissented were harsher than towards those of no or other faiths. Two aspects of the Muslim school were considered to be impacting on this view. One was related to the religious identity formation which, for reasons mentioned earlier, is not being discussed in this chapter. The second was related to the way that the school was less effective in developing its students' cognitive sophistication. This was seen to be directly related to the fact that the religious teaching in Al Medina did not allow any critical examination of the faith, nor was interpretation of the Qur'anic text encouraged. These restrictions can be seen to reflect wider Islamic understandings about the nature of the Qur'an and the nature of the faith (Bennett, 2005; Esack, 2005).

I have included this part of the research in order to raise two points. The first is that here is an example and an indication of where faith schools, through an aspect of their faith, can negatively affect tolerance. The connection with Islam means that it can be easily discounted as an 'Islamic issue'. To do so would be foolish as some Christian interpretations, such as Exclusive Brethren and Old Order Amish and Mennonites among others, would also take this very conservative view of critical engagement with faith or scripture.

The majority of Christian faith schools in England, though, would not take such an approach to the faith. Therefore the second point is to again highlight the link between cognitive sophistication and tolerance and this time to suggest that rather than faith being an impediment to developing cognitive sophistication, the mainstream Christian tradition provides an excellent means of increasing tolerance through the development of cognitive sophistication. The way that this can be achieved was evident in one of the faith schools in the research. This Roman

Catholic school, St Joseph's, took its faith very seriously. In this school teaching was almost exclusively focused on Roman Catholicism, but the approach taken was almost brutal in the way that the students were expected to examine and argue any claims they were making regarding their faith, or any other belief they held. An important aspect of this approach appeared to be the staff who were themselves not only religious education specialists, but who were also confident and secure in their own faith. Although this approach was being encouraged at KS4, it was most evident in the sixth-form religious studies lessons and this may account for no discernible difference being seen in tolerance between the Year 10 pupils in this and the other Christian faith schools. Rather than limiting the opportunity for developing the critical thinking skills the faith aspect of the school therefore can be seen to enhance them. Again this approach is not advocating that the faith teaching be diluted, rather that a rigorous approach is employed which is not afraid to explore alternatives.

I feel that this approach is harder to use within community schools. In these schools it would require that the claims of all faith groups, as well as secularism, be approached in this manner, something which would be controversial to say the least. In addition, there will be a limited number of staff who have the depth of knowledge in a range of faith to be confident enough to engage in such discussions about and challenges to the faiths. Again it can be seen that in the faith schools these elements are less of an issue as it is only critical engagement with one faith which is being advocated and the religious education teachers are likely to be practicing members of that faith, and therefore hopefully confident in discussing a wide range of aspects of the faith.

Conclusion

This chapter was framed around a question about whether Church schools can promote tolerance in the twenty-first century. Not only have I argued that they can, but I have suggested ways in which the faith aspect of Church schools, rather than being a hindrance, can actually be a resource. Critical examination of the faith can provide an opportunity to help the students to develop cognitive sophistication and as students are in an environment in which they experience faith as a lived reality they are potentially better placed to be able make an emotional connection with members of other religious groups. Both of these are seen to increase tolerance.

I have argued that Church schools can promote tolerance in the twenty-first century, whether they do is a different matter, and one which is not solely dependent on the school itself. Neither of the two suggestions can be considered straightforward or uncontroversial and it seems unlikely that these suggestions will have a marked impact unless they become embedded within the school ethos and are supported by parents and others associated with the school. Effective deep contact requires trust of the type which can really only be gained through prolonged contact. It also requires the school and the staff involved in this work to be confident and secure in their own faith and what they are trying to achieve in order that they can help students engage with underlying tensions and differences rather than gloss over them as Donnelly and Hughes (2006) found was the case in the integrated schools which they studied in Northern Ireland. The current climate in which schools, particularly faith schools, are under close scrutiny does not encourage schools to undertake potentially controversial initiatives of the type which have been suggested and yet I am confident that Church schools can, and will, rise to the challenge.

Key questions

1. Are Church schools better placed to critically examine various truth claims than community schools?
2. How practically can Church schools increase their students' contact with other faiths in a way which would positively impact on tolerance?
3. To what extent is Christian teaching on social justice a good foundation for teaching tolerance in the school context?
4. Should Church schools be promoting tolerance?

Notes

1 Although not very ethnically mixed nevertheless the Well did reflect the ethnic diversity of its location in a commuter town in the Home Counties. St Joseph's itself was situated in a predominantly monocultural area of England, but because of its boarding aspect it attracted about one-third of its students from outside the United Kingdom and thus was ethnically diverse.

2 Similarity was seen between the responses in the Christian faith schools and those from the community schools, although these are not being included in this discussion. This question was only asked to students who had indicated that they held a religious faith.

13

What Must Church Schools Do to Live Up to Their Rhetoric?

Julian Stern

Abstract

All schools have rhetorics. These are ways of describing, explaining and justifying their activities. Rhetoric is needed for internal audiences (the staff and pupils of the school) and for external audiences (local, regional and national organizations). Schools associated with the Church of England have often used versions of two rhetorics popular throughout the history of the church's involvement in education. These are the rhetoric of inclusive service, and the rhetoric of mission. This chapter presents findings from research in a number of schools with and without Church of England foundations. There are indications of some distinctiveness of the Church schools and, in those schools, of each of the two rhetorical traditions. What is argued here, is that there are some forms of research on the living reality of a school that can investigate separately, its rhetoric and (the rest of the school's) lived reality, and can therefore explore how those complement or contrast with each other.

Keywords
Church of England, mission, inclusion, Church schools, dialogue, rhetoric, research

Introduction

Every school uses rhetoric. Rhetoric refers to the art of influence and persuasion (Aristotle, 1984, p. 215), with which all schools and religious groups are familiar. The word has gained additional meanings, both positive and negative. Positively, rhetoric can mean eloquence and the skilful use of language; negatively, it can mean showy and insincere linguistic flourishes. Schools and religious groups may be familiar with these forms of rhetoric too. Rhetoric is used within institutions, often intended to create a particular ethos (which itself is one of the classical branches of rhetoric), or to persuade members of the institutions to accept a policy or practice. Beyond the institution, rhetoric is used to persuade others of the value of the institution, and to persuade people to join the institution. In those senses, rhetoric might be referred to in more modern language as 'marketing', although marketing implies a market, and this may be objected to by those who see education or religion as of value independent of, or additional to, its 'market' value. Rhetoric is therefore a more general term for persuasive activities, of describing, explaining and justifying roles and activities. The phrase 'living up to the rhetoric' could be misleading. Effective rhetoric persuades, it influences people; ineffective rhetoric fails to persuade. So if the life of an institution is distinct from its rhetoric, this indicates the failure of the rhetoric itself, rather than a failure to 'live up' to the rhetoric. An alternative title for this chapter might therefore be 'how effective is the rhetoric of Church schools'. The rhetoric, as it were, might be judged by whether it 'lives up to' the reality of Church schools. Nevertheless, as rhetoric is often the responsibility of the more powerful people in schools (notably, headteachers), it is worth considering the match between rhetoric and reality – whichever of those might be asked to 'live up to' the other. A great deal of time is spent, especially by school leaders, in fashioning specific examples of rhetoric – the more formal, systematic, attempts at persuasion. Along with formal speeches in assemblies or parents' evenings, school mottos, mission statements, logos, websites, uniforms and prospectuses can all be seen as rhetorical devices. Headteachers and other school leaders use these opportunities to persuade those in and beyond the school that the school is as they would like it to be.

The Church of England has a long and significant influence on schooling, reflected especially in the two centuries of activity of the National Society. It is beyond the scope of this chapter to describe this history. Instead, two of the elements of church school rhetoric are briefly presented, along with some of their implications. One is the rhetoric of education as part of the church's service to the community, and the nature of this service – of an *established* church – as inclusive, that is, providing service (a form of pastoral support) to all members of the community, whatever their religious beliefs, activities or membership. The other is the rhetoric of education as part of the church's mission including the wish to gain adherents to the religion itself. Those two rhetorics complement each other, of course, and there is much theological debate on their complementarity.

Schools may use both rhetorics, as in Wright's claim (in the Australian Anglican context) that the Church school 'has a duty to educate and a purpose of propagation of faith' (Wright, 2011). Yet the two rhetorics are treated as distinct, not least because it appears from the history of church school interaction, over the past two centuries, that one or other has had greater prominence.

This account of rhetorics is followed by an account of how schools may come to understand their own lived realities. There are many ways of researching schools. What is presented here is an approach intended to explore what is referred to as the 'spirit of the school' (Stern, 2009). By researching the spirit of the school, it is possible to investigate the extent to which the lived reality of that school and the rhetorics of the school match each other. Effective rhetoric is itself persuasive, and so a close match would be expected between rhetoric and lived reality. More than that, the rhetoric is itself one of the important 'lived realities' of the school's leaders. One of Aristotle's first surprises, to a modern audience used to the more negative and cynical use of the term 'rhetoric', is his insistence that rhetoric is effective to the extent that the good character of the speaker is itself exemplified in the speech. The first mode of persuasion, he says, 'depends on the personal character of the speaker' (Aristotle, 1984, p. 215). Being a good person should be demonstrated systematically, in rhetoric. This is therefore a second reason why 'living up to the rhetoric' could be misleading. School-based research can investigate the character of people within the school, especially its leaders, and in that sense, it can help in exploring the character-based qualities of the rhetoric itself.

Rather than a definitive account of church school rhetorics or of church school lived realities, this chapter provides examples of methods by which rhetoric and reality can be investigated, along with tentative examples of some such investigations.

Church school rhetorics

According to Murphy, the two education rhetorics of the Church of England – of inclusive service and of mission – can already be found at the origin of the National Society. The aim of the BFSS 'founded, in its embryonic form, in 1808' and inspired by the Quaker Joseph Lancaster, was to promote 'the Education of the Labouring and Manufacturing Classes of Society of every Religious Persuasion' (Murphy, 2007, p. 4). When the Church of England set up what Murphy refers to as a 'rival' association, in 1811, it was given 'the significant title' of 'The National Society for Promoting the Education of the Poor in the Principles of the Church of England' (Murphy, 2007, p. 5). Both organizations have inclusive service in their rhetorics. There was a stated emphasis in the BFSS's foundation on education itself being the aim, as a form of inclusive service. That is still today reflected in the society's current 'vision' and 'mission', 'to maximise educational opportunity for all' and 'to enhance the lives of people throughout the world by promoting the advancement of opportunity for education, that is the physical, intellectual, moral, religious and spiritual development of the whole person regardless of ethnicity, nationality or religious belief' (www.bfss.org.uk/about-us/vision-values-and-mission/). For the National Society, too, education was promoted as a form of service, and this was often described specifically as inclusive, at least for 'some members of the National Society' who felt that 'the true spirit and policy of the Church of England' should be 'comprehension and *not* exclusion' (Murphy, 2007, p. 38, quoting Best from 1956). That inclusive service rhetoric was recently restated by the Chair of the Church of England Board of Education, who said Church of England schools' 'main function should be serving the wider community' (BBC, 2011). He continued, 'I know that there are other philosophies that will start at the other end, that say that these are for our church families, but I have never been as convinced of that as others' (Marley, 2011). That long-standing rhetoric underpins the importance of the introduction of the somewhat controversial 'conscience clause' in the 1870 Education Act which 'implied officially restricting religious instruction to set times, and hence its separation from secular instruction, a principle hotly denounced by many Anglicans and particularly by the Tractarians' (Murphy, 2007, pp. 38–9; see also Louden, 2003).

Much of the rhetoric of the BFSS and the National Society was therefore similarly focused on educational service that was inclusive. However, what Murphy regards as the 'significant' addition to the founding aims of the National Society is the reference to the 'Principles of the Church of England', which indicated a form of religious mission. Since then, the society's name has been changed to the 'National Society for Promoting Religious Education', but its activities still include 'promoting the churches' policies'. In the context of the early nineteenth century, the differences between the rhetorics would have been less significant than they might be today, as 'the poor', for whose educational benefit both the BFSS and the National Society were set up, would at that time have been described as 'free or almost free of infidelity'. Even if '[t]he literature of the working man was violently anticlerical, antichurch, antimethodist, antechapel' and 'rollicked in abuse of the establishment', 'it was not usually heathen', and '[m]ost working men would have been horrified to be told that they were not Christians' (Murphy, 2007, p. 8, quoting Chadwick from 1966). So the 'mission' rhetoric was more about bringing people to the church, than it was about bringing people to religion in general. Yet it is worth exploring further the mission-oriented religious rhetoric.

What can be seen in these historical examples, is evidence of each of the rhetorics of the Church of England's National Society. Can those two rhetorics still be seen in Church schools today? A brief look at the front pages of eight Church of England secondary school websites chosen at random (through searching for schools nearest to eight addresses around the country, using the National Society website), suggest that both are alive and well, with different emphases in different schools. One school (with all schools remaining anonymous in this chapter), is 'led by God' and refers to the 'teachings of Christ' and 'the Psalmist' on its website, and in these ways emphasizes the 'mission' rhetoric, while also mentioning the 'poor' for whom the school was originally set up. Another, similarly, describes itself as 'A Christian Community Committed to Excellence', and refers to the diocese, to the 'Christian ethos', and the school community being 'created by God'. Three other school websites, in contrast, emphasize education and sometimes inclusion (as in the motto 'All different, All equal'), and can therefore be seen as examples of the educational inclusive 'service' rhetoric of the church, but mention nothing about religion – other than identifying (in one case, in smaller and fainter type than the school name) as a Church of England school. Of the eight websites, the remaining three schools in this very small and inevitably unrepresentative sample of schools, have both rhetorics in evidence, including a significant but not predominant reference to the 'mission' rhetoric. One, for example, has several different references to the Church of England, another has a picture of a cross as one of its two photographs (reflecting the recommendation to 'proclaim that it is a Church of England school on its external signboard and on its stationery and make appropriate use of Christian symbols inside and outside the school', Dearing, 2001, p. 20), and so on.

Research in living schools

There are numerous ways of researching schools, from the self-evaluation recommended by the National Society's 'Christian values for schools' website (www.christianvalues4schools.org.uk/) or the SIAS external evaluation and self-evaluation systems addressing the 'distinctive Christian character' of the school (www.churchofengland.org/education/national-society/ inspecting-our-schools.aspx). Those examples are useful, yet they tend to work from the rhetoric to the reality, generally working on the rhetorical statements and then finding evidence for them. Such an approach can give rather too much of an expectation that the rhetoric is 'right' and that evidence must be found to support it. To understand 'living schools', it may be helpful to have an approach to research that is independent of the stated rhetoric, that builds a distinct picture of the school which can then be compared with the rhetoric. As stated in the introduction, this might allow for an answer to the question 'does the rhetoric live up to the reality of the school?' It is a complex issue for researchers as well as for schools. What is described here is an approach based on that of a particular project that explored not only the complexities of schools, but many of the complexities of the research process itself. For three years, the *Spirit of the School* project (Stern, 2009) investigated primary and secondary schools with and without religious foundations – including Church of England foundations. The aim was to understand and promote the spirit of the school, with that spirit being generated by and in turn supporting three dimensions of humanity: community, learning and dialogue. Community is described by relationships, including opportunities for friendship. Learning is a creative process, with school learning centred on becoming human. Dialogue is how people come to be themselves by relating to others, making community and learning.

In order to explore these issues, a number of questions were asked of all the participants – pupils, teachers and headteachers. These included asking for descriptions of the three most recent or memorable times that the school 'made you feel good about yourself', 'how we can make the school more of a community?', 'what is typically said' in particular lessons and other situations, and a time in school 'when you talked about something important to you'. They were also asked 'who is closest to you in school', 'when do you feel most included', 'to what do you belong', 'what beliefs are most important to you', 'what from your life outside school is studied in school' and 'what would you say to someone in school who was troubled?'. By the end of the period of research, a definition of the spirit of the school had emerged, and the definition was reported (in the final chapter of the initial book of the project) in this way:

> The spirited school is an inclusive community with magnanimous leadership that enables friendship through dialogue in order to create and evaluate valuable or beautiful meanings, valuable or beautiful things, and good people. (Stern, 2009, p. 161)

A longer version of that definition, with some added explanation, is this:

> The spirited school is an inclusive (bringing in from past times and local and distant places) community (people treating each other as ends in themselves) with magnanimous leadership (aiming for the good of the led) that enables (but does not insist on) friendship (by overcoming fear and loneliness and allowing for solitude) through dialogue (not monologue) in order to create and evaluate valuable or beautiful meanings, valuable or beautiful things (including the environment), and good (real) people. (Stern, 2009, pp. 160–1)

Several people asked the project team, during and after the period of research, whether Church schools were different to non-Church schools. Were they more or less 'spirited', or were they spirited in different ways? There is not a single straightforward answer to that question, but attempting to answer the question illuminates the topic of this chapter on how Church schools live up to their rhetoric. Using the terminology of the definition of spiritedness given above, one issue was concerned with how inclusive the community was (who was 'brought in' to the school, and how were people treating each other as ends in themselves), and a second issue was how leaders expressed their magnanimity – and in particular their relationships to their own and their school's rhetorics.

How are Church schools inclusive communities?

In terms of bringing people in to the school and members of the school reaching out beyond the school – among the most important descriptors of the nature of community – Church and non-Church schools were similarly committed to bringing people in and to going beyond the school. The research therefore did not indicate that Church schools were more or less inclusive than were non-Church schools. Instead, the types of school appeared to be inclusive in slightly different ways: they 'included' somewhat different external groups and organizations. Church schools were more likely than other schools to make those connections with religious people and organizations. The ways in which they did this, and the implications for individual members of the school community (especially those who might not be members of the school's church), are illustrated by the interviews with pupils in a Church of England primary school (pseudonymously identified in Stern 2009 as 'Ruislip School'), who talked of one of the most 'memorable times . . . [that] your school has made you feel good' being a visit to York Minster, which included work on prayers, and a project that engaged the children in designing a stained glass window for the school hall. There were some other distinctive features of the evidence from Church schools with respect to religious education, and these are worth presenting in some more detail.

Religious education in a school with a religious foundation might be expected to involve some of the rhetoric of mission, as it might be thought that such a school would promote the sponsoring religion (i.e. in this case Christianity). In the following extract from a conversation about 'what is typically said in religious education?', there is some evidence of this mission rhetoric, in the emphasis given to 'God and Jesus' (repeated for further emphasis), and to prayers that fit Christian models of prayer:

Interviewer:	So, if it was a religious education lesson what might your teacher say to you then, for religious education?
Terence (aged 9):	As far as we're doing in religious education, we're doing,
Jonathan:	We are doing religion of God and Jesus. We're doing stuff about God and Jesus.
Interviewer:	So, what might the teacher mention about God and Jesus do you think? Would she ask you a question or ask you to do something? . . .
Lucia:	In our religious education lesson last week, Mrs . . . told us to think of a line to go in our prayer when we went to York Minster . . .
Terence:	and this was our prayer in the crypt
Interviewer:	Oh, lovely, lovely. So, did you think of something?
Lucia:	Yeah, . . . we each thought of a line.
Interviewer:	So, what sort of line did you come up with? What might the pupil, the child in the picture say? What sort of thing if she was asked, she was asked to put a line together? What sort of lines did you come up with? Can you remember any?
Terence:	I can, it was stuff like 'Thank you God for food and water' . . . 'Thank you God for letting us come to this wonderful place' . . . things like that

This account of prayer-writing, while in a Christian church, might be expected to end up being Christian. The school would then be living up to a rhetoric of mission and (in Wright's words) the 'propagation of faith'. This is useful evidence in itself. Yet there is evidence, later in the discussion, when Terence 'objectifies' the Christian nature of what he has said, suggesting he has understood and would therefore be in a position to reject mission rhetoric, in saying 'that's good' to his religious statement. Terence's position indicates that the mission rhetoric is not as powerful as it seemed at first. His view is complemented by Jonathan's clear rejection of Christianity, accompanied by an acceptance that he nevertheless 'believes'. In these ways – in the following transcript – there is evidence of a form of inclusive (service) rhetoric in this Church school, belied by the initial impression of more mission-oriented rhetoric:

Jonathan:	Because God is, he made everything and if you don't like appreciate him you, you're not nice because he, he built everything in the world.
Interviewer:	That's good.
Terence:	Some, that's what Christians believe
Interviewer:	Yeah, you're right. You're right Terence. Christians do believe that. Do you believe that?
Terence:	Yeah
Interviewer:	You do
Terence:	Yeah
Interviewer:	Jonathan do you believe what you've just told me? That's good. How about you Lucia?
Lucia:	Yeah
Jonathan:	I'm not Christian but I still believe

The statement 'I'm not Christian but I still believe' is one of the most intriguing of the whole project, but it is worth continuing with the transcript, as that provides some further evidence:

Interviewer:	Do you?
Jonathan:	Yeah
Interviewer:	That's interesting. That's good. So what else, who else do you learn about? Do you just learn about Christians here because it's a Christian school?
Jonathan:	No
Terence:	No, we learn about Jewish
Jonathan:	yeah about Jewish and

Interviewer: A Jewish lady came?

Terence: Yeah

Jonathan: Yeah and we were, what is the other kind of language?

Lucia:Hindi

Terence: Buddhism. We learnt a bit about that

Lucia:Yeah

Jonathan: Yeah, we learn about Jewish and I can't remember the rest
                what we've learnt about.

Such an exchange provides evidence of the influence or effectiveness of the school's rhetoric of inclusive service. It also provides evidence that the school is following the Church of England's own guidance (or 'rhetoric') on religious education, which says that pupils should 'reflect critically on the truth claims of Christian belief' (Hall and Taylor, 2005, p. 6), rather than accept such claims uncritically. That is, religious education should be relatively more inclusive and not restricted to the 'propagation of faith'. Religious education at Ruislip School also includes work on other religions (following the locally agreed syllabus, as well as the church's guidance), as Terence and Lucia refer to learning about 'Jewish', 'Hindi' and Buddhism. What is more, when Jonathan describes 'worship to God and Jesus' as special, the statement is subtly modulated by Terence who explains 'that's what Christians believe'. That adjustment would be a model of good practice for an adult, and is exceptionally subtle for a pupil, and leads eventually to the enigmatic statement of Jonathan 'I'm not Christian but I still believe'. Jonathan may follow another religion such as Judaism, given that this is the only religion he goes on to mention in the subsequent conversation, while the other pupils talk of Buddhism and 'Hindi'. Perhaps he is not religious, and the statement 'but I still believe' is an affirmation of the ability to believe outside religion. The word 'but' is particularly interesting, as it suggests an awareness of the challenge he presents to a 'Christian school': belief is possible *despite* being other than Christian. It is a more confident position than the rather sad statement beautifully analysed by Rudge, and providing the title for her article: 'I am nothing: does it matter?' (Rudge, 1998). The conversation including the assertive statement 'I'm not a Christian but I still believe' is therefore presented here as an example of how a Church school demonstrates its inclusive rhetoric. It exemplifies encouraging a pupil outside the foundation religion to work confidently with belief, and encouraging other pupils to recognize that Christianity is one way but not the only way of being in the world. The inclusive service rhetoric has proved more influential or effective, in this particular Church of England school, than the mission rhetoric.

How do heads of Church schools demonstrate magnanimity?

Magnanimity is a virtue. For Aristotle, magnanimity is the 'crown of the virtues', being possible and more likely for a person who already demonstrates other virtues (Aristotle, 1976, p. 154). The term 'points to the generous, unselfish, kind and benevolent aspects of human nature' (Nixon, 2008, p. 96). One of the central qualities of 'character', in Greek philosophy, magnanimity has been somewhat underused as a virtue-term in contemporary life, perhaps because it can be seen as a 'very upper-class' virtue (a note by the translators Thomson and Tredennick, in Aristotle, 1976, p. 153). Yet generosity of spirit is surely a significant characteristic of all people, and especially of those in leadership positions. Perhaps the best example from the research of a headteacher describing his relationship to the school's rhetoric, and at the same time demonstrating magnanimity, was from another primary Church of England school in the United Kingdom (pseudonymously identified in Stern 2009 as 'Afton School'). The headteacher said of himself that he was 'not a practising Christian', and was someone with 'a secular viewpoint'. This was therefore a good situation to investigate whether the church-related rhetoric was being used by the headteacher in a cynical way (e.g. using the rhetoric without believing it, perhaps in a self-serving way), pragmatically (e.g. using the rhetoric without believing it but as the best option for 'surviving' as a headteacher), or magnanimously (e.g. using the rhetoric with sincerity, believing it to be to the benefit of the people for whom the leader is responsible, even if parts of the rhetoric are of little direct value to the leader).

Afton School's 'statement of values' was discussed with the headteacher. The statement clearly formed a central element in the school's rhetoric, not least because it was printed on the entrance to the school. These values, developed during the same headteacher's time in charge, included the sentence 'As a community our best will only ever be good enough; the best we can be, the best we can do and the best we can offer to God'. The interview proceeded in this way (in a slightly edited transcript):

Interviewer: Is it [the statement of values] different to what you would
                have written on your own?

Headteacher: Possibly but the, in spirit, no, I mean I

Interviewer: Well, is it what you ended up thinking anyway because you had those discussions [mentioned earlier in the interview]?

Headteacher: I, I think it's just, well, I am but one, I keep saying that and ... it, it, it is just a statement of what the, all the stakeholders ... could, could buy up to it, so it's rather like –

Interviewer: You didn't sign up for it?

Headteacher: it's, it's rather the protocol that, that all the countries in the EU might have to sign up to it, it's not going to be perfect for any one country but the thrust of it certainly you know, that the God bit is, is there and that's not really there for me but, but the rest of it ... [At this point, the headteacher goes on to talk about the parts of the statement of values that he likes.]

It would be hard to script a better account of discomfort than the initial response of the interviewee, when he says 'possibly but the, in spirit, no, I mean I'. When challenged as to whether he was persuaded of the statement as a result of discussions with staff, governors, children and their families, he responds with a statement of humility or membership of a larger group: 'I am but one'. This is followed up with the statement that 'it is just a statement of what ... all the stakeholders could buy up to', and when this is further challenged, the agreement is described as like that of an international organization such as the European Union. 'It's not going to be perfect for any one country', that is, for himself as 'but one' person, yet 'the thrust ... is there'. Furthermore, there are other parts of the statement he is very happy with, notably the references to 'home'. The response of the interviewee in this case clearly suggests that the headteacher had considered the principles – the rhetoric – carefully before supporting them, and before describing this support in the interview. This indicates that he was not using the rhetoric cynically, as a self-serving pretence – especially given the sincere-sounding expression of humility. Whether his use of rhetoric was narrowly pragmatic or more magnanimous remains to be clarified in the light of later elements of the interview, a complex and subtle discussion of educational principles.

The interview went on to demonstrate the magnanimity of the headteacher, in a way that would clarify the evidence related to the school's statement of values. Magnanimity, or being 'great-souled' (Aristotle, 1976, p. 154), means working for the led, in contrast to working for yourself (being 'self-serving'), working for people external to the organization being led (perhaps being a pragmatist who bends to any external pressures), or being weak (offering little leadership).

Leaders who work for themselves, said Aristotle, were tyrants, and suffered from arrogance; leaders who thought themselves as equal in every way to those who are led, suffered from pusillanimity, or petty-mindedness. Those leaders who were able to lead in the interests of the led were, in contrast, magnanimous. Incidentally, because all leaders are themselves also followers (i.e. there is always someone with more power), it is possible and appropriate to combine magnanimity with humility. Statements such as 'I am but one' express a proper humility, in these circumstances, but the leadership given to the school to work out a proper set of values that 'all the stakeholders . . . could buy up to' is an example of what might be magnanimity – a generosity of spirit, one might say, of a less than religious headteacher of a Church of England school. Whether it is indeed magnanimous, rather than pragmatic, is explored in the following account of a later element of the interview.

At one point, the headteacher said – in a suitably rhetorical way as a clear statement of educational values – that he was 'absolutely, diametrically opposed in any way to any kind of selection on the basis of, you know, social background or culture or faith or skin tone or socio-economic, . . . profile or, or indeed level of attainment'. Later, he mentioned his own background as having been to a selective grammar school as a child. The transcript continues (in a slightly edited version) with the first response being the best example in the whole *Spirit of the School* project of a genuinely ambiguous response combining 'yes', 'no' and 'possibly':

Interviewer: You mentioned . . . going to the grammar school was the thing that made you, my feeling is from what you've said that you might not be in favour of creating grammar schools, as you've said you reject selection for this, that or the other

Headteacher: No, no, yeah you are right but it is . . . there's clearly a slight contradiction there yeah, thank you for picking it up.

Interviewer: Sorry!

Head: No, it is, it is and, I suppose hand on heart there's, there's, it's, it's easy to sit here and pontificate about values and vision and what's right for a community of the size of this school, when it comes down to oneself and in particular one's own children, sometimes one's values go out of the window,

Saying that your 'values go out of the window' suggests a cynical or perhaps pragmatic approach to rhetoric. Once again, however, the continuing exploration of the issue in this interview allowed a much more value-driven and magnanimous explanation to emerge. At this point in the interview, the headteacher talks about whether he might send his own child to a private school. Although he 'believe[s] in children being taught with their, the people they grow up with in their local communities', adding 'I, I honestly believe and I don't just say it because I want more children in the school, it's not self-serving', he justifies going against that principle by reference to principles of inclusion:

> I suppose going back to that same set of similar principles if we talk about community cohesion as being accepting . . . without you know being sort of lily-livered about it saying 'Well you can never, you can never disagree with anything then you know' it will be too open minded I suppose but grammar, grammar school suited me and . . . the grammars or the, or the high-performing private schools that, that will suit a certain kind of child who is very, very motivated and it's naïve to think that society doesn't need these high, high-flyers but, but there should be an alternative that is in many ways just as good but just better suits the, the skills of the other children.

This part of the interview is concluded with an admission of the complexity of the situation, recognizable by many educationists:

> I, I have my own internal conflicts on that, it's easy to paint a vision but the reality is that if we are being truly inclusive, I think, I think they have to, that they are you know, provide you know a range of provision to suit, to suit all sorts.

The interpretation put forward of this exchange is that the interviewee is not ignoring his values, but has a higher value of inclusion, along with an understanding of current educational institutions, which means that the value he attributes to non-selective schooling is overruled by the higher value given to inclusion. It might be more comfortable to ignore the conflict between values – it would avoid 'internal conflicts'. Yet the decision-maker in this case admits the discomfort and makes a decision on the basis of the educational needs of the child – his daughter – and not on the basis of what would be more comfortable or easier to defend. Being prepared to look after your child in this way is precisely the example given by Aristotle to illustrate the difference between a magnanimous and tyrannous leader – working 'for the led' rather than working 'for yourself', as a good father who 'is concerned for the welfare of his children' (Aristotle, 1976, p. 276). As a virtue is a 'character trait' of the person, rather than simply a characteristic of an action, it is appropriate to attribute the virtue of magnanimity to the earlier, even more ambiguous, situation of the school's statement of values. That is, at least, what is suggested here.

The self-awareness and moral complexity of the views of this respondent are presented here as an example of the complexity of education in general, the need to explore the relationship between 'headline' principles (often expressed in formal rhetoric) and lived reality, and also some of the complexity of researching education. Research that fails to allow for such nuanced and complex responses, as given here, may itself undermine the respondents (by encouraging an insincere separation of rhetoric and lived reality) and undermine the research process. It would have been easier, as a researcher, to have avoided such sensitive topics, or to have accepted the first responses rather than challenging them. However, such an approach is likely to generate a false picture of schools. It would also fail to recognize the magnanimity of the headteacher, as someone able to think through principles as they affect the people for whom he is responsible. He demonstrated an important aspect of his own character – his magnanimity – precisely through his description of work on the rhetorics of the school's statement of values and his own principle of non-selective education.

Conclusion

In the section 'Church school rhetorics' of this chapter, an account was given of some of the rhetorics used by Church schools and organizations supporting Church schools. This was followed by a brief account of how those rhetorics are exemplified on websites. Following this, the section 'Research in living schools' described methods of researching the lived reality of those schools. Some of the results of such investigations were presented, related to the issues of inclusive communities, the magnanimity of school leaders, and the complex relationship between rhetoric and lived reality of the schools. The research also illuminated some of the problems associated with educational research, and how those might be overcome by encouraging sincerity – a research virtue (explored in Stern, 2006 and 2009), and a virtue for those practising rhetoric and wishing to avoid the modern cynical understandings of the term. Indications are given of the distinctiveness of Church schools, including some of the specific rhetorics used by schools with Church of England foundations. This chapter does not describe the relationship between rhetoric and the lived reality of every Church of England school, but it raises questions that every school might try to answer. For example, what evidence is there of the rhetoric used in the school, and how is that rhetoric related to the traditions and rhetorics of the Church of England (as described in Murphy, 2007, or as currently described by the National Society's 'Christian values for schools' website, www.christianvalues4schools.org.uk/)? From the perspective of the lived reality of the school, what is typically said in particular situations (such as religious education lessons, other lessons, assemblies and collective worship, playtime and lunchtime) that might help describe the lived reality of the school, when do pupils and staff feel most included in school, and what would make the school more of a community? The intention is to understand the specifics of particular schools, just as a good architect will design a building suited to the particular site and needs of the building's users, while also recognizing historically and geographically wider contexts.

Where does this leave rhetoric? An understanding of the older uses of 'rhetoric' is helpful. The art of persuasion in more formal situations, used so much by professionals in education and especially by headteachers, is worth reviving as a study in its own right. Important 'performances' of headteachers – major speeches, policy documents, mission statements, websites – are all too easily regarded as no more than insincere marketing or 'spin'. Yet, as Aristotle describes it, such rhetoric is itself effective insofar as it provides evidence of the real character of the leader. The leader of a Church school may, like the head of Afton School, have a complex relationship even to the service-oriented rhetoric he has created for his own school. No doubt some church school heads would, instead, exemplify the more mission-oriented rhetoric expected by Wright: those of 'prophet, pastor, priest and king . . . as well as those of educational innovator and human resources manager' (Wright, 2011). It will certainly take high quality research to bring out, separately and independently, both the rhetoric and the lived reality of Church schools, and to describe the complex relationships between them. However, it is only with such research that the question can be answered, 'what must Church schools do to live up to their rhetoric?' May this chapter encourage such research.

Key questions

1. In the schools and other organizations you are familiar with, where would you find evidence of their 'rhetoric'?
2. Having discovered the rhetorics, what do they tell you about the traditions in Church of England involvement in education?
3. Within the schools you know, what is typically said in particular situations (e.g. religious education lessons, other lessons, assemblies and collective worship, play-time and lunchtime)?
4. When do you think pupils and staff in the schools feel most included?
5. What do you think would make the school more of a community?

14

Church School Identity beyond the Dearing Era

Tim Elbourne

Abstract

Two hundred years after the start of the church school movement by the National Society, our system stands at another crossroads. The 'decade of Dearing' (2001–11) achieved much to reinvigorate Anglican education, but its time draws to an end. A new Government introduces substantial change. The Church and its schools need fresh conceptual and theological resources for new times. After a concise overview of the decade past and the emerging context in education, this chapter proposes theological ideas to equip Church schools and those who support them. It offers and explores the concepts of *rootedness, belonging* and *narrative* as key ideas for developing the notion of distinctiveness in the new era. It urges the Church to prioritize theological reflection about its schools and their mission alongside its operational work.

Keywords
Theology, distinctive, rootedness, belonging, narrative

The Dearing era

The Dearing era is over. It was an exciting time for Church schools. In many respects the Church has rediscovered its schools, affirming them as standing at the 'centre of the Church's mission to the nation' (Dearing, 2001, p. 1). The *Church School Review Group* was established following a resolution by General Synod in 1998 and its report was the first major statement on Church of England schools since *The Future in Partnership* in 1984 (Waddington, 1984). The number of secondary schools has grown considerably – some say we have seen the greatest expansion of the sector since the Victorian age. Many of the new secondary schools which are Academies serve vulnerable families and needy urban areas, reconnecting the sector with its founders' intention to serve the poor. There has been greater and more systematic emphasis on the Christian character of Church schools and its implications, to which the embedding of SIAS (National Society, 2010b) has contributed significantly. Dioceses have developed their schools teams and their networks have improved. Their voice and joint enterprises have begun to flourish. Many of the waves of government initiatives during the last Labour administration offered the Church recognition and opportunity to make its contribution in local decision-making. Dearing invited his readers to reconnect with the notion of 'vocation'; both in terms of the teaching profession and ministerial formation and much has been achieved, although sometimes more patchily. Above all, there was a renewal of confidence and energy and the flowering of creativity and enterprise. I think 2001–11 will come to be seen as a remarkable decade.

Of course there were frustrations and failures along the way – there always are. Not all the initial burst of energy was sustained. Might it now, ten years on, be germane to revisit the 79 recommendations he made?

The Dearing era began in the age of 'education, education, education' in the first term of the 'New' Labour administration, when optimism was in the air. It also coincided with a period of economic growth and prosperity, evidenced, for example, by the renewal of so many school buildings which had long been neglected, smaller class sizes,[1] significant increase in the workforce through Teaching/Learning Assistants; Early Years expansion and Sure Start and Children's Centres. This was also the era of 'Every Child Matters' and the creation of 'Children's Services' departments in local authorities. The Department for Education and Employment became first the Department of Education and Skills and latterly the Department for Children, Schools and Families.

However, it concluded in a recession and with a new political landscape. The political agenda of the new coalition government represents not an ideological reversal of the direction of its predecessor in schools policy but a radical extension of some aspects of it. To signal a change in emphasis, the department was immediately renamed, Department for Education and the word 'teaching' stressed over what is regarded as the softer 'learning'. The system for teacher training is being changed with fewer PGCE places and the introduction of Teaching Schools to extend workplace-based teacher training. The Building Schools for the Future programme has gone and the James Review commissioned and published;[2] the English Baccalaureate has been introduced (omitting Religious Education to the consternation of the religious education community). The National Curriculum is to be reviewed. The new government's flagship policies were to be the introduction of a wave of 'Free' Schools and the radical extension of the Academy programme. Now all schools are to be encouraged to explore this independent status and those deemed to be 'failing' may have it thrust upon them under a new sponsor. The drive towards individual school autonomy is part of a wider rhetoric of 'localism' but has the paradoxical effect for the school of exchanging for its previous local relationship with its Town Hall a series of direct relationships with Whitehall and with private educational service providers unfettered by local democratic accountability. The 2010 White Paper *The Importance of Teaching* tellingly described Whitehall's education civil servants simply as 'officials' while those working in local government, many of whom have a professional background in schools, were dismissed as 'bureaucrats'.

The Chair of the Church of England's Board of Education/National Society was quoted as saying:

> In the long run there will be a major shift to academies because it is what the Government is determined shall be. The local education authority is going to wither on the vine in many cases. (Pritchard, 2011)

The role of local authorities had been shifted in the later years of 'New' Labour from 'provider' towards 'commissioner'. The clear implication now is that in some places they are to be almost written out of the picture altogether.

It is hard to exaggerate just how much time and attention the new Academies agenda and its implications are requiring, whether or not there are wholesale 'conversions' in progress or in prospect. *The Importance of Teaching* stated unequivocally that 'all schools will be able to become academies' (p. 57). The aspiration was clear; 'It is our ambition that Academy status should be the norm for all state Schools' (p. 55) and the first choice for new schools is to be an Academy or Free School (p. 65) and Academy chains are commended. While it also stated, 'we will not force any school to take on the increased autonomy if the headteacher and governors do not want to' (p. 59) (if it meets 'minimum standards') it is the central government which controls the financial levers and the ability of a local authority to retain its schools depends upon its financial and human resources. Where a significant number of schools leave the local authority, a 'tipping point' is reached and it becomes less viable for others to remain. It has been claimed that some £400m is to be 'top sliced' from the 'formula grant' that government gives to local councils. What was once an entirely secondary school option now exercises primary schools too. Since the large majority of the Church of England's 4,800+ schools are in the primary sector this has far-reaching implications for DBEs and their officers. As well as navigating the legal and organizational complexities, their attention is now absorbed in themselves developing mechanisms to be 'providers', held to account for provision and outcomes as well as supporting newly converted academies – perhaps through brokering arrangements with other service providers whose numbers are rapidly expanding. DBEs are developing a range of models including 'umbrella' and 'multi-academy' trusts to keep the family of Church schools together. They are seeking approval to become academy sponsors in their own right. In previous decades dioceses have considered their responsibility towards their schools to be mainly focused around Christian character and on areas such as religious education, building projects and admission arrangements in VA schools and participation in local authority committees. The Dearing era expanded their vision to include 'distinctiveness' as a whole, especially in areas such as leadership and management, vocational development, ministerial education and relationship with local churches. A main section of the report was focused on the expansion of provision and many new schools, especially secondary schools and 'old style' Academies serving disadvantaged communities, were created. Although capacity in diocesan teams was in many places increased to meet this challenge, the new era (if this is what it turns out to be) now considerably stretches those resources and expertise. There is a recognized danger that if they are not careful the current political realities will soak up all available energy in dioceses as it becomes directed into responding to technical and 'performance' focused considerations to the detriment of theological and missiological reflection.

The new 'era' poses new challenges in thinking through what the core and abiding identity of Church schools is to be into the future. This chapter cannot pretend to offer an extended commentary on the shifting sands of government education policies, nor to offer a critique of them from a Christian point of view. Instead it offers some thoughts and themes as pointers towards what may be helpful.

The first point is something of a lament. It is to note that the Church of England's education community has rarely sought to maintain a careful and continuing academic reflection on the nature and purpose of Anglican schooling amid a changing culture. Nor has it offered theological critique of government schooling policies and their underlying ideological suppositions except in fairly general terms.

Archbishop William Temple, in his negotiations with Rab Butler, was instrumental in establishing the settlement of the 1944 Education Act which created VA and VC schools and ensured that daily collective worship and religious instruction (later education) would play a part in the life of every maintained school in the land. In those days the Christian basis of the national culture was uncontested in ways that seem far distant today. Schooling was intended to provide basic skills and qualifications for people to take their place immediately in the workforce while preparing a small minority to proceed to further study and university. The postwar economic task seemed straightforward enough, if daunting.

Temple's biographer commented:

When the top rung of the educational ladder set up under the Act was reached, what would the climber have gained? He would be equipped, was Temple's hope, for Christian citizenship and for taking up the further duties that it involved. To widen that sense of citizenship and to Christianise it had been the burden of what he had said and taught for thirty years. (Iremonger, 1948, p. 578)

The ideal of a 'Christianised' citizenry would be keenly contested today. If Church schools are to continue as a significant part of the educational landscape they need to be confident and clear of their theological and practical purpose. They are offered as gift only for so long as the community as a whole wishes them. With the safety of a long-held 'dual system', consolidated by the 1944 Act, removed by the erosion of the VA/VC categories and the advent of a multiplicity of school providers in an era of Academies, Anglican schools need fresh tools to explore and deepen their core identity.

There may be a number of reasons why the Church has not yet developed sustained capacity to reflect on the theological and educational identity of its schools and the nature of the Christian education they seek to offer or to offer ongoing critique of prevailing secular orthodoxies in education. Diocesan education departments and Church House staff are fully engaged in making the best of whatever opportunities and challenges government policies create and may feel some reluctance to criticize a system of which they are a part and in which they seek to maintain their position. They may lack the confidence with which to analyse and criticize; they certainly lack the capacity and time to step back. Many are themselves products of the systems which have evolved and been recreated, whose skill-sets equip them well to be canny operators within, but less so to be reflectors about. Education policy is subject to continual technical change; one year's policy and reflection will be tomorrow's 'chip wrapper' in any case, so what's the point? The well-organized and persistent, if numerically few, secularist campaigners, and the constant war of attrition they wage against the place of the Church in the public sphere and in education and Church schools in particular, provoke defensiveness and squeeze the space for creative reflection.

Most significantly of all, perhaps, the Church did not use the post-1944 Education Act for decades or the momentum of the Dearing era to create and nurture an Anglican education academy or theological community. We lack an Anglican academy of educational theology or journals and societies. A few initiatives have been taken in recent years, such as the creation of the National Institute for Christian Education Research (NICER) at Canterbury Christ Church University, but it takes time for such programmes to take root to the extent that they develop the capacity to sustain continuing and lively conversation with an essential contribution to the centre of the Church's educational enterprise.

Dearing's report was pragmatic and while it made a number of recommendations about developing the Christian distinctiveness of Church schools, did not point to the importance of establishing an ongoing theological and reflective enterprise. Little was said about the Christian purpose of education or what may be the characteristics of 'Christian education' in the school context. The report limited itself to two paragraphs on the 'curriculum'; enjoining teachers to develop schemes of work that reflect the Christian character of the school and welcoming those engaged in developing methodologies for a distinctively Christian approach to the curriculum (while refraining from citing examples) (Dearing, 2001, S. 4.10–11)

The climate in which we find ourselves today requires that this reflection is now taken with the utmost seriousness and urgency for a number of reasons. Politically, the dismantlement of many of the organizational structures that have characterized postwar schooling creates a climate in which nothing can be taken for granted. The Church can no longer be assured a protected place at the table and will need to establish clarity of purpose and a clear rationale for what it seeks to offer in a new and rapidly expanding market-place. Culturally, economically and morally, we live in times of great uncertainty and insecurity of which the banking crisis and city disturbances of 2011 are poignant and shocking reminders. Globally, the next generations will face challenges – environmental, political and economic – which may have been visible on the horizon for some time but for which solutions are yet to be devised. Religiously, although the Church of England is far more robust and energetic than its many media critics allege, it faces urgent challenges in terms of its own demographics, resources and mission strategies which render simply maintaining the status quo as not an option. As one bishop expressed it baldly in prefacing a recent diocesan strategy document,

> Church attendance has been steadily declining for more than a century; decline in the attendance of children and young people has been particularly sharp; and the financial pressures are enormous. (Newcome, 2011, p. 5)

Distinctiveness, inclusiveness and Christian values

The Dearing era for Church schools saw the rise to prominence of a number of keywords and concepts that have come to characterize what the Church thought its schools were about during the period. *Distinctiveness, Inclusiveness* and *Christian Values* are perhaps the three concepts which have been used with greatest frequency during the period.

One reason these words became so embedded in the Church's rhetoric about its schools perhaps flows from the language of the Dearing Report itself. The report used the word, Distinctive, 31 times in its first three chapters and 64 times in all; Inclusive(ness) was mentioned 17 times and (Christian) Values 18 times. On the other hand words such as 'kingdom' (1 mention), gospel (6) and Jesus/Christ (3) featured much less. While much cannot be read into this and substance is not correlated to the use of certain vocabulary, here were clear signals that these concepts were ones on which Church schools should focus.

At times these words, repeated together, almost took on the flavour of a mantra among church school apologists and they continue to have widespread currency as denoting the desirable hallmarks of Church schools. Perhaps they have deserved greater detailed exposition than sometimes they have been given; the trouble with a mantra is that it can become so familiar that what was initially intended to be a gateway into the discovery of new meaning and depth becomes instead a substitute for further thought and development.

It could be argued that the profound implications of *distinctiveness* have often been glossed over; that *inclusiveness* has been employed simply as a defence against those critics who accuse Church schools of serving only a particular subcommunity (defined by religion or social class) and *Christian values* have been promoted only to the extent that they sit comfortably with those of a prevailing wider culture. Since Church schools belong to the maintained public system, the language used by those who promote them has to sit comfortably within a more secular mainstream. This is not just a matter of political reality; it stems also from theological conviction. Church schools are offered not as a kind of entryism into a hostile and alien secular world. They belong to a Church of England which understands its vocation to be service and Christian witness to the whole community and which occupies a place not apart from society but embedded – incarnated – within it.

However, undue emphasis on *Distinctiveness, Inclusiveness* and *Christian Values* also has its limitations as a summary for what Church schools are about. The era upon which we have now embarked requires us to reinvent and extend the vocabulary of what lies at the theological heart of Church schools.

As well as their overfamiliarity, the three concepts that have become so well used from the Dearing era, have their own built-in limitations. This is not to render them useless, but to suggest that they cannot necessarily bear the weight of alone summarizing the essential characteristics of Church schooling, especially in a system that is becoming more fragmented as the academy model is extended.

1) It has been noted that the notion of **Distinctiveness** has not been well developed or widely researched and that schools are not clear about how Christian distinctiveness relates to teaching, learning and the curriculum (Jelfs, 2008).

   Distinctiveness is often taken to mean 'difference'. What makes a Church school a Church school is taken to mean those elements which Church schools have and which other schools lack. These become 'unique selling points' in an educational market-place. To press the notion of distinctiveness can be to concentrate on lateral comparison and towards what distinguishes Church schools from other schools. Inevitably, such comparison can lead to a concentration on the most easily observable differences. The aspiration for distinctiveness can then easily become a quest for acquiring Christian-shaped 'fridge magnets' to decorate the plain white door of a school which would otherwise be identical to another school which claims no Christian identity. Such 'fridge magnets' might include elements that are indeed important parts of being a Church school such as relationships with the local church, collective worship, signs and symbols, proper time for religious education, etc. But the identity of a Church school should be more than being simply an 'ordinary' schools with a few add-ons, like fridge magnets. The limitation of overuse of the word distinctive is that it is apt to encourage such thinking since it commonly directs the attention laterally into making comparisons with others, rather than vertically towards considering the core of the school's Christian identity. Moreover '(Different conceptions of Christian distinctiveness result in) a lack of clarity around such concepts as values, ethos and spirituality' (Green, E., 2009, p. 83).

2) '**Inclusiveness**' can all too easily become a kind of defensive shorthand to provide assurance that the Church school's admissions policy does not discriminate religiously or socially and is there to serve the whole community. The extent to which a Church school is thought of as 'inclusive' therefore will depend upon the way in which its Admissions Policy is worded. A significant majority of Church schools, especially VC and Academies, offer their places to all children in their locality. A minority, mainly of VA schools, do not. Are they automatically to be described as less 'inclusive' for that reason? Perhaps, they understand their vocation within the local system as a whole to give preference to some pupils on religious grounds for whom there would otherwise be no opportunity of a Christian-based education? Or perhaps, their location would mean that a wholly distance based Admissions Policy would result in a very sociologically unbalanced pupil body, maybe exclusively of children from wealthier homes within the community? For them, there could be a very real tension between being religiously and socially inclusive. The challenges of trying to be 'inclusive' do not end with admissions. How is the curriculum to be structured, especially those aspects which have an explicitly Christian basis? And what of special-needs provision? And behaviour management policy? And staff recruitment? Quickly, the ideal of 'inclusiveness' has to be tempered by a whole series of practical issues and choices that can set limits on what may be possible or desirable. So in the sense that it means 'not blatantly prejudiced and exclusive' the word 'inclusive' may be useful, especially in countering the objections of secularist critics who make exaggerated claims that Church schools are by their very nature selective. But, I suggest, 'inclusive' is not a robust enough concept to be one of the *main* pillars of church school identity in the new era.

3) And what of '**Christian values**'? Who could argue against them as being at the core of Church school's life? Values have to be at the heart of any educational enterprise that intends to be formational and rather than simply concerned with imparting information (chosen on the what basis?). The *Christian Values for Schools* website explores a number of values that can be traced back to Scripture and are core principles in the Christian tradition. In a culture with Christian roots, unsurprisingly, a number feature also in

other publications and resources which have no explicit religious basis. The limitation is not that that many core values which can be derived from scripture and the Christian tradition are not exclusive to Christianity, rather that values are abstract derivations.

In my work with school leaders over the last 18 months I have introduced three different concepts to help explore and deepen the characteristics and practice of developing the Church school. One of my criticisms above of 'distinctive' and 'inclusive' has been that these words are often thought of by school leaders as comparative and tend to be used to defend Church schools from their critics. Although 'distinctive' may lead to a reflection about what lies at the heart of being a Church school, often the word points those who employ it towards concentrating on difference. Similarly, 'inclusive' can tend to point leaders to consideration of how to avoid being the opposite, 'exclusive'. I wanted therefore to explore concepts that helped them to concentrate on and deepen an appreciation of what they wish their Church schools to develop and deepen *in themselves;* to explore more deeply what might be the characteristic essence of being a Church school in the current situation. The feedback has been very positive and suggests that the concepts may be helpful as keys to creative and energizing reflection and development as we embark upon the new era.

The concepts I have used are 'Rootedness', 'Belonging' and 'Narrative'.

Rootedness, belonging and narrative

Rootedness

Rootedness expresses faithfulness both to the Gospel and our shared Anglican tradition. The Parable of the Sower (Matthew 13.1–9 etc.) speaks of the importance of sinking roots deeply enough to nourish faithful life. Roots nourish and feed. Unlike the seed sown on the path or the rock, the seed that falls on good soil puts down roots that enable it to hold fast and survive.

The root system of each plant is particular to it; it helps the plant to grow and sustain its authentic identity. So too with the school. Its rootedness in the Gospel secures its Christian identity. If it is an Anglican school, it may share many of the characteristics of other Christian schools, but it will remain identifiably Anglican for its roots remain Anglican. Its particular local 'flavour' will depend on its own context, the 'soil' in which it is planted.

Public education systems come and go and are subject to political fashion. The environment of the surface in which the school is planted is subject to change. The plant may need to bend according to the wind and the direction of the sun. It may need to accommodate from time to time changes to the system of which it is a part. But if it is deeply rooted it can endure.

If the notion of distinctiveness can encourage a tendency to compare Church schools with others, it can distract from nurturing the fundamental yet invisible roots that underpin the most visible differences. Rootedness is not about comparison with others; it is about faithfulness to and security in one's own identity; identity in the Gospel and the Church to which it belongs.

The Cambridge Theological Federation, an ecumenical federation of eleven theological and ministerial training institutions, expresses its ethos in the phrase 'Roots down, walls down'. This is a helpful expression for the Church school too. For as a root system is established, the plant above the surface no longer needs as much shelter as does a young sapling. It is possible to remove protective walls, secure in the knowledge that it can withstand and include and take its place as a mature plant in the garden or forest. A deeply rooted school is not easily threatened and is confident in its own identity.

The notion of being securely rooted, pointing towards a secure Christian and Anglican identity and knowledge of what the school exists for, and for whom, can also be a helpful way into a confident exploration of what was intended by those who first offered the idea that Church schools should be 'inclusive' as well as 'distinctive'. The corollary to 'roots down' of 'walls down' can helpfully apply to schools as well as theological institutions and mature trees. A deeply rooted school is not easily threatened. Nor does it need to be defensive or exclusive. It can serve the whole community, perhaps by admitting pupils of all faiths and none, precisely because it is secure enough in its Christian identity and ties to the Church, to become a hospitable and welcoming community to all who choose it, irrespective of background.

A school that is soundly rooted in its Anglican Christian identity will be neither tribal nor sectarian. Its purpose is not primarily to further the Church's place in the community, but rather to further God's mission in the community which the Church is called to join in. 'Mission is seen as a movement from God to the world; the Church is viewed as an instrument for that mission. There is a Church because there is mission, not vice versa' (Bosch, 1994, p. 390).

One can helpfully add the word 'school' after 'Church' in this sentence. Moreover, since Church schools are rooted in a faith that favours the poor (Luke

1.52–53; 4.18–19) they have a particular vocation to serve the neediest, faithful to the intentions of those who founded the National Society in 1811.

One important caveat. In July 2011 the first ever international gathering of Anglican school leaders took place in London and Cambridge.[3] The consultation focused on common identity and priorities using these concepts of 'Rootedness', 'Belonging' and 'Narrative' and found the framework they provided helpful and illuminating. However, a delegate from Australia pointed out to the gathering that although the metaphor of roots and the importance for schools of living roots which feed lively Anglican and Christian identity was helpful, the notion of 'rootedness' was not. In the Australian context, 'rooted' speaks of inertia and the inevitability therefore of decay and death. In British vernacular, the idea of being 'rooted in the past' would be a similar negative connotation. Perhaps, however, the possibility that the idea of being rooted can have negative as well as positive associations can be helpful in using the concept as a tool for schools to reflect on their identity. There are, indeed, forms of rootedness that are inimical to growth and confident development and the double edge that the concept has may assist schools to be discerning in what they identify as the healthy roots to which they might attend.

Belonging

If 'Christian values' tend towards the abstract, **'Belonging'** directs the attention to sets of specific relationships. Church schools and those who live and work in them belong to a number of communities; to the Church at local, diocesan, national and worldwide level; to the educational community in the local and wider context and, of course, to the neighbourhood or locality they serve, often as a crucial focus and resource for it. Sometimes these multiple belongings can be the source of tension. For example, belonging to a wider public education system can involve compromise with powers which have different priorities and educational philosophies. Church schools teach earthly as well as heavenly citizenship (cf. Philippians 3.20). Church schools are committed to the common good and the well-being of the wider culture and the economies which they serve and to which their pupils belong. They depend on a wider system for their funding, the supply of their teachers and their standing in the public eye. Although the first Church schools in England were originally independent of the state, which did not then offer free schooling for all, most became part of a universal state funded provision out of necessity and a conviction that partnership was a better way to live out their vocation to serve all irrespective of private means. However, belonging to a state-funded public provision brings challenges as well as opportunities. The removal of control by local authorities may remove one layer of institutional belonging, but dependence on funding directly from Westminster may lead to other tensions more difficult to resolve since they involve a more distant bureaucracy. It remains to be seen how valuable the various freedoms associated with Academy status will turn out to be, such as freedom from the National Curriculum and national pay and conditions agreements. There is a corresponding fear that the new freedoms might put at risk elements that dioceses and schools have worked hard to strengthen over recent years such as denominational inspection, religious education and collective worship. The hope is that Academy status will lead schools to strengthen their sense of belonging to their diocesan family and DBEs are working hard for this to be the case.

But belonging is more than just institutional. A school is a community to which people belong with each other. It is not simply a factory for the acquisition of knowledge and skills, but one of the contexts, alongside the family and friendship circles, in which young people discover and learn about personal relationships.

Amid talk of creating a 'big society' and the reflection that will surely follow the urban disturbance of August 2011, we might hope to expect to hear more of this theme and of the role that Church schools may play in that task, although it may be a challenge to maintain school spending on 'enrichment' in an era of austerity. Schools are contexts in which civic virtues are discovered and practiced (Mongoven, 2009); in a Church school, they are rooted in the Christian ideal of love and the Kingdom of God (Wright, A., 2010) and the rediscovery of the common life.

Narrative

The life of a Church school constitutes a **Narrative**. A Church school *lives out* and *tells* a story. The story is communicated through the school's common ethos and through the range of educational and formative experiences it offers its pupils. It is the narrative lived and experienced through the life of the school as a whole which makes the most important contribution to the unfolding story of its pupils' lives.

Of course, a Church school offers an educational narrative through the teaching and learning it offers its pupils and its formal curriculum. If there is no such thing as value-free education, the content of the curriculum, what is taught and how it is taught, is crucially important. Despite the restrictions imposed by the National Curriculum (if the school is not an Academy) and formal assessment and public examinations there remain choices to be made about content and method.

Smith (2009) employs the notion of 'liturgy' to describe the whole formative narrative conveyed by a context, exploring by example, the formative influence of the 'liturgy' played out by the experience of visiting a shopping mall; a liturgy which people regularly repeat and which, alongside the supporting narrative of advertising, can have a formative influence on human desires and priorities.

> Liturgies, whether 'sacred' or 'secular' shape and constitute our identities by forming our most fundamental desires and our most basic attunement to the world. In short, liturgies make us certain kinds of people, and what defines us is what we *love*. (Smith, 2009, p. 25)

> The liturgy of the school can be similarly formative and 'real formation cannot be effected by actions that are merely episodic. There must be a rhythm and a regularity to formative practices in order for them to sink in ... directing our passion to the kingdom of God and thus disposing us to action that reflects such a desire. (Smith, 2009, p. 226)

He cites George Orwell's experience of a public school in the early twentieth century as one example of a negative 'liturgical formation' experienced in a school:

> I suppose there is no place in the world where snobbery is quite so ever-present or where it is cultivated in such refined and subtle forms as in an English public school. You forget your Latin and Greek within a few months of leaving school but your snobbishness, unless you persistently root it out like the bindweed it is, sticks by you till your grave. (Orwell, 1937, p. 128)

More positive, is this striking testimony by one of the children who contributed to the evidence base of *A Good Childhood*, 'People showed me love. So I copied them.'

The task of the Church school is therefore to examine the formational 'liturgy' or narrative it conveys as a whole and the shaping of desire that is the result and to do so beyond as well as through its formal religious life. If the desire it seeks to inculcate – for the Kingdom of God, rooted in love understood as 'commitment to others' well-being' – can feel countercultural, the task may be a daunting one. However, not to attempt it would be to depart from the raison d'etre of continuing to offer Church schools in the mainstream public system.

Many Church schools have in fact become quite sophisticated in taking seriously the narrative as a whole – the liturgy – they offer their pupils by conscious enrichment of their hidden and extended curricula as well as attending to the formal liturgy of their patterns of collective worship, learning environment and community engagement. From a Christian perspective:

> Before we articulate a worldview, we worship. Before we put into words the lineaments of an ontology or an epistemology, we pray for God's healing and illumination. Before we theorize the nature of God, we sing his praises. Before we express moral principles, we receive forgiveness. Before we codify the doctrine of Christ's two natures, we receive the body of Christ in the Eucharist. Before we think, we pray. That's the kind of animals we are, first and foremost: loving, desiring, affective, liturgical animals who for the most part, don't inhabit the world as thinkers or cognitive machines. (Smith, 2009, p. 34)

Conclusion

Church schools are not simply institutions that the Church establishes and manages from a distance. I have written elsewhere about the challenge to the Church of coming to appreciate that after 200 years its school are part of what the Church of England now *is*, not simply one of the projects it *does* (Elbourne, 2009). This is an ecclesiological issue as well as a practical and missiological one and this reflection is in its infancy.

People glimpse something of what the *whole* Church is about by the narrative/ liturgy lived out by Church schools day by day. The life and work of the Church school is seen and heard by those who know it as belonging to the mission and ministry of the Church; indeed in many cases the school is the single point of contact with the Church for those who belong to the school or have dealings with it.

I began with a brief overview of the Dearing era, which I contend is now ended, and some brief observations on the new landscape. Although the positive legacy of Dearing remains, I have pointed to some of the limitations of three of the defining concepts offered by that report and have offered three different concepts to aid that process for the current landscape. More important is that the task of theologizing about Church schools and offering them reflective tools with which to explore their purpose and identity is not one which is done once and for all, but needs to be continuous and creative and liberating of the imagination. Such a project will require resourcing and tenacity; my hope is that a commitment to this will be one of the fruits of the current bicentennial celebrations of the National Society, regardless of whether or not that body is God's chosen vessel for continuing reflection on the next era of Church schooling.

Key questions

1. What have been the key successes of the Dearing era and what hopes are as yet unfulfilled?
2. How can we develop our capacity to reflect theologically and creatively on the nature and continuing purpose of Church schools?
3. What theological concepts can robustly underpin Church schooling as a more diverse system develops?
4. How can the various Anglican trusts and bodies which exist to support Anglican education learn to work in more effective and strategic collaboration?
5. What do we mean by 'distinctiveness' when we speak of Church schools and how can we express and explore what it might mean in new ways that can inspire and enrich?

Notes

1 For example, the ceiling of 30 pupils in Infant Class Sizes.

2 The Review, chaired by Sebastian James, Group Operations Director at Dixons Retail plc, was published in April 2011 and advocated centralized design and procurement of school buildings. Since it sits somewhat opposed to the Government's professed 'localism' agenda, it remains to be seen, at the time of writing, how its recommendations will be adopted.

3 The 2011 Consultation issued *The Cambridge Declaration on Anglican Schooling*:

As Anglican school educators from across the world, we are gathered in Cambridge, UK, on the Two hundredth anniversary of the church school movement initiated by Joshua Watson.

1) We celebrate our roots and hope in the Gospel and in our Anglican identity.

2) We affirm our Anglican schools as being central to God's mission in the world.

3) We resolve to establish a worldwide network of Anglican schooling to promote our common witness.

4) We ask our bishops to affirm and strengthen the network of Anglican schools throughout our worldwide communion by prayer, encouragement and active support.

15

Conclusion

Howard J. Worsley

No movement remains static, certainly not if it is alive and effective in engaging with the society in which it operates. So it is with the current growth of Anglican Church schools in terms of their number, impact and value after two centuries of being established. This final chapter offers a reflection on the material offered to the Watson Symposium, taking a practical lens to consider implications for those involved in Church schools. At heart, most educators are intensely practical because education is all about finding new insight to effect change in the present. Therefore, this part will take the previous chapters and suggest how they might be applied in Church schools in ways that affect the personal and professional lives of staff and pupils, governors and parents, clergy and diocesan officers.

First, however, it will comment on the current context of how Church schools are often negatively perceived in contemporary culture, before inviting analysis of particular schools. Further to this it will detail the recommendations of the Watson Symposium. Finally, it will suggest a vision of how those Church schools can further develop with theological insight in the twenty-first-century education system of England and Wales:

1. objections to Church schools in current culture
2. analysis of a specific school context
3. recommendations of the Watson Symposium to Church schools
4. theological vision for Church schools in the twenty-first century.

Since the National Society was started in 1811, Church of England schools have passed through various phases from being the originators of free education for all children, to being co-partners with the state in delivering education to children and young people. The dawn of the second millennium has more recently brought with it a new optimism for Church schools with the publication of the Dearing Report (in 2001) which encouraged those schools to not only be inclusive but to be distinctively Christian. However, contemporary society continues to articulate certain objections.

Objections to Church schools in current culture

Church schools have always had factions of opposition surrounding them from their initial birth and throughout their development. Initially, the National Society under the guidance of Joshua Watson had to establish the schools as being under the particular influence of the high church and not under the control of the evangelical wing of the Church of England, nor of the dissenters. This struggle for the dominance of the Hackney Phalanx within the Established Church is detailed in the chapter 'The High Church and Evangelical Legacies to Mission in Church of England Church School Education since the Nineteenth Century' (Chapter 2). The struggle for the survival of Church schools during the nineteenth and twentieth centuries is detailed in Chapters 1 and 3 by Robert Wickham and Priscilla Chadwick respectively. Webster (1954) further records Watson's wider struggle for dominance in which he wrestled with four groups within and without the Church:

> Watson was fighting for his policy against four different enemies: against the Secularists who would banish religion from the schools, against Dissenters who either wanted their own schools or State control with undenominational Christian teaching, against those Churchmen who considered the National Society too exclusive and welcomed State assistance, and against many squires, manufacturers, farmers and parents who objected to the increasing cost of education in any form. (p. 41)

Today the objections to Church schools are very different in that the battle for widespread education has been won and the competition with other denominations or faiths is no longer the battle place it was. Although there still remain sceptics of Church schools found within the Church of England or the free churches, the most vehement and widespread opposition is linked around the notion that twenty-first-century society is secular and, if not secular, then pluralist. This is detailed in Chapter 10 by Trevor Cooling. In response to T. S. Eliot's *The Idea of a Christian Society* written in 1939, the economist theologian D. Munby wrote *The Idea of a Secular Society* in 1963 in which he identified six marks of a secular society, all of which he deems to be contrary to the way a Church school operates.

Munby describes secular society as being one that

1. refuses to commit itself to any particular view of the nature of the universe
2. is pluralist
3. is tolerant
4. operates by minimum structure
5. solves problems by examining empirical facts
6. has no official images.

While these objections can be challenged and shown to be far more tribal and ideological (by writers like Grace Davie and her work in *Religion in Modern Europe: A Memory Mutates* (2000)), they have remained in the popular psyche and reappear in populist debates concerning Church schools, deeming them to be inadequate for current society. The Canadian philosopher of education, Elmer Thiessen, develops the argument by articulating his own catalogue of seven more recent objections to the idea of a Christian university in his article so titled of 2004. They surround the issues of:

- tradition and particularity
- liberation and free enquiry
- relativism and the battle for truth
- academic freedom
- indoctrination
- the question of the possibility of Christian Scholarship
- tolerance and social cohesion.

In these he details how a twenty-first-century society deeply mistrusts the intentions of a faith tradition which offers education and is suspicious of its ability to be professional or open in finding a pathway for the future.

If the combined condemnation of creeping secularization or of pluralism is not sufficiently damning, the alternative objection is simply that Church schools make no practical difference at all (as Leslie J. Francis suggests in Chapter 8 and Helen Everett in Chapter 12) – they are merely a bland residue left over from a previous age. Clearly, this argument is entirely the opposite to the former one in that Church schools cannot be both dangerously contrary to current secular society and also irrelevant at the same time.

To refute these objections, I could draw on a similar rhetorical style of argument and reference Baron Friedrich Von Hügel from the twentieth century (1908) who spoke of Christian education being holistic, without a secular/sacred divide, and one that offers balance between the authority of past tradition and openness to a new age, but this would keep the debate at an ideological level. In this vein is the more recent work of the educational theologians Andrew Walker and Andrew Wright, who joined forces to write a defence for the concept of a Christian university in 2004 by drawing on the classical Greek notion of Paideia – the formative task of transmitting a cultural heritage to school which adds virtue and cultivates character. The defence is well offered in different contexts, namely in Wales (Lankshear, Chapter 4) through learning (Cooling in Chapter 10) through philosophy and theology (Walsh in Chapter 5, Astley in Chapter 6, Terry in Chapter 7, Brown in Chapter 9 and Wright in Chapter 11) and through aspiration (Stern in Chapter 13 and Elbourne in Chapter 14).

Analysis of your school context

In order to focus reflection onto the particular context of a given school, it is useful to use the tool of the 'pastoral cycle'. This is very simply a staged process of focusing on one issue or one context and pursuing a sequence of evaluation which enables a development in both thought and action.

The reflection could be on anything from the purpose of church school education, the content or delivery of the curriculum in the school, the degree of community cohesion, to the specific leadership or governance of a given school.

In the context of leading a particular Church school, the pastoral cycle determines that you start from current experience. The first stage is to reflect on the current experience of leadership in that school, the second is to analyse the experience, the third is to consider that analysis via a theological lens and the fourth is to proceed to action which is informed by the previous reflection, analysis and thought. The cycle can then be repeated.

For further reading as to how this is applied, Bishop Laurie Green offers many examples in his seminal book, *Let's Do Theology* (2009).

To help in understanding the initial experience (in this example of leading a Church school), it is of value to have an understanding of the model of the Church school. Models of school need not only be technical descriptions (e.g. VA, VC, Academy, Foundation, Federated), nor geographic descriptions (e.g. rural, urban), nor be concerned with size but may be more visual and non-technical as suggested in the depictions overleaf. Those who think visually can interpret such

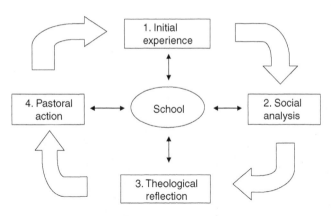

Figure 15.1 Pastoral cycle

models to mean that if the Church school is like a tent, it is fragile but flexible; if it is like a marquee it is more stable and imposing but still transitional; if it is like a house it is like a home where pupils are safe and nurtured; if it is like a castle, it has a long and imposing tradition that is not easily changed. It may be difficult to get admission. If it is like a supermarket, the school embodies the consumerist culture, but delivers what is wanted; if it is like a leisure centre, it is a place of holistic enterprise and where people want to be. If it is like a church, it is where Christian teaching is offered and values are lived out in a worshipping community; and if it is like a hospital, it exists for those who are most in need. (Other models can be offered, for example, a lighthouse, a windmill, the Houses of Parliament, the O2 Arena, a football stadium.) If this book is being used to enable reflection in a given context (such as a governors' training event or a staff away day), these visual models can be used as a discussion starter in the initial task of analysing what the school is like now and what it is intended that the school becomes in the future.

The pastoral cycle (from the previous page) details the movement of reflection as the school experience is examined more closely.

Recommendations of the Watson Symposium to Church schools

Taking the chapters one by one, recommendations are now offered based on each of the symposium writers' insights.

Part	Chapter	Recommendations for church school leaders	Recommendations for church school authorities
I: The Historical Story	1. The Political Theology of Joshua Watson (Joshua Watson and his understanding of Church/State relations) by Robert Wickham	Become familiar with the theologically reflected politics that enabled Church schools to be initially founded Are encouraged by the historic influence of lay movements in the Church	Recover confidence in focusing education for the poor Recover confidence in speaking to government
	2. High Church and Evangelical Legacies to Mission in Church Schools (the ecclesiastic struggle for mission in schools since the nineteenth century) by Howard J. Worsley	Foster non-partisan church links with schools Draw on both high church inclusivity and low church enthusiasm in forming distinctively Christian ethos	Offer guidance as to how Church schools might nurture young people in the Christian faith Think theologically in focusing mission on the poor
	3. Conflict and Consensus in the Dual System (Anglican schools through the twentieth century) by Priscilla Chadwick	Are encouraged by Anglicanism's partnership with government in education. Work in an increasingly collaborative way as current resources reduce	Create a clear long-term Church of England strategy for schools Develop a better understanding of Church schools (legal frameworks and funding) in parliament and in the DfE
	4. Anglican Education in Wales (serving Christ through education in Wales) by David W. Lankshear	Replicate how the Anglican Church in Wales has tested the outcome of 'Serving Christ through Education' Develop strong links with the local parish church	Are mindful of the wider context of Wales Use research to drive outcomes in education
II: Current Policy and Philosophy	5. Philosophy, Theology and the Christian School by Paddy Walsh	Create a curriculum that enables students to respond to the call of Christ Cultivate historical sensibility in students	Apply the insights of philosophy as well as theology in creating school policy Focus on the dignity of personhood in education

	6. Church Schools and the Church's Service to the Poor by Jeff Astley	Build school communities that benefit young people both spiritually and materially	Resist the historical trend of gentrification within education
		Invest in 'social capital' and in 'spiritual capital'	Beware the current commodification of education and implement a preferential option for the poor
	7. Church schools and Anglican identity (Anglican schools seen in the context of Anglicanism) by Ian Terry	Draw on Anglican heritage by deeper connection with the parish church	Embrace the legacy of critical partnership with the State
		Draw on Anglican heritage by encouraging diversity of belief	Make 'Trinitarian relationships the heart of education and spirituality'
	8. Pupil Voice in Anglican Secondary Schools (the ethos of Anglican secondary schools reflected through pupil values: an empirical enquiry among 13–15-year-olds) by Leslie J. Francis and Gemma Penny	Listen to the voice of their pupils	Note the current negligible impact of Anglican ethos on adolescent values
		Reflect on how to be more effective in influencing adolescent religious attitude	Use empirical enquiry to find out what Church schools are actually like
III: Reflection on Current Practice	9. The Church Schools as 'Safe' School (stepping stones to inclusion and imagination) by Alan Brown	Be inclusive of wide religious exploration	Beware of religious radicalism as a threat to 'safe place'
		Allow the school to be 'a stepping stone' to and from the local community	Encourage Church schools to be places of enquiry and openness
	10. The Distinctiveness of Christian Learning in Church of England Schools by Trevor Cooling	Learn to 'think faithfully' as Christians	Identify 'distinctively Christian learning' for church school education
		Consider the value of 'What If Learning' for Christian pedagogy	Adopt a distinctively Christian approach to the curriculum
	11. Church School Ministry as Contextual Theology by Andy Wright	Become more aware of theological relativism	Create a policy whereby Church schools teach and nurture the nation's children in the Christian faith
		Draw on the Anglican Communion as a model of engagement with culture	Offer the vision that the Church can yet transform the nation through a holistic mission of social service and evangelism

(Continued)

Part	Chapter	Recommendations for church school leaders	Recommendations for church school authorities
Part IV: Instrumental in Shaping the Future	12. Can Church Schools Promote Tolerance in the Twenty-First Century? by Helen Everett	Lead their school to be 'a beacon of excellence in promoting tolerance'	Encourage faith schools to be proactive in promoting tolerance
		Create opportunities for students to examine faith critically within a 'lived faith' environment	Demonstrate faith to be a resource (not a hindrance) by wider empiric research
	13. What Must Church Schools Do to Live up to Their Rhetoric? by Julian Stern	Investigate (and become aware of) the rhetoric of their school	Research both the rhetoric and lived reality of Church schools
		Encourage sincerity	Provide guidelines as to how schools can live up to the 'inclusive service' rhetoric as well as the 'mission' rhetoric
	14. Church School Identity Beyond the Dearing Era (context and change) by Tim Elbourne	Develop school policy using the concepts of 'Rootedness', 'Belonging' and 'Narrative' to develop Christian distinctiveness and inclusiveness	Offer theological critique of government schooling policies and their underlying ideological suppositions
		Reflect on the nature and purpose of Anglican schooling in a changing culture	Identify a vision for Church schools in the post-Dearing era

Recommendations are divided between those offered to church school leaders and those offered to church school authorities. The former are considered to be headteachers and staff for whom the research will have personal and practical implications. The latter are considered to be National and DBEs and school governing bodies for whom the research will have strategic and professional implications. Undoubtedly there will be considerable overlap in these categories.

Theological vision for Church schools in the twenty-first century

As a summative reflection, following on from an overview of objections to Church schools, a focus on a particular school and the compilation of 56 recommendations from 14 research articles, a theological vision for Church schools is now offered. This takes the form of 3 models, each derived from the wider Christian narrative. These themes are reflected in some of the previous chapters.

- Church school as family
- Church school as meeting place
- Church school as threshold place.

The Church school as family

In his book, *Politics, Theology and History* (2001), Raymond Plant speaks of a 'hotel' model, rather than a 'family model' of organization being used in a secular university. Such an institution insists that all faiths are permitted as long as the host organization is ideologically free, creating a public zone within which private beliefs might exist. This line of thinking draws on the eighteenth-century enlightenment thinking of John Locke (as developed by John Stuart Mill) who argued that the state tolerates diversity in the private realm as long as it does not undermine the conditions in the public realm.

Therefore, the hotel model insists on neutrality in the public space so that individuals can behave as they wish in the privacy of their own rooms. While this seems entirely plausible in a hotel, in educational circles it creates a vacuum dominated by a language of political correctness when issues of personal difference take place. It also allows a culture to breed which values individualism, personal desires and customized needs which are met within an atmosphere of accepted consumerism and market forces.

By contrast, I wish to argue for a family model where expectations of shared values, cultures and faith are all out in the open as being key features of the host organization.

To take this further, and to reflect other stated objections to the Church school, it is the family environment that is conceivably the most open and safe place in which to learn, because it is a place of love. Where love exists and the individual is accepted with all their differences, gifts and foibles, then there is the potential for growth. The zone of learning is, of course, protected by the framework of the family, its traditions and its hopes.

This model of family must be understood as being neither narrowly nuclear and tribal nor with a dominant patriarchy or matriarchy. It is an open extended family which has got the security of normative reflected culture and the openness of incorporating new customs. Such a model of family draws more from the traditions of the Old Testament hospitality laws than from the recent tribal formulation commonly referred to in the West.

The Church school as family can draw on tradition not only for the sake of future transmission, but in order to learn from the failings of the past. The Christian faith is one of significant complexity that has a literature base which bluntly shows human error, failure, restitution and healing, so in a Church school it is the narrative of repentance, forgiveness and new starts that can flow through an understanding of the school's structures and practices.

To fail to draw on the deep veins of cultural learning that come from the embedded story held in the family would be to ignore the ancient wisdom of a previous generation. The Church school as family is the place where former knowledge is adopted into a new culture. It is, of course, not a place to be dominated by ancient certainties nor to be manipulated by new fads.

It is in the arms of the nurturing family of the Church school that children of the Christian faith can be expected to explore, challenge and own their faith, in the context of children of other faiths and of no faith. Similarly, those from other faith traditions or from homes that are more secular can learn in the contextual awareness of the Christian faith, knowing it is not proselytizing but nurturing them as world citizens.

The model of family fits readily within the model of 'Church as sacramental', as analysed by the ecclesiastical sociologist Avery Dulles in 1974. This is reflected on at some length by the Catholic educationalist O'Brien in his book *The Idea of a Catholic University* (2002) because it is the sacraments that hold the church together, even as mealtimes and key events preserve a family's sense of unity. The sacrament of Holy Communion is not seen as an unusual celebration any more than is a special meal within a family, and the celebration of Christmas, like a birthday celebrated at home, is an explicit re-enactment on an ongoing relationship.

Another valuable aspect of a functional family is its ability to reflect on its lived memory and its previous history in order to make sure of its present and future. In encountering the long list of objections to Christianity as an educational sponsor (listed earlier by Thiessen (2004)), it is hugely important to emphasize this aspect of the need to reflect on history. Christianity is clearly a religion with an ideology and with a flawed history and these are both present in the canons of scripture as well as in the long-term and short-term histories of faith expression across the world. It is Christianity's ability to reflect on its historic perpetuation of slavery and patriarchal oppression and its current ambiguity towards homosexuality and the free market that actually qualifies it to offer academic freedom and the pursuit of free enquiry. It is a case study of an institution learning to be relevant to the evolution of society. For the emergent child, the freedom to think within the cultural context of the family is what allows new learning to take place.

To further explore the vision of Church school as family, it is important to disassociate it from not only the exclusiveness of the nuclear family, but also from the notion of tribalism. In his book, *Belonging: Challenge to a Tribal Church* (1994), Bishop Peter Selby says, 'Human groups and communities cannot avoid creating a boundary around themselves and seeking their identity at the expense of those who are not members' (p. 23). In qualifying this human observation as regards the Church, he says, 'The Church, however, is not an ethnic community: it is required to assume always that the stranger may be an angel of God, bearing some new word or some new gift' (p. 43). When this is explored in relationship to Church schools, the notion of Church school as meeting place can be identified.

The Church school as meeting place

The concept of a Bedouin tent of meeting has been seized upon by St Ethelburga's in the city of London. This church established a place of dialogue after the church was devastated by an IRA bomb in 1993. It is a place where people of different perspectives, convictions and ideas can meet to find their common ground.

The idea was borrowed from the nomadic tribes who wander in the Sahara seeking to make sacred that place where they pitched tent. They would find an oasis and make that a sacred space for the period of their encampment, and it was a place of hospitality, welcome and respectful engagement, following the code of the Bedouin family.

Reflecting on this tent of meeting now erected in the grounds of St Ethelburga's, as a symbol of reconciliation and peace for groups to get involved with interfaith dialogue, Trevor Cooling (2010b) sees it to be a place that is sacred and mutual, but not neutral. In other words, the desert of the city has found itself an oasis, but it is one where the host community is not neutral to its own Christian values while being genuinely open to the free expression of engagement with the values of other faiths.

Cooling is clear that education must be transparent about its purpose and that the purpose is never neutral. Whether it is religious or secular, the rationale behind education needs to be explicit. To illustrate this he quotes the evocative letter purported to have been written by a holocaust survivor who wrote to the United Nations about the importance of studying history.

> Dear Teacher,
>
> I am a survivor of a concentration camp. My eyes saw what no man should witness: Gas chambers built by learned engineers; children poisoned by educated physicians; infants killed by trained nurses; women and babies shot by high school graduates; so I am suspicious of education.
>
> My request is: help your students to become human. Your efforts must never produce learned monsters, skilled psychopaths, educated Eichmanns.
>
> Reading, writing and arithmetic are important only if they serve to make our children more human. (2010a, pp. 13–14)

As a meeting place, the Church school is clear about its Christian ethos as a place from which it derives its values. It draws on a deeply embedded culture of hospitality taken from ancient Jewish laws that order the edges of the fields to remain unharvested, so that the stranger can glean (Ruth 1) and that allowed for the host to expect a blessing in the act of welcoming a traveller. This is supremely noted of Abraham (in Genesis 18) who offered an act of hospitality on the occasion when he was promised the gift of a son, and inferentially the survival of his name and the establishment of Israel as a nation.

> The Lord appeared to Abraham at the sacred trees of Mamre. As Abraham was sitting at the entrance of his tent during the hottest part of the day, he

looked up and saw three men standing there. As soon as he saw them, he ran out to meet them. Bowing down with his face touching the ground he said, 'Sirs, please do not pass by my home without stopping; I am here to serve you. Let me bring some water for you to wash your feet, you can rest here beneath this tree. I will also bring a bit of food; it will give you strength to continue your journey. You have honoured me by coming to my home, so let me serve you.' They replied, 'Thank you, we accept.' (Genesis 18.1–5, Good News Bible)

The early Church generally understood this meeting to be the occasion when Abraham met with the triune God as became famously depicted in Rublev's icon.

The Church of England's engagement in interfaith dialogue expects a broader perspective to emerge as a result of such hospitable relationships. It will not wish to polarize debates after terrorist attacks, but to seek to understand, almost as a form of faith seeking understanding.

The network of Church schools is a fine place to continue this practice of hospitality and of open tolerance. Interestingly, it is well known to the Association of Diocesan Directors of Education that Muslims looking for school places for their children tend to be far more content with Anglican provision than with the more neutral community schools on offer because they are places that accept the premise of faith as being foundational.

In its role as meeting place, the Church school operates at the boundaries of church and society, neither completely the tool of the church nor the instrument of government. It is a transitional place of contact reflecting both the outreach interests of church and the institutional edicts of government, yet to some extent critiquing both, and maintaining the tension of healthy dialogue. It is at this place that learning occurs because transition takes place alongside learning. This gives rise to the notion of the Church school as a threshold place.

The Church school as threshold

The Latin word for threshold is *limen*, denoting the bottom part of a doorway that must be crossed when entering a building. Any transition into the building will entail the movement prior to the threshold, the actual movement of crossing from outside to inside and the final movement on the other side of the threshold. These three stages have been reflected upon by the anthropologist Arnold Van

Gennep in his influential book titled *Rites of Passage*. In this he noted that rites of passage, such as coming-of-age rituals and marriage all have a three-part structure:

1. separation
2. luminal period
3. reassimilation.

The person undergoing the ritual is first stripped of the social status that he or she possessed before the rituals, inducted into the liminal period of transition, and finally given his or her new status and reassimilated into society.

Van Gennep's work can be developed to describe communities that are 'betwixt and between' and might be used to view a Church school as being a marginal community.

This metaphor has been picked up by Jeff Astley (2002) in relation to Church schools, where he notes that the Church school neither offers the characteristics of tribal church nor the hallmarks of institutional government. The Church school is not merely about the Church's influence in finding a new generation of people to boost its own membership, but offers a threshold of free entry and free exit. People can travel in either direction. At the threshold, assumptions are not made about membership to the tribe and nor is there any subtle pressure made for people to join.

Astley further cites a French catechetical scholar, Jean Boutellier, who describes people on the edge of church life as 'threshold Christians'. He wrote:

> Church is still visited, frequented, questioned, explored, loved, criticised by a crowd of people who call themselves more of less Christians. . . . many encamped at the Church's doors are willing to be recognised as being of the church and to be linked to it, but they are very hesitant about being recognised as being integrally within the Church. (1979, pp. 65–80)

In the same way, the Church school is a place where people with a religious worldview and people without such reference can reposition themselves and rub shoulders. Clearly the Church school maintains the historic compass point by offering a Christian framework but it is one that is open and hospitable.

If it is possible to use the threshold metaphor to operate as an exit as well as an entrance to a new state of being, it becomes even more interesting. In a post-modern world of flux, the threshold positioning of the Church school is attractive to those seeking understanding of the Christian narrative and it is a place of comfort and challenge for those moving away from Christian thinking.

To the one it adds an engaged and contextualized expression of the Christian faith to enable a way in. To the other, it allows for a relevant relationship as they depart from the structures of faith. The school as a threshold place allows for those on the edges to transit in various directions.

And from the aspect of education, which is the context of any school, movement across threshold is an ongoing process for the learning person.

Bibliography

Adie, M. (1990) 'Restoring Responsibility'. *Education* 14 December.

Ajegbo, K. (2007) *Curriculum Review: Diversity and Citizenship.* London: DfS.

Allen, R. and West, A. (2009) 'Religious Schools in London: School Admissions, Religious Composition and Selectivity?' *Oxford Review of Education* 35 (4), 471–94.

Allport, G. W. (1954) *The Nature of Prejudice.* Reading, MA: Addison-Wesley.

Anderson, D. S. (1971) 'Do Catholic Schools Cause People to Go to Church?' *Australian and New Zealand Journal of Sociology* 7, 65–7.

Anderson, D. S. and Western, J. S. (1972) 'Denominational Schooling and Religious Behaviour'. *Australian and New Zealand Journal of Sociology* 8, 19–31.

Anderson, G. (1961) *The Theology of Mission.* London: McGraw-Hill Books.

Archbishop's Council (1985) *Faith in the City.* London: Church House Publishing.

— (2004) *Mission Shaped Church.* London: Church House Publishing.

— (2010) *Going for Growth.* London: Church House Publishing.

Archer, M. S., Collier, A. and Porpora, D. V. (2004) *Transcendence: Critical Realism and God.* London: Routledge.

Aristotle (1976) *Nichomachean Ethics.* London: Penguin.

— (1984) *The Complete Works of Aristotle: The Revised Oxford Translation:* Edited by J. Barnes. Princeton, NJ: Princeton University Press.

Arthur, J. (2003) *Education with Character: The Moral Economy of Schooling.* London: RoutledgeFalmer.

— (2006) *Faith and Secularisation in Religious Colleges and Universities.* London: RoutledgeFalmer.

— (ed.) (2010a) *Citizens of Character: New Directions in Character and Values Education.* Exeter: Imprint-academic.

— (ed.) (2010b) *Of Good Character: Exploration of Virtues and Values in 3–25 Year Olds.* Exeter: Imprint-Academic.

Astley, J. (1992) 'Growing into Christ: The Psychology and Politics of Christian Maturity', in J. Astley and D. Day (eds), *The Contours of Christian Education.* Great Wakering: McCrimmons.

— (1994) *The Philosophy of Christian Religious Education.* Birmingham, AL: Religious Education Press.

— (1996) 'The Role of Worship in Christian Learning', in J. Astley, L. J. Francis and C. Crowder (eds), *Theological Perspectives on Christian Formation: A Reader on Theology and Christian Education.* Leominster: Gracewing Fowler Wright; Grand Rapids, MI: Eerdmans.

— (1998) 'Christian Values and the Management of Schools', in W. K. Kay and
   L. J. Francis (eds), *Religion in Education 2*. Leominster: Gracewing.
— (2002) 'Church, Schools and the Theology of Christian Education'. *Journal of the
   Association of Anglican Secondary School Heads* 10.
— (2005) 'Religious Schooling and the Challenge of the Poor'. *Journal of Empirical
   Theology* 18 (1), 41–7.
Astley, J., Francis, L. J., Sullivan J. and Walker, A. (eds) (2004) *The Idea of a Christian
   University*. Paternoster: Milton Keynes.
Audit Commission (1991) *Home to School Transport: A System at the Cross Roads*.
   London: HMSO.
Avis, P. (1989) *Anglicanism and the Christian Church*. London: T&T Clark.
— (2000) *The Anglican Understanding of the Church*. London: SPCK.
Bailey, J. (2002) 'Religious Education in Church Schools', in L. Broadbent and A. Brown
   (eds), *Issues in Religious Education*. London: RoutledgeFalmer.
Baker, K. (1993) *The Turbulent Years*. London: Faber.
Baker, L. (2002) *Lords Hansard* Volume 632, Part No. 103 Columns 560–2, 11 March.
Barker, R. and Anderson, J. (2005) 'Segregation or Cohesion', in R. Gardner, D. Lawton
   and J. Cairns (eds), *Faith Schools: Consensus or Conflict?* London: RoutledgeFalmer.
Bayes, J. (1994) *William Wilberforce: His Impact on Nineteenth Century Society*,
   Churchman 108/2.
BBC (2011) 'Bishop: "Cut Priority School Places for Churchgoers"'. www.bbc.co/news/
   education-13158380 (accessed 22 April 2011).
Beeson, T. (1999) *Rebels and Reformers, Christian Renewal in the Twentieth Century*.
   London: SCM.
Bell, D. (2005) 'What Does It Mean to Be a Citizen?' *Guardian* 17 January. (Online)
   Available at www.guardian.co.uk/education/2005/jan/17/faithschools.schools
   (accessed 19 November 2008).
Bennett, C. (2005) *Muslims and Modernity: An Introduction to the Issues and Debates*.
   New York: Continuum.
Berkeley, R. (2008) *Right to Divide? Faith Schools and Community Cohesion* (Online)
   Available at www.runnymedetrust.org/uploads/publications/Summaries/
   RighToDivide-Summary.pdf
Bethge, E. (1985) *Dietrich Bonhoeffer*. London: Fount.
Bevans, S. B. (1992) *Models of Contextual Theology*. Maryknoll, NY: Orbis.
Bicknell, E. J. (1955) *A Theological Introduction to the Thirty-Nine Articles of the Church
   of England*, 3rd edn rev. H. J. Carpenter. London: Longmans, Green & Co.
Biggar (2009) *Religious Voices in Public Places*. Oxford: Oxford University Press.
Birmingham Agreed Syllabus of Religious Education. www.birmingham-asc.org.uk/
   agreedsyl1.php (accessed 22 September 2011).
Blackburn Diocesan Board of Education (1994) *Going Grant Maintained?* Blackburn: DBE.
Bobo, L. and Licari, F. C. (1989) 'Education and Political Tolerance: Testing the Effect of
   Sophistication and Target Group Effects'. *Public Opinion Quarterly* 53 (5), 285–308.

Bosch, D. (1994) *Transforming Mission.* Orbis: New York.

Bottery, M. (1990) *The Morality of the School: The Theory and Practice of Values in Education.* London: Cassell.

— (1992) *Ethics of Educational Management: Personal, Social and Political Perspectives on School Organization.* London: Cassell.

Boutellier, J. (1979) 'Threshold Christians: A Challenge for the Church', in W. J. Reedy (ed.), *Becoming a Catholic Christian.* New York: Sadlier, pp. 65–80.

Bradley, I. (1993) *The Celtic Way.* London: DLT.

— (1999) *Celtic Christianity.* Edinburgh: Edinburgh University Press.

Bragg, M. (2011) *The Book of Books: The Radical Impact of the King James Bible 1611–2011.* London: Hodder & Stoughton.

Bretherton, L. (2009) *Hospitality as Holiness.* Aldershot: Ashgate.

— (2010) 'Big Society and the Church'. *The Guardian,* 7 October.

Bridges, D. and Husbands, C. (eds) (1995) *Consorting and Collaborating in the Education Market Place.* London: Falmer.

Bridges, D. and McLaughlin, T. H. (eds) (1994) *Education and the Market Place.* London: RoutledgeFalmer.

Brierley, P. (2000) *The Tide Is Running Out.* London: Christian Research.

— (2006) *Pulling Out of the Nose Dive.* London: Christian Research.

Brothers, J. (1964) *Church and School: A Study of the Impact of Education on Religion.* Liverpool: University of Liverpool Press.

Brown, A. (1987) *Religious Education and the Pupil with Learning Difficulties.* Cambridge: Cambridge University Press.

— (1992) *The Multi-Faith Church School.* London: National Society.

— (1997) *Secondary School Inspections.* London: National Society.

— (2002) 'The Statutory Requirements for Religious Education 1988–2001: Religious, Political and Social Influences', in L. Broadbent and A. Brown (eds), *Issues in Religious Education.* London: RoutledgeFalmer.

— (2003) 'Church of England Schools: Politics, Power and Identity'. *British Journal of Religious Education* 25 (2), 103–16.

— (2011) *Reassessing the Culture of Assessment: Weighing Pigs Does Not Make Them Heavier.* Grove: Cambridge.

Brown, A. and Lankshear, D. W. (1995) *Inspection Handbook: for Section Thirteen Inspections in Schools of the Church of England and the Church in Wales.* London: National Society.

Brown, C. K. (1942) *The Churches Part in Education 1833–1941.* London: SPCK.

Brown, S. (2001) *The National Churches of England, Ireland and Scotland 1801–1846.* Oxford: Oxford University Press.

Bryk, A. S., Lee, V. E. and Holland, P. B. (1993) *Catholic Schools and the Common Good.* Cambridge, MA: Harvard University Press.

Burgess, H. (1958) *Enterprise in Education.* London: SPCK.

Burns, A. (2000) 'Whigs and Revolutionaries', in H. Chadwick (ed.), *Not Angels, but Anglicans.* Norwich: SCM Canterbury Press, pp. 200–1.

Butler, R. A. B. (1971) *The Art of the Possible*. London: Hamish Hamilton.

— (1982) *The Art of Memory*. London: Hodder & Stoughton.

Callan, E. (1985) 'McLaughlin on Parental Rights'. *Journal of Philosophy of Education* 19 (1), 111–18.

Cantle, T. (2001) *Community Cohesion: A Report of the Independent Review Team*. London: Home Office.

Carey, G., Hope, D. and Hall, J. (1998) *A Christian Voice in Education: Distinctiveness in Church Schools*. London: National Society.

Carpenter, E. (1991) *Archbishop Fisher*. Norwich: Canterbury Press.

Casson, A. E. (2011) 'Perceptions of Catholicity in a Plural Society: An Ethnographic Case Study of Catholic Secondary Schools in England'. Ph.D. dissertation, University of Warwick.

Catholic Education Service (CES) (1997) *The Common Good in Education*. London: Catholic Education Service.

Cavanaugh (2004) 'Church', in Scott and Cavanaugh (eds), *The Blackwell Companion to Political Theology*. Oxford: Blackwell.

Chadwick, P. (1994) *Schools of Reconciliation: Issues in Joint Roman Catholic-Anglican Education*. London: Cassell.

— (1997) *Shifting Alliances (Church and State in English Education)*. London: Cassell.

Churton, E. (1855) *The Gifts of God to the Good*. Oxford: Rivington.

— (1861) (and 1963) *Memoir of Joshua Watson*, 2 vols. Oxford: JH Parker.

Cochrane, C. N. (1944) *Christianity and Classical Culture*. Oxford: University of Oxford Press.

Coleman, J. S. and Hoffer, T. (1987) *Public and Private High Schools: The Impact of Communities*. New York: Basic Books.

Coleridge, S. T. (1830) (1972) *On the Constitution of the Church and the State*. London: JM Dent and Sons.

Congregation for Catholic Education (2007) *Educating Together in Catholic Schools: A Shared Mission Between Consecrated Persons and the Lay Faithful* (Rome).

Conroy, J. C. (2004) *Betwixt and Between*. Oxford: Peter Lang.

Cooling, T. (2005) 'Curiosity: Vice or Virtue for the Christian Teacher? Promoting Faithfulness to Scripture in Teacher Formation'. *Journal of Education and Christian Belief* 9 (2), 87–104.

— (2010a). *Called to Teach: Teaching as a Mission Vocation*. Cambridge: Grove Books.

— (2010b) *Doing God in Education*. London: Theos.

— (2010c) 'Transforming Faith: Teaching as a Christian Vocation in a Secular, Worldview-Diverse Culture'. *Journal of Education and Christian Belief* 14 (1), 19–32.

— (2011) '*Is God Redundant in the Classroom?*' 9 June. www.canterbury.ac.uk/ education/nicer/ (accessed 22 September 2011).

Copley, T. (1999) *Teaching Religion: Fifty Years of Religious Education in England and Wales*. Exeter: University of Exeter Press.

Copson, A. and Norman, R. (2011) *Trevor Cooling, Education and Doing God*. London: British Humanist Association.

Cox, J. (2011) *Beyond Caring and Sharing*. Stowmarket: Kevin Mayhew.

Creppell, I. (2003) *Toleration and Identity: Foundations in Early Modern Thought*. New York, London: Routledge.

Crick, R. D. (2002) *Transforming Visions: Managing Values in Schools*. London: Middlesex University Press.

Cruickshank, M. (1963) *Church and State in English Education*. London: Macmillan.

Cupitt, D. (1980) *Taking Leave of God*. London: SCM.

D'Costa, G. (2005) *Theology in the Public Square: Church, Academy and Nation*. Oxford: Blackwell.

Daniels, H. (2001) *Vygotsky and Pedagogy*. London: RoutledgeFalmer.

Davie, G. (2000) *Religion in Modern Europe: A Memory Mutates*. Oxford: Oxford University Press.

Davies, L. (2008) *Educating against Extremism*. Stoke-on-Trent: Trentham.

DCSF (2010) *Working Together to Safeguard Children*. London: DCSF.

de Botton, A. (2004) *Status Anxiety*. London: Hamish Hamilton.

de Witte, H. (1999) 'Everyday Racism in Belgium. An Overview of the Research and an Interpretation of Its Links with Education', in L. Hagendoorn and S. Nekuee (eds), *Education and Racism: A Cross National Inventory of Positive Effects of Education on Ethnic Tolerance*. Aldershot: Ashgate.

Dearing, R. (2001) *The Way Ahead*. London: Church House Publishing.

Dennis, N. (2001) *The Uncertain Trumpet*. Trowbridge: Cromwell Press.

Dennis, R. (1984) *English Industrial Cities of the Nineteenth Century*. Cambridge: Cambridge University Press.

Dewey, J. (1916) *Democracy and Education. An introduction to the Philosophy of Education*. New York: Free Press.

DfE (2010) *The Importance of Teaching*. London: HMSO.

DfEE (1997) *Excellence in Schools*. London: Stationery Office.

DfES (2003) *Every Child Matters*. London: DCSF.

Dika, S. L. and Singh, K. (2002) 'Application of Social Capital in Educational Literature: A Critical Synthesis'. *Review of Educational Research* 72 (1), 31–60.

Dixon, J., Durrheim, K. and Tredoux, C. (2005) 'Beyond the Optimal Contact Strategy: A Reality Check for the Contact Hypothesis'. *American Psychologist* 60 (7), 697–711.

Donnelly, C. and Hughes, J. (2006) 'Contact, Culture and Context: Evidence from Mixed Race Faith Schools in Northern Ireland and Israel'. *Comparative Education* 42 (4), 493–516.

Driel, B. V. (2004) *Confronting Islamophobia in Educational Practice*. Stoke-on-Trent: Trentham.

Dronker, J. (2004) 'Do Public and Religious Schools Really Differ?' in P. J. Wolf and S. Macedo (eds), *Educating Citizens: International Perspectives on Civic Values and School Choice*. Washington, DC: Brookings Institution Press.

Dulles, A. (1974) *Models of the Church*. Dublin: Gill & Macmillan.

Duncan, G. (1990) *The Church School*. London: National Society.

Durham Report (1970) *The Fourth R: The Report of the Commission on Religious Education in Schools.* London: National Society and SPCK.

Durka, G. (2002) *The Teacher's Calling – A Spirituality for Those Who Teach.* Mahwah, NJ: Paulist Press.

Elbourne, T. (2009) *Church Schools: A Mission Shaped Vision.* Grove: Cambridge.

Eliot, T. S. (ed.) (1982) *The Idea of a Christian Society* (2nd edn). London: Faber and Faber.

Ellison, M. and Herbert, C. (1983) *Listening to Children: Fresh Approaches to Religious Education in the Primary School.* London: CIO Publishing.

Erricker, C. (2010) *Religious Education.* London: Routledge.

Erricker, C. and Erricker, J. (2000) 'The Children and Worldviews Project: A Narrative Pedagogy of Religious Education', in M. Grimmitt (ed.), *Pedagogies of Religious Education.* Great Wakening, Essex: McCrimmons.

Erricker, C. and Erricker, J., Ota, C., Sullivan, D. and Fletcher, M. (1997) *The Education of the Whole Child.* London: Cassell.

Erricker, C., Lowndes, J. and Bellchambers, E. (2011) *Primary Religious Education: A New Approach.* London: Routledge.

Ertman, T. (2010) 'The Great Reform Act of 1832 and British Democratization'. *Comparative Political Studies* 43 (8/9), 1000–22.

Esack, F. (2005) *The Qur'an: A User's Guide.* Oxford: Oneworld.

Everett, H. (2011) 'The Effect of Faith Schools on Their Students' Attitudes of Tolerance'. Unpublished Ph.D. dissertation, University of London, London.

Fahy, P. S. (1976) 'School and Home Perceptions of Australian Adolescent Males Attending Catholic Schools'. *Our Apostolate* 24, 167–88.

— (1978) 'Religious Beliefs of 15,900 Youths: Attending Australian Catholic Schools, Years 12, 10, 8, 1975–7'. *Word in Life* 2, 66–72.

— (1980a) 'The Effectiveness on Christian Criteria of 17 Australian Catholic High Schools'. Unpublished Ph.D. dissertation, Boston College, Massachusetts.

— (1980b) 'The Religious Effectiveness of Some Australian Catholic High Schools'. *Word in Life* 28, 86–98.

Fergussen (2004) *Church, State and Civil Society.* Cambridge: Cambridge University Press.

Field, J. (2003) *Social Capital.* London: Routledge.

Fisher, J. W. (2000) 'Being Human, Becoming Whole: Understanding Spiritual Health and Well-Being'. *Journal of Christian Education* 43, 35–52.

— (2001) 'Comparing Levels of Spiritual Well-Being in State, Catholic and Independent Schools in Victoria, Australia'. *Journal of Beliefs and Values* 22, 99–105.

— (2004) 'Feeling Good, Living Life: A Spiritual Health Measure for Young Children'. *Journal of Beliefs and Values* 25, 307–15.

Flannery, A. (1981) *Vatican Council II: The Conciliar and Post-Conciliar Documents.* Leominster: Fowler Wright.

Flynn, M. F. (1975) *Some Catholic Schools in Action.* Sydney: Catholic Education Office.

— (1979) *Catholic Schools and the Communication of Faith*. Sydney: Society of Saint Paul.

— (1985) *The Effectiveness of Catholic Schools*. Homebush, New South Wales: Saint Paul Publications.

Ford, D. (2011) *Christianity and Universities Today: A Double Manifesto*. Third Lord Dearing Memorial lecture given to Cathedrals Group Universities on 1 November. http://cathedralsgroup.org.uk/Uploads/Dearing2011.pdf (accessed 17 November 2011).

Forster, G. (1997) *Education: Vision, Ethos and 'Values'*. Cambridge: Grove Books.

Fosnot, C. T. (ed.) (2005) *Constructivism: Theory, Perspectives, and Practice* (2nd edn). New York: Teachers College.

Francis, L. J. (1986a) 'Denominational Schools and Pupil Attitude towards Christianity'. *British Educational Research Journal* 12, 145–52.

— (1986b) *Partnership in Rural Education: Church Schools and Teacher Attitudes*. London: Collins.

— (1987) *Religion in the Primary School: Partnership between Church and State?* London: Collins Liturgical Publications.

— (2001) *The Values Debate: A Voice from the Pupils*. London: Woburn Press.

— (2005) 'Independent Christian Schools and Pupil Values: An Empirical Investigation among 13–15 Year Old Boys'. *British Journal of Religious Education* 27 (2), 172–41.

Francis, L. J. and Carter, M. (1980) 'Church Aided Secondary Schools, Religious Education as an Examination Subject and Pupil Attitudes towards Religion'. *British Journal of Educational Psychology* 50, 297–300.

Francis, L. J. and Grindle, Z. (2001) 'The Changing Ethos of Church Schools: A Survey of Teacher Attitudes in 1982 and 1996'. *Research in Education* 65, 1–19.

Francis, L. J. and Jewell, A. (1992) 'Shaping Adolescent Attitude towards the Church: Comparison between Church of England and County Secondary Schools'. *Evaluation and Research in Education* 6, 13–21.

Francis, L. J. and Stone, E. A. (1995) 'School Governors and the Religious Ethos of Church of England Voluntary Aided Primary Schools'. *Educational Management and Administration* 23, 176–87.

Francis, L. J., Penny, G., and Baker, S. (2012) 'Defining and Assessing Spiritual Health: A Comparative Study among 13- to 15-Year-Old Pupils Attending Secular Schools, Anglican Schools, and Private Christian Schools in England and Wales'. *The Peabody Journal of Education* 87, 351–67.

Gamarnikow, E. and Green, A. (2005) 'Keeping the Faith with Social Capital: From Coleman to New Labour on Social Justice, Religion and Education', in R. Gardner, J. Cairns and D. Lawton (eds), *Faith Schools. Consensus or Conflict?* London: RoutledgeFalmer.

Gardner, R., Cairns, J. and Lawton, D. (eds) (2005) *Faith Schools: Consensus or Conflict?* London: RoutledgeFalmer, pp. 90–101, 99.

General Synod Board of Education (1996) *Youth A Part: Young People and the Church*. London: Church House Publishing.

Gert, B. (1998) *Morality.* New York: Oxford University Press.

Gilbert P. (1992) *Depression: The Evolution of Powerlessness.* New York: Guildford Press.

Gilley (1990) *Newman and His Age.* London: DLT.

Glanzer, P. L. (2000) 'Finding the Gods in Public School: A Christian Deconstruction of Character Education'. *Journal of Education and Christian Belief* 4 (2), 115–29.

— (2003) 'Did the Moral Education Establishment Kill Character? An Autopsy of the Death of Character'. *Journal of Moral Education* 32 (3), 291–306.

— (2005) 'The Impact and Implications of Faith or Worldview in the Classroom'. *Journal of Research in Character Education* 3 (1), 25–42.

— (2008a) 'Searching for the Soul of English Universities: An Analysis of Christian Higher Education in England'. *British Journal of Educational Studies* 56 (2), 163–83.

— (2008b) 'Why We Should Discard "the Integration of Faith and Learning": Rearticulating the Mission of the Christian Scholar'. *Journal of Education and Christian Belief* 12 (1), 41–51.

Goldman, R. (1964) *Religious Thinking from Childhood to Adolescence.* London: Routledge.

— (1965) *Readiness for Religion: A Basis for Developmental Religious Education.* London: Routledge Kegan Paul.

Grace, G. (1995) *School Leadership: Beyond Educational Management – An Essay in Policy Scholarship.* London: Falmer.

— (2000) *Catholic Schools and the Common Good: What This Means in Educational Practice.* London, University of London Institute of Education, Centre for Research and Development in Catholic Education.

— (2002) *Catholic Schools: Mission, Markets and Morality.* London: RoutledgeFalmer.

— (2011) 'Renewing the Catholic School Curriculum', in K. Chappell and F. Davis (eds), *Catholic Social Conscience.* Leominster: Gracewing, pp. 221–39.

Graham, E. L. (1996) *Transforming Practice: Pastoral Theology in an Age of Uncertainty.* Eugene: Wipf and Stock.

Greeley, A. M. (1998) 'The Future of the Catholic School: An American Perspective', in J. Matthew Feheney (ed.), *From Ideal to Action: The Inner Nature of a Catholic School Today.* Dublin: Veritas.

Greeley, A. M. and Rossi, P. H. (1966) *The Education of Catholic Americans.* Chicago: Aldine Publishing Company.

Greeley, A. M., McCready, W. C. and McCourt, K. (1976) *Catholic Schools in a Declining Church.* Kansas City: Sheed and Ward.

Green, E. (2009) *Mapping the Field: A Review of the Current Research Evidence on the Impact of Schools with a Christian Ethos.* London: Theos.

— (2010) 'An Ethnographic Study of a City Technology College with a Bible-Based Ethos'. D.Phil. dissertation, University of Oxford.

Green, E. and Cooling, T. (2009) *Mapping the Field: A Review of the Current Research Evidence on the Impact of Schools with a Christian Ethos.* London: Theos.

Green, L. (ed.) (2009) *Let's Do Theology* (2nd edn). London: Continuum.

Griffiths, M. (2009) *One Generation from Extinction: How the Church Connects with the Unchurched Child*. Oxford: Monarch.

Grimmitt, M. (2000) 'The Captivity and Liberation of Religious Education and the Meaning and Significance of Pedagogy', in M. Grimmitt (ed.), *Pedagogies of Religious Education*. Great Wakening, Essex: McCrimmons.

Gunton, C. (1983) *Yesterday and Today: A Study in Continuities in Christology*. London: Darton, Longman and Todd.

— (1998) *The Triune Creator: A Historical and Systematic Study*. Edinburgh: Edinburgh University Press.

Hall, J. and Taylor, J. (eds) (2005) *Excellence and Distinctiveness: Guidance on RE in Church of England Schools*. London: National Society.

Hand, M. (2003) 'A Philosophical Objection to Faith Schools'. *Theory and Research in Education* 1 (1), 89–99.

Hardy, D. W. (2001) *Finding the Church: The Dynamic Truth of Anglicanism*. Oxford: Berghahn Press.

Hauerwas, S. (1983) *The Peaceable Kingdom*. Notre Dame, IN: University of Notre Dame Press.

— (2007) *The State of the University: Academic Knowledges and the Knowledge of God*. Oxford: Blackwell.

— (2010) *Hannah's Child*. London: SCM.

Healy, G. (1999)'Catholic Education and Self-Esteem', in J. W. Feheney (ed.), *Beyond the Race for Points: Aspects of Pastoral Care in a Catholic School Today*. Dublin: Veritas.

Heelas, P. and Woodhead, L. (2005) *The Spiritual Revolution: Why Religion Is Giving Way to Spirituality*. Oxford: Blackwell.

Heenan, J. (1944) *Cardinal Hinsley*. London: Burns and Oates.

Hella, E. and Wright, A. (2009) 'Learning "About" and "From" Religion: Phenomenography, the Variation Theory of Learning and Religious Education in Finland and the U.K.' *British Journal of Religious Education* 31 (1), 53–64.

Henson, H. H. (1939) *The Church of England*. Cambridge: Cambridge University Press.

Herriot, P. (2007) *Religious Fundamentalism and Social Identity*. London: Routledge.

Hesselgrave, D. and Rommen, E. (1989) *Contextualization: Meanings, Methods and Models*. Leicester: Apollos.

Hick, J. (ed.) (1977) *The Myth of God Incarnate*. London: SCM.

Higton, M. (2004) *Difficult Gospel: The Theology of Rowan Williams*. London: SCM.

Hill, B. (2004) *Exploring Religion in School*. Adelaide: Openbook Publishers.

Hill, W. S. (1997) 'Richard Hooker in the Folger Edition', in Arthur Stephen McGrade (ed.), *Richard Hooker and the Construction of Christian Community*. Tempe, AZ: Medieval & Renaissance Texts & Studies, pp. 3–20.

Hirst, P. (1971) 'Christian Education: A Contradiction in Terms'. *Faith and Thought* 99 (1), 43–54.

— (1974) *Moral Education in a Secular Society*. London: University of London Press.

Hoggart, R. (1996) *The Way We Live Now*. London: Pimlico.

Holt, M. (2002) 'It's Time to Start the Slow School Movement'. *Phi Delta Kappan* 84 (4), 264–71.

Hornsby-Smith, M. P. (1978) *Catholic Education: The Unobtrusive Partner.* London: Sheed and Ward.

Horsley, S. (1813) *The Charges of Samuel Horsley,* cited in Varley, *The Last of the Prince Bishops* (2002).

Houlden, L. (1977) 'The Creed of Experience', in John Hick (ed.), *The Myth of God Incarnate.* London: SCM.

House of Commons (2007) *Report on Citizenship Education.* London: HMSO.

Howley, W. (1832) *A Charge Delivered at His Primary Visitation.* Oxford: Rivington.

Huelin, G. (1986)'Innovation: The National Society 1811–1934', in Joanna Yates (ed.), *Faith for the Future.* London: National Society and Church House Publishing.

Hull, J. (1995) 'The Holy Trinity and Christian Education in a Plural World', National Society's Annual Lecture 1994. London: National Society.

Humanist Philosophers Group (2001) *Religious Schools: The Case Against.* London: British Humanist Association.

Hunter, J. (2000) *The Death of Character: Moral Education in an Age Without Good or Evil.* New York: Basic Books.

Hursthouse, R. (1999) *On Virtue Ethics.* Oxford: Oxford University Press.

Iremonger, F. A. (1948) *William Temple Archbishop of Canterbury. His Life and Letters,* London: Oxford University Press.

Jackson, P. (ed.) (1993) *The Moral Life of Schools.* San Francisco: Jossey-Bass.

Jacob, W. M. (1996) *Lay People and Religion in the Early Eighteenth Century.* Cambridge: Cambridge University Press..

— (2007) *The Clerical Profession in the Long Eighteenth Century 1680–1840.* Oxford: Oxford University Press.

James, O. (1998) *Britain on the Couch.* London: Arrow Books.

— (2004) 'School of Hard Knocks', *Observer Magazine,* 3 October.

Jamison, C., OSB (2013) 'God Has Created Me to Do Him Some Definite Service' (Cardinal Newman): Vocation at the Heart of the Catholic Curriculum. *International Studies in Catholic Education* 5 (1).

Janmaat, G. J. (2010) *Classroom Diversity and Its Relation to Tolerance, Trust and Participation in England, Sweden and Germany.* London: Centre for Learning and Life Chances Knowledge Economies and Societies. Available at: www.llakes.org.uk

Jelfs, H. (2008) '"Is It the Dance of Life Miss?" An Exploration of the Educational Paradigm and Pedagogical Practice in Church of England Schools'. Ph.D. dissertation, University of Bristol.

— (2010) 'Christian Distinctiveness in Church of England Schools'. *Journal of Beliefs and Values* 31, 29–38.

Jeynes, W. H. (2004) 'A Meta-Analysis: Has the Academic Impact of Religious Schools Changed over the Last Twenty Years?' *Journal of Empirical Theology* 17 (2), 197–216.

— (2005) 'The Impact of Religious Schools on the Academic Achievement of Low-SES Students'. *Journal of Empirical Theology* 18 (1), 22–40.

Kay, W. K. (2001) *Religious Education Syllabus for Primary Schools.* Cardiff: Church in Wales.

Kay, W. K. and Francis, L. J. (1996) *Drift from the Churches.* Cardiff: University of Wales Press.

— (eds) (1997) *Religion in Education,* Volume 1. Leominster: Gracewing.

Kelly, J. N. D. (1950) *Early Christian Creeds.* London: Longman, Green and Co.

Kirby, T. (1997) 'Richard Hooker as an Apologist of the Magisterial Reformation in England', in A. S. McGrade (ed.), *Richard Hooker and the Construction of Christian Community.* Tempe, AZ: Medieval & Renaissance Texts & Studies, pp. 219–33.

Lancaster, J. (1803) *Improvements in Education.* London: Darton and Harvey Grace-Church-Street; J. Mathews, Strand 5 and W. Hatchard, Piccadilly.

Lankshear, D. W. (1996) *Churches Serving Schools.* London: National Society.

— (2003) 'The Way Ahead – Context: Developments between 1969 and 1998', in W. K. Kay, L. J. Francis and K. Watson (eds), *Religion in Education* Volume 4. Leominster: Gracewing.

— (2005) 'The Influence of Anglican Secondary Schools on Personal, Moral and Religious Values', in L. J. Francis, M. Robbins and J. Astley (eds), *Religion, Education and Adolescence: International Empirical Perspectives.* Cardiff: University of Wales Press, pp. 55–69.

— (2009) *The Church in Wales Education Review* (2nd edn). Cardiff: Church in Wales.

Lankshear, J. F. (1997) *Denominational Inspection in Primary Schools.* London: National Society.

Lawlor, M. (1965) *Out of This World: A Study of Catholic Values.* London: Sheed and Ward.

Lawton, D. (ed.) (2005) *Faith Schools: Consensus or Conflict?* London: RoutledgeFalmer.

Layard, R. and Dunn, J. (2009) *A Good Childhood.* London: Penguin.

Leavey, C. (1972) 'The Transmission of Religious Moral Values in Nine Catholic Girls Schools'. *Twentieth Century* 27, 167–84.

LeDoux, J. (1999) *The Emotional Brain: The Mysterious Underpinnings of Emotional Life.* London: Phoenix.

Lessing, G. (1957) *Theological Writings,* ed. and trans. Henry Chadwick. Stanford, CA: Stanford University Press.

Likert, R. (1932). 'A Technique for the Measurement of Attitudes'. *Archives of Psychology* 140, 1–55.

Lindbeck, G. A. (1984) *The Nature of Doctrine: Religion and Theology in a Postliberal Age.* Louisville, KT: Westminster John Knox Press.

Locke, J. and Gough, J. W. (1966) *The Second Treatise of Government: An Essay Concerning the True Original, Extent and End of Civil Government, and, A Letter Concerning Toleration* (3rd edn). Oxford: Blackwell.

Louden, L. (2003) *The Conscience Clause in Religious Education and Collective Worship: Conscientious Objection or Curriculum Choice?* Oxford: Culham Institute (and www.culham.ac.uk/Res_conf/conscience_clause.pdf).

Lowther, C. (1959) *A History of the SPCK*. London: SPCK.

McAdoo, H. (1997) *Anglican Heritage: Theology and Spirituality* (rev. edn). Norwich: Canterbury Press.

McClendon, J. W. (1990) *Biography as Theology*. Harrisburg, PA: Trinity Press.

MacEoin, D. (2009) *Music, Chess and Other Sins*. London: Civitas.

McGrath, A. (1994) *Christian Theology*. Oxford: Blackwell.

MacIntyre, A. (1985) *After Virtue: A Study in Moral Theology* (2nd edn). London: Duckworth.

— (1999) *Dependent Rational Animals: Why Human Beings Need the Virtues*. London: Duckworth.

McLaughlin, T. H. (1985) 'Religion, Upbringing and Liberal Values: A Rejoinder to Eamonn Callan'. *Journal of Philosophy of Education* 19 (1), 119–27.

MacMullen, I. (2007) *Faith in Schools?: Autonomy, Citizenship, and Religious Education in the Liberal State*. Princeton, NJ: Princeton University Press.

Mander, D. (1993) *St John at Hackney, a Story of a Church: The Parish of Hackney*. London: Hackney Society.

Markham, I. (2011) 'Trends and Directions in Contemporary Theology: Anglican Theology'. *The Expository Times* 122 (5), 209–17.

Marks, J. (2001) 'Foreword', in J. Burn, J. Marks, P. Pilkington and P. Thompson (eds), *Faith in Education*. London: Civitas.

Marley, D. (2011) 'C of E Opens School Gates to Non-Believers'. *Times Educational Supplement* 22 April; www.tes.co.uk/article.aspx?storycode=6078734&navcode=94 (accessed 22 April 2011).

Marsden, G. M. (1997) *The Outrageous Idea of Christian Scholarship*. New York: Oxford University Press.

Matheson, W. (1923) *English Church Reform 1815–1840*. London: Longmans Green and Co.

Mayfield, G. (1963) *The Church of England, Its Members and Business*. London: Oxford University Press.

Meirose, C. E. (ed.) (1994) *The Preamble to the Constitution of the New Jesuit Secondary Education Association*. Washington, DC.

Milbank, J. (1990) *Theology and Social Theory: Beyond Secular Reason*. Oxford: Blackwell.

Mol, J. J. (1968) 'The Effects of Denominational Schools in Australia'. *Australian and New Zealand Journal of Sociology* 4, 18–35.

Mongoven, A. (2009) *Just Love; Transforming Civic Virtue*. Bloomington: Indiana University Press.

Morris, A. B. (2008) *Fifty Years On: The Case for Catholic Schools*. Chelmsford: Matthew James Publishing.

Munby, D. (1963) *The Idea of a Secular Society.* London: Oxford University Press.

Murphy, J. (1971) *Church, State and Schools in Britain, 1800–1970.* London: Routledge.

— (2007) *Church, State and Schools in Britain, 1800–1970.* London: Routledge.

Nagel, T. (1986) *The View from Nowhere.* Oxford: Oxford University Press.

National Assembly (2000) *The Professional Headship Induction Programme.* Cardiff: National Assembly Government.

National College for School Leadership (2000–present) *Leadership and Faith: Working With and Learning from School Leaders.* www.nationalcollege.org.uk/download?id=1 7234&filename=leadership-and-faith.pdf (accessed 22 September 2011).

National Office for Vocations: CBCEW (2011) Forthcoming (2013) in International Studies in Catholic Education, London.

National Secular Society (2011) Available at: www.secularism.org.uk/faith-schools.html (accessed 11 July 2011).

National Society (1988) *Children in the Way.* London: Church House Publishing.

— (1991) *All God's Children.* London: Church House Publishing.

— (1996) *Youth A Part: Young People and the Church.* London: Church House Publishing.

— (1997) *Inspection Handbook: for Section Thirteen Inspections in Schools of the Church of England and the Church in Wales.* London: National Society.

— (2009) *Self-Evaluation Toolkit for Church Schools.* London: National Society.

— (2010) *Statutory Inspection of Anglican Schools Report on Section 48 Inspections Cycle 2005–2009.* London: National Society.

— (2011) *Admissions to Church of England Schools: Advice to Diocesan Boards of Education, June 2011.*

Neill, S. (1958) *Anglicanism.* Harmondsworth: Pelican.

Neuwien, R. A. (ed.) (1966) *Catholic Schools in Action.* Notre Dame, IN: University of Notre Dame Press.

Newcome, J. (2011) *Growing Disciples: Vision and Strategy: 2011–2020.* Diocese of Carlisle.

Newman, J. H. (1899) *The Idea of a University.* London: Longmans Green.

NFER (National Foundation for Educational Research) (2006) *Active Citizenship and Young People: Opportunities, Experiences and Challenges in and Beyond School.* London: www.nfer.ac.uk/research-areas/citizenship.

Nichols, A. (1993) *The Panther and the Hind: A Theological History of Anglicanism* Edinburgh: T&T Clark.

Nixon, J. (2008) *Towards the Virtuous University: The Moral Bases of Academic Practice.* New York: Routledge.

Nockles, P. (1994) *The Oxford Movement in Context.* Cambridge: Cambridge University Press.

— (2004) 'Joshua Watson', in *Oxford Dictionary of National Biography* Volume 57. Oxford: Oxford University Press, pp. 636–9.

Norman, E. (2004) *Anglican Difficulties: A New Syllabus of Errors.* London: Continuum/ Morehouse.

Norman, R. (2004) *On Humanism*. London: Routledge.

O'Brien, G. D. (2002) *The Idea of a Catholic University*. Chicago: University of Chicago Press.

O'Donovan, J. L. (2004) 'The Church of England and the Anglican Communion: A Timely Engagement with the National Church Tradition?' *Scottish Journal of Theology* 57 (3), 313–37.

Ofsted (2002/3) *National Curriculum Citizenship: Planning and Implementation*. London.

— (2006) *Towards Consensus? Citizenship in secondary schools*. London.

— (2009) *Independent Faith Schools*. London.

O'Keefe, J. (2003) 'Catholic Schools as Communities of Service: The US Experience', in N. Prendergast and L. Monahan (eds), *Reimagining the Catholic School*. Dublin: Veritas.

Orwell, G. (1937) *The Road to Wigan Pier*. London: Gollancz.

Padmore, C. (2005) *Aspects of Anglican Identity*. London: Church House Publishing.

Palmer, P. J. (1998) *The Courage to Teach: Exploring the Inner Landscape of a Teacher's Life*. San Francisco: Jossey-Bass.

Partners in Mission Consultation (1981) *To a Rebellious House?* London: CIO Publishing.

Pascarella, E. T. and Terenzini, P. T. (2005) *How College Affects Students* (2nd edn). San Francisco: Jossey-Bass.

Percy, M. (2006) 'In My Fathers House There Are Many Rooms', in Stephen Croft (ed.), *The Future of the Parish System*. London: Church House Publishing, pp. 3–15.

Peshkin, A. (1986) *God's Choice: The Total World of a Fundamentalist Christian School*. Chicago and London: University of Chicago Press.

Pike, M. (2009) 'Transaction and Transformation at Trinity: Private Sponsorship, Core Values and Christian Ethos at England's Most Improved Academy'. *Oxford Review of Education* 35 (2), 133–46.

— (2010) 'Christianity and Character Education: Faith in Core Values?' *Journal of Beliefs and Values* 31 (3), 311–21.

Pilkington, P. (2001) 'The Church in Education', in J. Burn, J. Marks, P. Pilkington and P. Thompson (eds), *Faith in Education*. London: Civitas.

Pirsig, R. (1974) *Zen and the Art of Motorcycle Maintenance*. London: Bodley Head.

Plant, R. (2001) *Politics, Theology and History*. Cambridge: Cambridge University Press.

Pope Paul VI (1996) 'Pastoral Constitution on the Church in the Modern World (Gaudium et Spes)', in A. Flannery (ed.), *Vatican Council II: Constitutions, Decrees and Declarations*. Northport, NY: Costello Publishing.

Popper, K. (1966) *The Open Society and Its Enemies, Volume One: Plato*. London: Routledge and Kegan Paul.

Pring, R. A. (1996) 'Markets, Education and Catholic Schools', in T. H. McLaughlin, J. O'Keefe and B. O'Keefe (eds), *The Contemporary Catholic School: Context, Identity and Diversity*. London: Routledge.

— (2000) *Philosophy of Educational Research*. London: Continuum.

— (2005) 'Are Faith Schools Justified?' in R. Gardner, J. Cairns and D. Lawton (eds), *Faith Schools. Consensus or Conflict?* London: RoutledgeFalmer.

Pritchard, R. (2011) Interview in *Times Educational Supplement*, 6 May, London.

Pugh, G. and Telhaj, S. (2008) 'Faith Schools, Social Capital and Academic Attainment: Evidence from TIMSS-R Mathematics Scores in Flemish Secondary Schools'. *British Educational Research Journal* 34 (2), 235–67.

Putnam, R. D. and Campbell, D. E. (2010) *American Grace: How Religion Divides and Unites Us.* New York: Simon & Schuster.

QCA (2008a), *KS3 Citizenship Curriculum Guidance* [Online]. Available at https://curriculum.qca.org/key-stage-3-and-4/subjects/citizenship/keystage3/index.aspx (accessed 2 January 2009).

— (2008b), *KS4 Citizenship Curriculum Guidance* [Online]. Available at http://curriculum.qca.org.uk/key-stage-3-and-4/subjects/citizenship/keystage4/index.aspx (accessed 2 January 2009).

Quash, B. (2003) 'The Anglican Church as a Polity of Presence', in D. Dormer, J. McDonald and J. Caddick (eds), *Anglicanism: The Answer to Modernity.* London: Continuum.

Quillen, C. (2005) *In Defense of Tolerance, Emerson Unitarian Church 24/4/05.* Huston, TX: Emerson Unitarian Church.

Quinn, P. V. (1965) 'Critical Thinking and Openmindedness in Pupils from Public and Catholic Secondary Schools'. *Journal of Social Psychology* 66, 23–30.

Ramsey, I. (ed.) (1970) *The Fourth R: The Report of the Commission on Religious Education in Schools.* London: National Society and SPCK.

Ray, J. J. and Doratis, D. (1971) 'Religiocentrism and Ethnocentrism: Catholic and Protestant in Australian Schools'. *Sociological Analysis* 32, 170–9.

Rayment-Pickard, H. (2011) *How to Avoid Descending into Theological Cliché*, 12 August. London: Church Times.

Rich, E. E. (1970) *The Education Act 1870.* London: Longmans.

Rivington Reports of the National Society 1812, 1813 etc.

Rivington, R. (1867) 'Memoir of the Last Joshua Watson Esq', in *The Church Builder* XXIV.

Robinson, J. A. T. (1963) *Honest to God.* London: SCM.

Rudge, L. (1998) '"I Am Nothing: Does It Matter?": A Critique of Current Religious Education Policy and Practice on Behalf of the Silent Majority'. *British Journal of Religious Education* 20 (3).

Rutter, J. (2005) 'Understanding the Alien in Our Midst: Using Citizenship Education to Challenge Popular Discourses about Refugees', in A. Osler (ed.), *Teachers, Human Rights and Diversity: Educating Citizens in Multicultural Societies.* Stoke-on-Trent: Trentham Books.

St Augustine (1976) *Confessions*, trans. R. S. Pine-Coffin. Harmondsworth, Middlesex: Penguin Books.

Scanlon, T. M. (1996) 'The Difficulty of Tolerance', in D. Heyd (ed.), *Toleration: An Elusive Virtue.* Princeton, NJ: Princeton University Press.

Schagen, S. and Schagen, I. (2001) 'Faith Schools and Specialist Schools: The Way to Raise Standards?' *Education Journal* 62, 30-2.

Scruton, R. (1998) *An Intelligent Person's Guide to Modern Culture.* London: Duckworth.

Searle, J. R. (1996) *The Construction of Social Reality.* London: Penguin Books.

Seierstad, Å. (2004) *The Bookseller of Kabul.* London: Virago Press.

Selby, P. (1991) *Belonging: Challenge to a Tribal Church.* London: SPCK.

Shepherd, P. (2004) 'Who Are Church Schools For? Towards an Ecclesiology for Church of England Voluntary Aided Schools'. Unpublished Ph.D. dissertation, Open University.

Sheppard, D. (1983) *Bias to the Poor.* London: Hodder & Stoughton.

Shklar, J. N. (1984) *Ordinary Vices.* Cambridge, MA: Harvard University Press.

Short, G. and Lenga, R.-A. (2002) 'Jewish Primary Schools in a Multicultural Society: Responding to Diversity?' *Journal of Beliefs and Values* 23 (1), 43-54.

Smith, D. (2005) 'Scripture, Speech Acts and Language Classes'. *Journal of Christianity and Foreign Languages* 6, 71-4.

— (2011) 'Reading Practices and Christian Pedagogy: Enacting Charity with Texts', in D. Smith and J. Smith (eds), *Teaching and Christian Practices: Reshaping Faith and Learning.* Grand Rapids, MI: Eerdma.

Smith, D. I. and Carvill, B. (2000) *The Gift of the Stranger: Faith, Hospitality and Foreign Language Learning.* Grand Rapids, MI: Wm. B. Eerdmans.

Smith, D. I. and Shortt, J. (2002) *The Bible and the Task of Teaching.* Stapleford: Stapleford Centre.

Smith, D. I. and Smith, J. K. A. (eds) (2011) *Teaching and Christian Practices: Reshaping Faith and Learning.* Grand Rapids, MI: Wm. B. Eerdmans.

Smith, J. K. A. (2009) *Desiring the Kingdom: Worship, Worldview and Cultural Formation.* Grand Rapids, MI: Baker Academic.

Smith, J. T. (2008) *A Victorian Class Conflict: Schoolteaching and the Parson, Priest and Minister 1837-1902.* Eastbourne: Sussex Academic Press.

Smyth, C. (1961) *Joshua Watson and the National Society.* London: National Society. www.natsoc.org.uk/society/history/jwatson.html

Solomon, R. C. (1993) 'Business Ethics', in Peter Singer (ed.), *A Companion to Ethics.* Oxford: Blackwell.

Spencer, A. E. C. W. (1968) 'An Evaluation of Roman Catholic Educational Policy in England and Wales 1900-1960', in P. Jeff (ed.), *Religious Education: Drift or Decision?* London: Darton, Longman and Todd.

Stern, L. J. (2006) *Teaching Religious Education: Researchers in the Classroom.* London: Continuum.

— (2009) *The Spirit of the School.* London: Continuum.

— (2010) 'Research as Pedagogy: Building Learning Communities and Religious Understanding in RE'. *British Journal of Religious Education* 32 (2), 133-46.

Street, R. (2005) 'Religious Education in Anglican Voluntary Aided Secondary Schools: Moving from Transmission to Transformation'. Ph.D. dissertation, Kings College, University of London.

Sullivan, J. (2001) *Catholic Education: Distinctive and Inclusive*. London: Springer.

— (2003) 'Scholarship and Spirituality', in David Carr and John Haldane (eds), *Spirituality, Philosophy and Education*. London: RoutledgeFalmer, pp. 123–36.

Tajfel, H. and Turner, J. C. (1986) 'The Social Identity Theory of Intergroup Behaviour', in S. Worschel and W. G. Austin (eds), *Psychology of Intergroup Relations*. Chicago: Nelson-Hall.

Taylor, C. (1989) *Sources of the Self.* Cambridge: Cambridge University Press.

— (2007) *A Secular Age*. London: Belknap Press.

Taylor, J. V. (1972) *The Go-Between God*. London: SCM.

Temple, W. (1942) *Christianity and Social Order*. London: Penguin.

Thatcher, A. (2004) 'The Curriculum of a Christian University', in J. Astley, L. Francis, J. Sullivan and A. Walker (eds), *The Idea of a Christian University*. Milton Keynes: Paternoster.

Thiessen, E. J. (1993) *Teaching for Commitment: Liberal Education, Indoctrination and Christian Nurture*. Montreal, QC: McGill-Queen's University Press.

— (2001) *In Defence of Religious Schools and Colleges*. Montreal, QC: McGill-Queen's University Press.

— (2004) 'Objections to the Idea of a Christian University', in J. Astley, L. Francis, J. Sullivan and A. Walker (eds), *The Idea of a Christian University*. Milton Keynes: Paternoster.

Thiessen, E. (2011) *The Ethics of Evangelism: A Philosophical Defence of Ethical Proselytizing and Persuasion*. Milton Keynes: Bucks, Paternoster.

Thirty-Nine Articles of Religion (1563) Article 21 'On the Authority of the General Councils'. Church of England.

Thomas, R. S. (1996) *Collected Poems 1945–1990*. London: Phoenix.

Thompson, P. (2001) 'How the Will of Parliament on Religious Education was Diluted by Civil Servants and the Religious Education Profession', in J. Burn, J. Marks, P. Pilkington and P. Thompson (eds), *Faith in Education*. London: Civitas.

Three Faiths Forum (2011) Available at: www.threefaithsforum.org.uk/ (accessed 20 July 2011).

Tillich, P. (1978) *Systematic Theology*, 3 vols. London: SCM.

Tomkins, S. (2010) *The Clapham Sect: How Wilberforce's Circle Changed Britain*. Oxford: Lion.

Torney-Purta, J. V. (2001) *Citizenship and Education in Twenty-Eight Countries: Civic Knowledge and Engagement at Age Fourteen*. Amsterdam: International Association for the Evaluation in Educational Achievement.

Torrance, T. F. (1996) *The Christian Doctrine of God, One Being Three Persons* Edinburgh: T and T Clark.

Treston, K., Whiteman, R. G. and Florent, J. G. (1975) 'Catholic School Religious Training versus Adolescent Background and Orientation: Two Comparative Studies'. *Notre Dame Journal of Education* 6, 59–64.

Van de Weyer, R. (ed.) (1997) *Bede: Celtic and Roman Christianity in Britain.* Berkhamsted: Arthur James.

Van Engen, C. E. (ed.) (1994) *God so Loves the City. Seeking a Theology for Urban Mission.* Monrovia, CA: MARC.

Van Gennep, A. (1909) *Les Rites de Passage.* Translated in English in 1960. Chicago: University of Chicago Press.

Varley, E. A. (2002) *The Last of the Prince Bishops.* Cambridge: Cambridge University Press.

Vogt, W. P. (1997) *Tolerance and Education. Learning to Live with Diversity and Difference.* Thousand Oaks, CA: Sage Publications.

Volf, M. (1996) *Exclusion and Embrace.* Nashville, TN: Abingdon Press.

Von Hügel, F. (1908) *The Mystical Element of Religion.* London: Dent.

Waddington, R. (1984) *A Future in Partnership.* London: National Society.

Walker, A. and Wright, A. (2004) 'A Christian University Imagined: Recovering Paideia in a Broken World', in J. Astley, L. Francis, J. Sullivan and A. Walker (eds), *The Idea of a Christian University.* Milton Keynes: Paternoster.

Walsh, P. (1993) *Education and Meaning: Philosophy in Practice.* London: Cassell.

Walzer, M. (1997) *On Toleration.* New Haven: Yale University Press.

Wannenwetsch, B. (1996) 'The Political worship of the Church'. *Modern Theology* 12 (3), 269–99.

Wax, T. (2010) *The Rebirth of Virtue: An Interview with N.T. Wright* on 5 January. http://trevinwax.com/2010/01/05/the-rebirth-of-virtue-an-interview-with-n-t-wright/ (accessed 22 September 2011).

Weatherell, M. (2004) *Identities, Groups and Social Issues.* London: Sage Publications.

Webster, A. B. (1954) *Joshua Watson (The Story of a Layman 1771–1855).* London: SPCK,

Weil, S. (1952) *The Need for Roots.* London: Routledge Kegan Paul.

Weissberg, R. (2008) *Pernicious Tolerance: How Teaching to 'Accept Differences' Undermines Civil Society.* New Brunswick, NJ; London: Transaction.

Wells, S. (2002) 'How Common Worship Forms Local Character'. *Studies in Christian Ethics* 15, 66–74.

Wenger, E. (1998) *Communities of Practice: Learning, Meaning and Identity.* Cambridge: Cambridge University Press.

White, M. (2009) 'God's "brush strokes" in science'. *ACT NOW* 77.

White, S. R. (1996) *Authority and Anglicanism.* London: SCM.

Wilberforce, R. I. and S. (1838) *The Life of William Wilberforce,* 5 vols. London: John Murray.

Wilkinson, R. and Pickett, K. (2010) *The Spirit Level: Why Equality Is Better for Everyone.* London: Penguin.

Williams, R. (2000) 'Richard Hooker: Anglican Logic', in H. Chadwick (ed.), *Not Angels, but Anglicans.* Norwich: SCM Canterbury Press, pp. 149–52.

— (2003) *A Culture of Hope? Priorities and Vision in Church Schools*, Lecture to the
   Association of Anglican School Heads, Exeter, 11 September.
— (2006) 'Theological Resources for Re-examining Church', in Stephen Croft (ed.), *The
   Future of the Parish System*. London: Church House Publishing.
Williams, S. (2011) 'Thinking in Christ'. Paper presented at the Knowing in God's World
   Conference on 12 March. www.christianacademicnetwork.net/2011Conference/
   reports/KeyNotePaper.pdf (accessed 22 September 2011).
Wolterstorff, N. (1989) 'On Christian Learning', in P. A. Marshall, S. Griffioen and
   R. J. Mouw (eds), *Stained Glass: Worldviews and Social Science*. Lanham, MD:
   University Press of America.
Worcester Division of Education (2007) *Everyfaithmatters: Contributing to Community
   Cohesion in Church Schools*. Worcester: Diocese of Worcester.
Worcestershire Agreed Syllabus for Religious Education (2010) *Questions Children Ask*.
   Edulink: Worcester: Worcestershire Local Authority.
Worsley, H. J. (2006) 'The Development of Anglican Schools as Places of Mission'.
   Journal of the Anglican Association of Secondary Schools Heads 16 (February), 18–22.
Wright, A. (2003) 'Freedom, Equality, Fraternity? Towards a Liberal Defence of Faith
   Community Schools'. *British Journal of Religious Education* 25 (2), 142–52.
— (2004) *The Future of Spirituality in Education*: Dare to Engage Symposium.
— (2010) 'The Spiritual Education Project: Cultivating Spiritual and Religious
   Literacy through a Critical Pedagogy of Religious Education', in M. Grimmitt (ed.),
   Pedagogies of Religious Education. Great Wakening, Essex: McCrimmons.
Wright, A. and Hella, E. (2009) 'Learning "About" and "From"'. *Religion British Journal
   of Religious Education* 31 (1), 53–64.
Wright, T. (2007). *Surprised by Hope*. London: SPCK.
— (2010) *Virtue Reborn*. London: SPCK.
— (2011) 'The Traditional Anglican Grammar School'. Paper for the Anglican
   Archbishop of Sydney, July.
Yablon, Y. B. (2011) 'Religion as a Basis for Dialogue in Peace Education Programs'.
   Cambridge Journal of Education 40 (4), 341–51.
Yates, J. (1986) *Faith for the Future*. London: Church House Publishing.
Young, D. (1994) *Fifty Years Forward TES* and Institute of Education.
Young, F. (ed.) (1997) *Encounter with Mystery: Reflections on L'Arche and Living with
   Disability*. London: DLT.
Zull, J. E. (2002) *The Art of Changing the Brain: Enriching Teaching by Exploring the
   Biology of Learning*. Sterling, VA: Stylus Publishing.
Zumthor, P. (2006) *Thinking Architecture: Second Edition*. Basel, Switzerland:
   Birkhäuser.

Index